WHY
PENN STATE:

WHY THE 1980s GAVE NITTANY LIONS A
COMMON CAUSE, CULTURE AND SHARED VALUES

GREG WOODMAN

©Affinity Connection

ISBN: 978-1-7370253-0-6

Disclaimer: *Why Penn State: Why The 1980s Gave Nittany Lions A Common Cause, Culture And Shared Values* is in no way affiliated, endorsed or sanctioned by Penn State University. Unless otherwise noted, the collection of articles within have been curated from Happy Valley Promotions' Penn State Football Annuals that were published from 1983 through 1992, and have been reprinted herein with the express permission of the publisher.

Affinity Connection
P.O. Box 296, State College, PA 16804
814 -237-0481 | affinityconnection.com

CONTENTS

Thank you to the writers who contributed to the Penn State Football Annuals in the 1980s and made these years come alive:

Ron Bracken
Jim Carlson
Joan Kurilla
Chris Lindsley
Scott Ott
Mike Poorman
G.R. Severine

Thank you to these photographers and artists for their exemplary work that has created a snapshot into this decade for us.

Richard Ackley
All State Sugar Bowl
Chuck Andrasko
AP/World Wide Photos
Barash Advertising
Jill Behler
Blue-White Illustrated
Gregory P. Bullock
Jeff Bustraan
Paul Chiland
Bill Cramer
Harry DiOrio
Jason Ebersol
Sara Eichmiller
Micah Grabenstein
Eric C. Hegedus
Jeff Hixon
Jeff Holmes
Craig W. Houtz
Steven P. Kerner
Tony Kurdsjak
Nathan Lader

George Lavanish
Harvey Levine
Pat Little
Mark McIntyre
Dave Mengle
Tom Mosser
Dan Oleski
Mike Palski
Barb Parkyn
Kitty Patterson
Penn State Room
Penn State Sports Information
Al Pinanaschi
Christy Rickard
Dave Shelly
Paul Silvie
Melodee Snoke
Sports Pix International
Jody Stechler
Thomas Swarr
The Daily Collegian
Brent Warner
Scott Wilkerson
WPSX
Cris Yarborough
Gregg Zelkin
Leslie Zuck

PUBLISHER
Affinity Connection

AUTHOR/CURATOR
Greg Woodman

PROJECT MANAGER
Cara Aungst

DESIGNERS
Melissa Hombosky
Patti Worden

CONTRIBUTING WRITERS
Christen Bell
John Patishnock

ARCHIVAL PHOTO CONTRIBUTORS
Chuck Fong
Sophie Kandler

COPY EDITOR
Leah Jackson

EDITORIAL INTERNS
Aletheia Fitch
Chara Fitch
Ellie Aungst

Don't Ask How Penn State Got to Where It is Today.

THE PENN STATE ALMA MATER

For the Glory of Old State
For her founders strong and great.
For the future that we wait,
Raise the song, raise the song.

Sing our love and loyalty,
Sing our hopes that bright and free
Rest, O Mother, dear with thee
All with thee, all with thee.

When we stood at childhood's gate,
Shapeless in the hands of fate,
***Thou didst mold us dear
old State***
Dear Old State, dear old State.

May no act of ours bring shame
To one heart that loves thy name,
May our lives but swell thy fame,
Dear old State, dear old State.

ASK 'WHY.'

Don't Ask How Penn State Got to Where It is Today. Ask 'Why.'

As it turns out, the secret to Penn State's success all comes down to values and the art of associating together

A few years ago, ESPN College Game Day analyst Kirk Herbstreit said, "If my kids could grow up to be like Penn State football players, I'd be a proud dad." That was the day that I knew that Herbstreit saw Penn State as more than just a place where athletes won awards and researchers made discoveries. He saw its true essence: shared vision and shared values that fostered tremendous success, making Penn State a place that's driven by values, tradition, success with honor, and fun with a purpose.

After all, every university is about graduating students, but over the years, Penn State has become so much more than that. It's described in heart-filled superlatives: home of the largest student-run philanthropy on the planet, the greatest show in college football, the happiest place on earth.

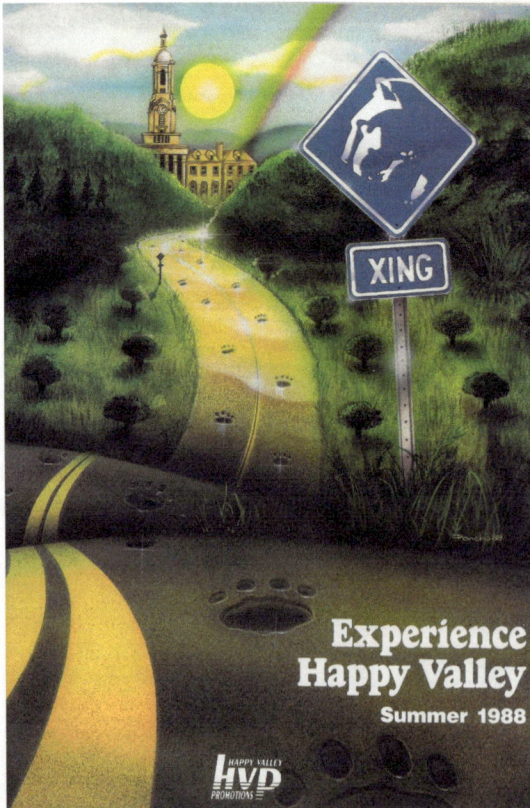

Experience
Happy Valley
Summer 1988

HVP HAPPY VALLEY PROMOTIONS

How did this happen? How did a land-grant state school in central Pennsylvania with students from steel and coal towns like Scranton and Pittston and Johnstown end up winning the hearts and souls of its fans while it went on to become a two-time national champion, leading fundraising university, and research powerhouse? And more importantly, why?

As a marketer, these transformations have always fascinated me. I've studied how startups like Blue Ribbon Sports turned into Nike and, powered by the hero story of runner Steve Prefontaine, embodied the essence of triumph through hard work. I've watched outdoor gear company Patagonia define itself through environmental activism and build fierce brand loyalty with its fans, while selling its products for more than twice the sticker price of its competitors. It's impossible to fully grasp successes like these through spreadsheets and numbers because they are defined in ideology and story. In other words, their success lies in their motivation—in their 'why.' And it's through their 'why' that these brands became the problem solvers and guides that they are today.

Every company, university and person has a 'what' and a 'how' that serves as the framework for winning. But it's each person's 'why' that steers their destiny. Combined with expectations, memories, stories and relationships, that 'why' becomes a North Star. It determines success and guides through hard times.

That's what Kirk Herbstreit was talking about when he said, "If my kids could grow up to be like Penn State football players, I'd be a proud dad." He knew that the story of Penn State was more than tailgates and Joe Paterno, headlines and comebacks. Instead, the true heart of the university boiled down its people and the vision and values that all Penn Stater share.

The French philosopher Alexis de Tocqueville said this kind of association was the bedrock of successful democracy. He said, "Among the laws that rule human societies there is one which seems to be more precise and clear than all others. If men are to remain civilized or to become so, the art of associating together must grow and improve in the same ratio in which the equality of conditions is increased."

"Associating together" sounds like an 1830s version of WE ARE to me. It sounds like that old clip of John Cappelletti as he breaks down in tears, dedicating his Heisman to his little brother dying of leukemia. It sounds like Wally Triplett's 1946 football team when they made history by refusing to play a game against the then-segregated University of Miami, refusing to leave their black players at home and instead unanimously agreeing, "We play all or none. We are Penn State." It sounds like Joe Paterno when he used Penn State's first national championship in 1982 as a catalyst to encourage the board of trustees to transform Penn State to be number one in academics, saying "Who we are, what we are, and I think that basically comes down to soul." And it definitely sounds like the era of the 1980s as we embraced success with honor right along with a love for fun with a purpose.

> **"**
> *Every company, university and person—you reading this right now—has a 'what' and a 'how' that serve as the framework for winning. But it's our 'why' that steers our destiny.*
> **"**

THE ART OF ASSOCIATING TOGETHER

To fully understand how Penn State became this place of heart—where infused values and vision have been such a catalyst of shared success—we need to go back to its early days.

Started as the only land-grant school in Pennsylvania, Penn State was strategically built in the exact center of the Commonwealth. It was equidistant from Pittsburgh and Philadelphia, and

closer still to hardworking towns like Johnstown, Altoona and Harrisburg. For its first 100-plus years, it was largely attended by Pennsylvanians. Some had grown up watching the Pittsburgh Steelers and the Pirates while their peers grew up cheering for the Philadelphia Eagles and Flyers and Phillies. (Knowing this, it comes as no surprise that Penn State's most enduring rival was Pitt, since the games were against Pennsylvanians who chose Penn State, and those who didn't.) They'd spent their early years in Catholic school or small public schools. Many of the boys had wrestled—Pennsylvania is the state for wrestling after all—and then moved on to college football. These students had parents who worked with their hands—coal miners, steelworkers, farmers. Coming from small towns around Philadelphia and Pittsburgh, they took on the persona of their respective cities: gritty and scrappy, wholesome and optimistic. And they all came together in the melting pot of transformation: Penn State.

The raw ingredients for greatness were there, in other words, the 'how' and 'what' were established. Penn State was good at what it did: preparing Pennsylvania's young people for their future. As it turned out, it was the 'why' that made all the difference to propel its student-athletes, students, fans, alumni, faculty and staff from good to great.

Penn State's coaches had a hand in turning Penn State into a guide for success with honor. Volleyball coach Russ Rose started in 1979, and his team has been the only program in the nation to appear in every NCAA volleyball tournament since its inception in 1981, winning it seven times. Harry Groves served as the head coach of track and field/cross country from 1968 until his retirement in 2006, and was named National Coach of the Year five times and Regional Coach of the Year a combined 26 times. Gillian Rattray was head coach of the Penn State field hockey program from 1974-86 and women's lacrosse team from 1974-85, guiding her programs to a combined five national championships. During the span of seven months in 1980, she directed two national championship squads, the first in May with the women's lacrosse team and the second in November with the field hockey squad.

> "
> *What is the cost when you trade values for wins?*
> "

For these legendary coaches, life was about much more than winning. It was about excellence in living. The athletes who were guided and mentored by these coaches still live by the mantras that impacted them decades later. *What is the cost when you trade values for wins?*

Joe Paterno was another coach who had a lot to do with that 'why.' Born in Brooklyn, raised with strong Jesuit values and educated at Brown, Paterno planned to go to law school before he got hired at Penn State as an assistant coach in 1950. In 1966, he was hired as head coach, and he set to work infusing everything he did with the value of Traditional Old School Lombardi-esque 'why.'

It was not all about football, first of all. He saw his role as training his student athletes for future success. "It was about faith, family and education," Jimmy Cefalo said at Paterno's funeral in 2012. "When he recruited me, he sat down with my mom and said 'Your son will go to class, he will get an education, and Gertie, he'll go to church every Sunday." Cefalo said that Paterno would tell his team over and over: "Today you are either going to get better or you are going to get worse, but you aren't going to stay the same. So what's it going to be?" It was soon clear that he wasn't talking about football at all. He never had been. If these players learned to hustle and succeed at life, they would also succeed on the football field.

It seemed modest and counter cultural in the days leading up to the 1980s. Culture was focused on individualism, and collegiate sports were increasingly becoming a win-at-any-cost war. But Paterno kept at his 'Grand Experiment' with football as a metaphor for life. "Keep hustling, something good will happen."

> **But Paterno kept at his 'Grand Experiment' with football as a metaphor for life. 'Keep hustling, something good will happen.'**

And good things did happen. During the 1960s and 1970s, the football team won 79 percent of their games since Joe Paterno assumed head coaching duties in 1966. The university as a whole was hitting a stride, starting the Materials Research Library with a grant from the U.S. Defense Department, establishing Milton Hershey Medical Center with a $50 million allocation from the M.S. Hershey Foundation and later developing the first lifelong rechargeable heart pacemaker. Student-run philanthropies like Sy Barash Regatta and Phi Psi 500 fueled fun-with-a-purpose at Penn State, which is still seen today with THON, the largest student-run philanthropy in the world. The college town that had once been derided for its 'sleepy' persona was seen for what it really was: a Happy Valley with the perfect mix of small city fun and stress-free living.

Just as this momentum was building, a TV show publicized Penn State to the rest of the country. In 1978, America's number one TV show, "60 Minutes," featured Paterno and his team. The interview took place only days before the Nittany Lions played at the Sugar Bowl against Alabama. They lost that game, but by the time they played, it hardly mattered. America had already fallen in love with Penn State's 'why.'

"Winning is part of the game, but I can't get excited about losing a football game. We lose, we lose," Paterno said matter-of-factly, pacing away from the camera in his too-short pants, socks sticking out a fair few inches. The shot cuts from him and pans over the locker room. His players sit on the benches, hunched over textbooks. "If we bring a kid into college and we don't think he can do the work and he doesn't graduate, we are really exploiting him," he says.

Even by the time of the broadcast, more than five years before their first national championship, he'd already been recruited by five NFL teams. "I'm happy here. I don't see any reason to move just for money."

About halfway through the landmark interview, he speaks the phrase that Jimmy Cefalo went on to use as his life motto in the four decades after he played on Paterno's team. "You either get better or get worse. You can't stay in the same place." And with his help, Penn State was about to get better. Much better.

IT ALL COMES DOWN TO VALUES

In today's world of 24-hour news coverage and myriad broadcasters, it's difficult to fully appreciate the weight that this single "60 Minutes" episode had on the American psyche. As Penn State, with its access to the New York market, became a popular ABC Saturday afternoon Game of the Week showcase, they were able to showcase student-athletes like Todd Blackledge, Shane Conlan, Curt Warner, Kenny Jackson, D.J. Dozier, John Shaeffer and Blair Thomas as they won both on the field, and in life.

> *During this decade fixated on TV, Penn State would become a top-watched sports icon, an example of how things should be, and could be.*

During this decade fixated on TV, Penn State would become a top-watched sports icon, an example of how things should be, and could be. Just as Nike was building its brand of innovation and empowering athletes, illustrated through indomitable runner Steve Prefontaine in the '70s and burgeoning star Michael Jordan in the mid-'80s, Penn State was illustrating success with excellence with its athletes.

The University dominated college football airtime. In fact, the 1986 National Championship was rated the number one college football telecast ever—and it clearly broadcast Penn State's 'why.' The game was a fable for the ages, portraying the philosophical 'good' Penn State pitted against 'evil' Miami, Pennsylvania down home values battling against Miami Vice and battle fatigues.

By the time of the 1986 Championship, this message was understood by everyone who gathered around their TV set in their living room and roared as Penn State made their final point. It was a moment tied to the *Sports Illustrated* Sportsman of the Year and the Century of Excellence, a mountaintop moment in a meteoric rise for Penn State.

There was no spin or marketing money spent in trying to create a narrative. It had all been accomplished by hard work and a

commitment to 'why,' and was seen as the way things ought to be. When Joe Paterno received the SI Sportsman of the Year award, he said just that: "This award meant so much to me, not because of me but because I really feel this was an award for the university and our intercollegiate program… it's a direct complement to Penn State's belief in the way intercollegiate athletics should be."

That's what OSU-alumnus Kirk Herbstreit was talking about. He recognized that being part of Penn State is to be part of this shared vision and values, prioritizing growth and teamwork over exploitative winning at any cost.

By the time he'd said it, players like John Cappelletti, Shane Conlan and Curt Warner were joined thirty years later by players like Saquon Barkley and Trace McSorley who understood teamwork, success with honor, and the value of teamwork.

After these pivotal wins and awards, Paterno kept on with his Grand Experiment, reminding players that winning wasn't their biggest aim, rather becoming successful people was the goal. Each time he put the strength of the team over that of an individual player, emphasizing a strict code of conduct over selfish exhibitions, or training his players for whole-person success rather than allowing them to be exploited, he was going back to those values again and again. His beliefs rippled through the psyche of the entire university, and over this decade, that collection of values solidified into a brand—into a 'why'—that made Penn State and its people stand apart from its peers, and rise, and rise again.

Penn State's commitment to education before athletics was recognized in the 1980s and has carried on through today. Penn

> " *This award meant so much to me, not because of me but because I really feel this was an award for the university and our intercollegiate program… it's a direct complement to Penn State's belief in the way intercollegiate athletics should be.* "

State's student-athletes were recognized by the College Football Association from 1985-87-88-89 for having a graduation success rate (GSE) of over 90%, joining an elite ranking with Notre Dame, Stanford and Duke. Today's Penn State student-athletes continue to maintain a 92% GSE.

Over the decade of the '80s, Penn State hit the magical essence of being both relatable and aspirational. In the middle of a recession, with the state dramatically reducing appropriations, Penn State learned and showed how to fundraise. In the midst of football dominated by showoffs and 'bad boys,' Penn State traded hot shot talent for 3-star players who displayed integrity and teamwork and created a football team that would go on to win two national championships and utterly dominate Pitt, the number one ranked team in the nation in 1981, at a score of 48-14. Ground was broken for a research park that would foster companies who continue to make headlines for global innovation and research today.

THOU DIDST MOLD US DEAR OLD STATE

Just like in the cases of Nike and Patagonia, these successes were after effects of 'why.' In a time of self discovery, self fulfillment and self expression, Penn State flipped the script and showed people that if they lived their life serving others, working hard and rising together, they'd find success. It was a grand experiment and a drive for excellence that wasn't just for Penn State. It was for the

> "
> *In a time of self discovery, self fulfillment and self expression, Penn State flipped the script and showed people that if they lived their life serving others, working hard and rising together, they'd find success.*
> "

community made up of you and me: fans and alumni, donors and staff, faculty and fans. And it worked.

In 2012, during the height of the Sandusky scandal, a survey went out to people who comprised the collective heart of Penn State. They were asked to evaluate Penn State, their mentor and guide, and assess the current situation, helping to chart a course for the future. When asked the question, "Describe the core values of Penn State," the responses were almost unanimous. Even in the shadows of tragedy, Penn State still embodied success with honor. And remembering those core values would prove to be an integral part of rebuilding the Penn State culture and community over the upcoming years.

"'Success with honor,' and 'The grand experiment,' pretty much describes the community's core values," answered one contributor. "It gave me a solid foundation, values and an education," said another.

"Positive, kind, caring community with integrity and honesty. It showed me values like love your neighbor, support your local business, honesty, integrity and hard work."

"Academics first, integrity, service to others, innovation, research, provide opportunities for excellence."

In the face of Penn State's biggest tragedy, these people were remembering that Penn State was raising people for life, raising them for excellence, and that it would emerge from the dark times stronger than ever. And it has. The idea and concept of Penn State is the enduring philosophy that fuels progress.

This book relives all of those golden moments: the wins and the speeches, the downtown hangouts and favorite traditions. But it digs deeper—into the 'why' of Penn State that beats in each of our hearts. Because the integrity, service to others and success with honor has crafted Penn State into a university and a brand like no other, and bonded all of us into an association that's like nothing else on earth. And this is the story of 'why' that happened.

> " *In the face of Penn State's biggest tragedy, these stakeholders were remembering that Penn State was raising people for life, raising them for excellence, and that it would emerge from the dark times stronger than ever.* "

Penn State alumnus Greg Woodman is an Instructor of Entrepreneurial Leadership at Penn State University and CEO of Affinity Connection that is based, of course, in Happy Valley—the greatest place on earth to live, work and play. Affinity Connection, in name and mission, promotes human connectedness and purpose. Greg learned the meaning of connection to an affinity group the first day he tailgated at Penn State. He turned that memory into a National Tailgate Champion T-Shirt and sold the shirts from tailgate to tailgate. Greg can be reached at Greg@ AffinityConnection.com.

Previous page: Old Main photo courtesy of Sophie Kandler

2

The '80s at
Penn State

In 1980:

President Carter's failure to resolve the Iran hostage crisis contributes to Ronald Reagan's win in the November 1980 election.

The football team finishes the season ranked 8th in the AP poll, garnering an invite to Fiesta Bowl X in Tempe, Arizona, winning 31-19.

Student football tickets cost $4 each and are so valuable that they're locked in the university's vault before they go on sale.

Beaver Stadium was renovated in 1978 and now seats 76,639, up from 60,000.

Penn State's Lady Lions gymnastic team defeats Utah to bring home the national title. Throughout the '80s, fans would pack Rec Hall to watch them compete.

Alternate plans are made for Phi Psi 500, Penn State's legendary road race, including a new route and a limit of 1,800 participants.

1980 THON raises more than $86,000.

A rash of fires cause destruction on campus and downtown. A dorm room in McElwain Hall was gutted, and three students escaped serious injury. Delta Tau Delta house was totally destroyed and a midnight blaze at the Garden Theatre building at 114 S. Allen gutted apartments, leaving 20 residents homeless. Arson was suspected.

In July, Congress reinstates draft registration for eligible men aged 19 and 20. The draft had been abolished in 1974, close to the end of the Vietnam War.

In December, John Lennon is shot five times in front of his apartment. On campus, Eisenhower Chapel overflows with students showing up for a candlelight memorial service.

Top movies for 1980 included "Caddyshack," "The Empire Strikes Back," "The Blues Brothers," "The Blue Lagoon," "The Shining," "Somewhere in Time," "Urban Cowboy," "The Elephant Man" and "American Gigolo."

Top songs included "Another One Bites the Dust" by Queen, "Celebration" by Kool & The Gang, "Hit Me with Your Best Shot" by Pat Benatar, "All Night Long" by Joe Walsh, "It's Still Rock and Roll to Me" by Billy Joel, "9 to 5" by Dolly Parton, and "Any Way You Want It" by Journey.

Live performers on campus include comedian and activist Dick Gregory, The Talking Heads, Johnny Cash and the Marshall Tucker Band.

Nov. 28, 1981
Penn State 48, Pitt 14

The rivalry spans 127 years, 100 meetings and 22 U.S. presidents, but one Pitt-Penn State game stands above all the rest. The Nittany Lions completed one of the biggest upsets in Penn State's history, and it was less about their rival than how they won. They took on the number one-ranked Pittsburgh Panthers, and even though they found themselves trailing 14-0 after the first quarter, they ended up winning 48-14.

Some fans might have stopped watching at that point, after all, Penn State wasn't supposed to rally over Pitt, who was riding a 17-game winning streak, and poised for the national championship. But then, something happened. The game turned on the first play of the second quarter when Penn State defensive back Roger Jackson intercepted a Marino pass from the Penn State 31 in the end zone. And just like that, the great Pitt team crumbled. There would be three more Marino interceptions, three lost Pitt fumbles ... and a total of 48 unanswered Penn State points.

The 1980s Were the Golden Era of Penn State Football

BY JOHN PATISHNOCK

Let's say something up front.

Penn State football has been wildly successful nearly from the start of its program. There were down years, and average stretches—common to every team—but success defines Penn State football in nearly every single era. Throughout the 1950s and 1960s, especially, the Nittany Lions gradually built themselves into a regional power, also impressing on the national scene when given the opportunity.

But the 1980s is the decade when the Nittany Lions roared onto the national scene in a mainstream way.

Here's a rundown of what every Nittany Lion fan should know about the 1980s, a decade that further cemented Penn State's excellence on the gridiron.

1980-81

Penn State won 10-plus games five times in the 1980s, including in three straight seasons at the beginning of the decade. The Nittany Lions started the decade 20-4, including two wins in the Fiesta Bowl, defeating Ohio State and USC. Special mention should be made for how Penn State played a major role in transforming the Fiesta Bowl from a fringe game into one of the more popular and relevant bowls in college football. From 1977-86, the Nittany Lions played in the contest four times, winning all four, culminating in the epic clash with Miami.

As Penn State rose to even more national prominence, the Fiesta Bowl enjoyed a similar trajectory, as fans traveled well, gave the bowl good ratings, and the presence of Paterno also led to increased interest and media coverage. To this day, Penn State still remains undefeated in the bowl at 7-0, after defeating Washington to cap the 2017 season.

Also, any conversation about these seasons deserves to include the 1981 upset of No. 1 Pitt on the road. After falling behind 14-0, Blackledge and Co. stormed back for a 48-14 victory. You can read about the game on The New York Times' website, which includes an all-time memorable quote from Paterno.

When asked about his team winning as an underdog, he

PENN STATE'S WHY

The '80s was the decade when the Nittany Lions were no longer thought of as "only" an eastern power or a program solely worthy of consideration after midwestern and southern schools. They received top billing in the national polls and launched into living rooms across the country with national television appearances and extended media coverage.

replied, "I didn't think this was an upset. Who says so?"

Seriously, can't you just imagine Paterno, squinting through his glasses and offering an incredulous look to the question? It almost makes you laugh.

Also, in the article, Blackledge said, "This was the best game of my life," as he finished 12-for-23 for 262 yards, two passing touchdowns, and one rushing touchdown. As a sophomore, he out-dueled Panther quarterback and NFL Hall-of-Famer Dan Marino.

There was plenty of talent on these teams, and even an expectation that 1981 would lead to a national title, but losses to Miami and Alabama sidetracked the Nittany Lions, who then finished by handling Notre Dame (24-21), upending Pitt, and beating the Trojans (26-10) in the Fiesta Bowl.

Penn State handily beat USC. The Trojans had aspirations to play in the Rose Bowl that season, though those hopes vanished with two losses themselves in the regular season. Plus, the Nittany Lions were motivated to shut down Heisman Trophy recipient Marcus Allen, who started for USC. That happened, as Penn State's Curt Warner out-rushed Allen 145-85. It was Allen's lowest performance of the season and came in his last collegiate game.

After the '81 season, offensive lineman Mike Munchak declared for the NFL Draft and began a career that would end in Canton, Ohio, with him in the NFL Hall of Fame. He's one of six Nittany Lions enshrined in Canton and the lone player who played at State in the '80s.

1982

When Paterno visited Todd Blackledge's family in Ohio in the recruiting process, Paterno told the young signal-caller that he thought Blackledge could be the quarterback to lead Penn State to a national title. As outlined in Jordan Hyman's book, "Game of My Life," Blackledge recalled the story, saying, "And four years after that, we did exactly that."

Penn State finished the previous season with three impressive wins against Notre Dame, Pitt (ranked No. 1 at the time), and USC in the Fiesta Bowl. The clear goal for '82 was to be the top team in the country at the end of the season, and for the most part, the Nittany Lions aptly played that role during the year. The lone blemish was a 42-21 setback to Alabama in the Tuscaloosa heat in early October, after which Penn State rolled to six consecutive victories in mostly convincing fashion. The lone single-digit victory during that stretch was a 19-10 victory over the fifth-ranked Panthers.

Penn State was ranked second leading into the traditional Friday-after-Thanksgiving clash with Pitt, which led the Nittany Lions to New Orleans for a Sugar Bowl matchup with top-ranked Georgia and Heisman Trophy winner Herschel Walker.

The setting and game were the same as the 1979 Sugar Bowl (to cap the '78 season), where Alabama and Bear Bryant denied Paterno and the Nittany Lions a national title with a late goal-line stand. In the years following, Paterno acknowledged that the game stayed with him, maybe even haunted him in some ways, especially since he looked up to Bryant.

While the opponent differed this time, the stakes were the same: beat an SEC opponent and return to Happy Valley with the program's first national title.

Paterno and Co. delivered, thanks to a defense that stymied Walker, a clutch offense that included running back Curt Warner, who left school as Penn State's all-time leading rusher, and a fly route that still has fans remembering an undersized receiver who first came to Penn State as a walk-on.

The Nittany Lions took control early, taking a 20-3 lead over Georgia before the Bulldogs, who won the national title two years earlier, closed the gap to 20-17. Then early in the fourth quarter, Blackledge launched an aerial that Gregg Garrity caught in midair before falling in the end zone for the eventual winning margin.

Garrity's father played at Penn State, and actually was Paterno's first recruit when he was an assistant. The younger Garrity toured University Park during what could loosely be called a recruiting visit, when Paterno said he could walk on. Essentially, he'd be treated the same as everyone on scholarship, though no free ride. And if it turned out Garrity proved he could play at the Division I level, he'd earn the scholarship later on.

That happened, and his grab in the Sugar Bowl still serves as one of the most iconic images in Penn State football history. He landed on the cover of *Sports Illustrated*, with the caption "No. 1 At Last," with the text serving as a reminder that Penn State had been plenty good for a while.

This wasn't the case of an up-and-coming program breaking through. Penn State had broken through decades earlier, though because of all the intricacies that make college football wonderful, weird, and even sometimes confusing—remember, Paterno led his teams to five unbeaten, untied seasons with two national titles to show for it—the Nittany Lions hadn't previously been recognized as national champions.

Now, that happened, and in a big-time moment that was befitting such a powerful program.

Letterman Bill Contz lays out a convincing argument that this squad is one of the best college football teams ever, especially when factoring in the last three games from the '81 season, in his book, "When the Lions Roared." It's a compelling case, and one that takes into account that teams of that era played fewer games than now. And of course, Penn State was an independent with no conference championship game to play in before the bowl season.

After the victory in the Sugar Bowl that finally clinched the program's first national title, Paterno said, "I kind of felt it would happen. I hope nobody doubts we're No. 1 after today. ... This is the best football team I've ever had."

Both Blackledge (sixth) and Warner (10th) placed in the Top 10 for the Heisman Trophy, splitting votes among regional voters and finishing behind Walker. We think it's safe to assume both Blackledge and Warner would take that trade-off every time around. Two days after the victory, the duo accompanied Paterno on a private jet to New York for an appearance on Good Morning America.

"It was a whole different feel to Joe that day," Blackledge told Frank Fitzpatrick in Pride of the Lions. "It was more personable, friendly, relaxed. I think both Curt and I got to see a side of him we had never seen before."

Call it relief, satisfaction, joy, or a combination of all three. Either way, Paterno and the Nittany Lions were finally national champions, and the

Golden Era of Penn State football was just getting started.

1983-84

What makes this decade both successful and also a little atypical is that this two-year stretch represented one of the two down periods for Penn State. Paterno and the Nittany Lions finished 14-9, though they ended the '83 campaign with a win in the Aloha Bowl over Washington in the program's lone appearance in the island contest.

1985

Penn State's third most successful season of the decade, the 1985 squad stands as one of the program's more memorable and perhaps also overlooked teams of the last half-century. The Nittany Lions didn't score more than 30 points in a game until the season's ninth contest, when the team eclipsed that mark three straight times to end the regular season at 11-0 by beating Cincinnati, Notre Dame, and Pitt in succession. Only once in the team's first eight victories did Penn State win by double digits (West Virginia 27-0), and the other level victories all came by one score or less, including three separate two-point victories.

Many of the stars from the '86 championship were on this team, which ended the season with its only loss to Oklahoma in the Orange Bowl, in the national title game.

1986

Paterno had long admired the Greek classics. In part, perhaps in large part, by his own acknowledgment, that's what interested him in college football in the first place. Two teams entering the field of play. The bands playing. Fans cheering. A sense of competition and leaving it all out on the field. Paterno saw it as a modern-day retelling of gladiators battling in the Roman Colosseum.

Well, the 1987 Fiesta Bowl offered all that, and then some. Most fans know the storylines that elevated the game and tran-

scended it from a sports story to a national story: Miami's players wearing Army fatigues upon arriving in Arizona, walking out of a pregame meal, and the overall boldness of a Miami program juxtaposed against Penn State and Joe Paterno, whom many saw more as an educator than a coach. Or at the very least, both.

Penn State alumnus and college football author Michael Weinreb's in-depth article, "The Night College Football Went to Hell," offers a good summary. We pick up the story during the pre-game streak fry, where both teams were supposed to perform a comedy skit:

So now it was Miami's turn. Jerome Brown stood up and unzipped his sweat suit to reveal his fatigues. "Did the Japanese sit down and eat with Pearl Harbor before they bombed them?" he said. "No. We're outta here."

Out toward their buses went the men in the fatigues, cementing a reputation that Miami still cannot shake, 14 years after Brown's death in a car accident. Bauer (Trey Bauer, Penn State linebacker) started to laugh. Bruno (John Bruno, Penn State punter) stood up, made some crack about Miami having to leave so the players could begin filming "Rambo III," and then delivered a quote that Penn State football fans still evoke, 14 years after Bruno's death from melanoma:

"Excuse me," he said. "But didn't the Japanese lose the war?

In "Game of My Life," linebacker Shane Conlan offered an apt comparison between the Hurricanes' ability to act so brashly and Paterno's approach:

1980: The 1980s Were the Golden Era of Penn State Football

"I know for a fact that no Joe Paterno-coached team would have ever walked out of there. They'd be on the next plane ride home if they tried to pull that. So from that sense it was good. And it was good in the media. They pitted good versus evil, which was kind of cool."

Also leading up to the game, *Sports Illustrated* named Paterno "Sportsman of the Year" at a time when the magazine was the leading authority in sports journalism. In some ways, it's difficult to understand the importance of this honor in today's digital age. Paterno was the first college football coach to receive the honor (and still the only one). A complimentary column from Rick Reilly, back when he was one of the top columnists in the country, flattered Paterno and his program, extolling the virtues of Penn State's commitment to the true ideal of the student-athlete.

Coming off a near title the previous year, there was laser focus on getting back to the national title game. Unlike '82, the Nittany Lions didn't suffer a loss the entire year, nor did the Miami Hurricanes, setting up a made-for-TV clash on Jan. 2, 1987.

Offensively, the Nittany Lions were balanced, methodical at times, and always clutch. There was athleticism, to be sure, with guys like running back D.J. Dozier, who finished eighth in the Heisman Trophy voting that season. Dozier also had plenty of toughness, a quality shared by quarterback John Shaffer, who knotted the Fiesta Bowl at 7-7 right before halftime with a touchdown scramble.

Defensively, Penn State cemented its legacy as Linebacker U throughout the '80s, and especially this year. Conlan personified this position as well as anyone. He wasn't recruited by anyone other than Penn State, and yet, he rose as a leader seemingly through sheer will, grit, and determination. Conlan played like he was almost personally offended that the opposition thought they could score, dared to even try to score.

Against the Hurricanes, he finished with eight tackles and picked off two passes. The second was especially memorable, as he dropped back in coverage and picked off Heisman Trophy winner Vinny Testaverde—who threw five picks in the Fiesta Bowl—in the fourth quarter and nearly scored. His return set up Dozier's late game-winning score.

Just like Garrity, Dozier provided an iconic image, as he spun off tackled, dashed into the end zone, and immediately knelt to pray.

After Miami converted a clutch fourth down on its last drive, Testaverde marched the Canes down the field, connecting a few times with Michael Irvin—who was rocked early in the contest by safety Ray Isom—only to throw his final pick. With only seconds remaining and Miami needing a touchdown in the waning seconds, linebacker Pete Giftopoulos intercepted a pass near the goal-line and returned it for a few yards before wisely going down to secure Penn State's second national title.

1980s BY THE NUMBERS

70 million
TV audience for the 1987 Fiesta Bowl, still the most-watched college football game of all time

1986
Year that JoePaterno was named *Sports Illustrated* Sportsman of the Year; Paterno was the first and remains the only college football coach to receive the honor

220
Career wins for Paterno at end of 1989 season

89
WINS

10
Times ranked in the **AP preseason poll**

6
Times ranked in the **final AP poll**

6
Different bowl games played in (Fiesta, Sugar, Aloha, Orange, Citrus, Holiday)

6
Bowl wins
('80, '81, '82, '83, '86, '89)

5
Seasons with **at least 10 wins** ('80, '81, '82, '85, '86)

3
Appearances in the **Fiesta Bowl** ('80, '81, '86)

3
Heisman Trophy finalists (Todd Blackledge '82, Curt Warner '82, Blair Thomas '89)

2
National championships ('82, '86)

Two national title games, and twice the defense shut down a Heisman winner. Pretty impressive, and the second feat came in front of what remains to this day, the largest-ever audience to watch a college football game on TV: 70 million people.

After the 1986 season and 1987 Fiesta Bowl, there would never be any doubt again about Penn State's true place as one of the most prestigious college football programs in the country.

1987-89

Penn State stumbled again toward the end of the '80s, at least by its own standards, finishing 21-13-1 in the last three seasons, including missing a bowl during a rare losing season in 1988 (5-6). The Nittany Lions did close out the decade successfully, defeating future Heisman Trophy winner Ty Detmer and BYU in the Holiday Bowl, 50-39, in one of the more entertaining games of the decade, and perhaps in all of Paterno's tenure as coach.

Individually, one of the bright spots for the program occurred in 1989, when Blair Thomas was a Heisman Trophy finalist, finishing in a tie for 10th with Notre Dame receiver Raghib "Rocket" Ismail.

Thomas graduated from Penn State with 3,301 rushing yards, which was second-best ever in program history at the time to Curt Warner. Thomas' career yardage is still good for fifth, with future Nittany Lions Evan Royster, Saquon Barkley, and Tony Hunt surpassing him.

YEAR	RECORD	FINAL AP RANKING	BOWL
1980	10-2	8	Fiesta (W)
1981	10-2	3	Fiesta (W)
1982	11-1	1	Sugar (W)
1983	8-4-1	not ranked	Aloha (W)
1984	6-5	not ranked	no bowl
1985	11-1	3	Orange (L)
1986	12-0	1	Fiesta (W)
1987	8-4	not ranked	Citrus (L)
1988	5-6	not ranked	no bowl
1989	8-3-1	15	Holiday (W)

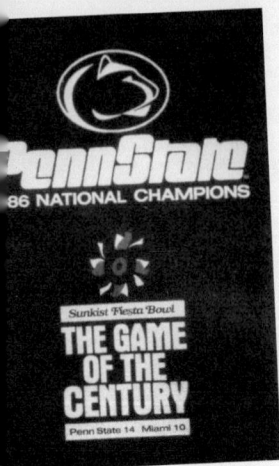

The Drive to Excellence

Reprinted from 1986 Football Preview

1980

The Lions finish the season 10-2 as they defeat Ohio State in the Fiesta Bowl.

1981

Penn State finishes 9-2 in the regular season, including a 48-14 rout of unbeaten Pitt in the last game of the season.

1982

Lions defeat USC in the Fiesta Bowl. Curt Warner outrushes Heisman Trophy winner Marcus Allen in that game.

Lions finish 10-1 in regular season and gained a berth in the Sugar Bowl against unbeaten and top-ranked Georgia. The season was highlighted by an exciting 27-24 comeback win over Nebraska at Beaver Stadium.

1983

Penn State wins its first national championship by defeating Georgia 27-23. The key play of the game occurred early in the fourth quarter when quarterback Todd Blackledge lofted a 48-yard touchdown pass to Greg Garrity. For the second year in a row, Warner outrushed a Heisman Trophy winner, Herschel Walker. This was the first team ever to win a national championship that gained more passing yards than rushing yards.

1984

Penn State established a Paterno Library Endowment Fund to which Paterno donates $20,000.

1985

Behind a solid defense and some breaks, the Lions finish 11-0 on the season.

1986

Penn State defeated by Oklahoma 25-10 in the Orange Bowl. Paterno donates $100,000 to the Paterno Library Endowment Fund and $50,000 for minority student scholarships.

ARTS FEST

By the 1980s, the Central Pennsylvania Festival of the Arts, or as Penn State students called it, Arts Fest, was in its second decade. The popular summer festival brought Happy Valley's biggest fans into downtown State College, where they enjoyed musical performances both downtown and on campus, along with a sidewalk sale and exhibition. The Arts Fest Race, which was started in 1976 which was started by Marie Doll as American distance running was in its heyday, began as a 10-mile race and was modified to a 10k by the end of the '80s.

CENTRAL PENNSYLVANIA
FESTIVAL OF THE ARTS 88

Join us for . . .
The 22nd Annual
SUMMER EXPLOSION
OF THE ARTS

Downtown State College
and the campus of
The Pennsylvania
State University

July 6 - 10, 1988

This year the Festival celebrates it's 22nd year of transforming both town and campus into a breathtaking outdoor visual and performing arts EXPLOSION! Come join in the excitement July 6 -10!!

• 370 Juried Sidewalk Artists.
• More than 200 performances.
• Exhibitions in Crafts, Sculpture, Photography and other visual arts.
• A daily roster of Children's Events plus Children's Day July 6.
• All Festival events are free.

Central Pennsylvania Festival of the Arts
P.O. Box 1023
State College, Pennsylvania 16804

Above right: Stolyn Hours playing at Alpha Sig during Arts Fest. *Photo courtesy Sophie Kandler.*

1981

In 1981:

The "New College Diner" changes hands and is renamed "Ye Old College Diner." Grilled stickies remain constant.

Through 1980-81, Penn State had won more major college national championships (nine) in women's sports than any other institution in the nation.

Throughout the decade, approximately nine out of ten Penn State students were residents of the Commonwealth, although virtually every other state in the union and its territories were also represented. New Jersey, New York, and Maryland accounted for the majority of out-of-state students. There were also in residence nearly 2,000 foreign students from 105 nations, mostly at University Park.

Beaver Stadium's maximum capacity increased from 76,639 to 83,770.

Wimpy the Gerbil announces his candidacy for Undergraduate Student Government, finishing second in the election.

Both Ronald Reagan and Pope John Paul II are shot; Egyptian president Anwar Sadat assassinated.

Students wake before dawn to watch the televised fairytale wedding of Prince Charles and Lady Diana Spencer.

Sandra Day O'Connor is the first woman named to the Supreme Court.

Top movies included "Raiders of the Lost Ark," "Endless Love, "The Great Muppet Caper," "Stripes, Reds," "Chariots of Fire," "Nine to Five," and "Time Bandits."

Top songs included "Endless Love" by Lionel Richie, "Bette Davis Eyes" by Kim Carnes, and "Slow Hand" by the Pointer Sisters.

Acid washed jeans started in the 1960s when Californian surfers used chlorine bleach instead of letting their jeans soak up the sun's rays. In the '80s, companies started to use their method, and a trend was born.

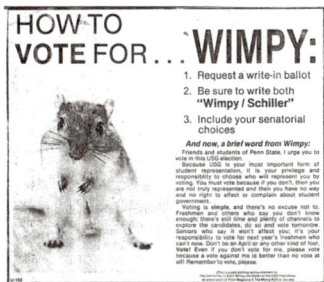

BUBBA did you Bubba today?

Players Who Epitomized Paterno's Grand Experiment

BY JOHN PATISHNOCK

In one way or another, coaches have said that when individuals give themselves over to the team, everyone wins.

At Penn State, that's an interesting dynamic. Recruit the best athletes who are incredibly successful on an individual level and have them fit into a team dynamic. And at the same time, have the players commit themselves to success off the field.

Joe Paterno was quite possibly the best ever to do that. Assistant coaches over the years have said that they were sometimes limited in who they could recruit because Paterno wouldn't accept subpar students or players unwilling to buy into the team concept.

Paterno also once said: "I don't want any hot dogs on my team. If you're a hot dog, you tend to get careless in the clutch."

He and Penn State always recruited student-athletes who truly embodied that term, and the 1980s are certainly no exception. With the benefit of time and perspective, many student-athletes from that period have gone on to become just as successful after college as they were at Penn State. And along the way, their success became Penn State's success, both when they were in school, and now, decades later.

Below, in alphabetical order, are 11 players who helped elevate Penn State onto the national scene on the field and also admirably represented the blue and white off the field.

Todd Blackledge

Todd Blackledge (1980-82)

Originally, Blackledge thought his path to college would land him on the basketball court. But after attending a camp with future NBA stars, he realized the football field offered a better option. Good choice, both for him, and Penn State.

Likable and dependable, Blackledge battled through an injury that held him out his freshman season, and then he replaced Jeff Hostetler as starter early in the 1980 season. He led Penn State in passing for three straight seasons from 1980-82 and his 22 touchdown throws in '82 was a school record at the time. He also graduated with 41 career passing touchdowns, also a school record then. The Kansas City Chiefs selected Blackledge in the first round, and he played five seasons for them and two more with the Pittsburgh Steelers.

With Blackledge as quarter, Paterno opened up the playbook and Blackledge delivered. In leading Penn State to a national title in '82, Blackledge helped the Nittany Lions score more than 30 points five times, total more than 40 points on three occasions, and surpass 50 points twice.

His pass to Greg Garrity on a fly route in the 1983 Sugar Bowl helped provide the winning margin in Penn State's 27-23 victory over Georgia for the national title. He finished 13-of-23 for 228 yards and that score, receiving the game's Miller-Digby Award for most outstanding player.

Blackledge also was named an Academic All-American in 1982 and was inducted into the GTE Academic All-America Hall of Fame in 1997.

Nowadays, Blackledge is familiar even to fans who never saw him play since he serves as one of the top college football analysts for ESPN, regularly calling premiere games each week. For a number of years, he also hosted a popular segment titled, "Taste of the Town," where he'd visit college football's best places to eat. He co-authored a book of the same name, and at Penn State, he showcased the Berkey Creamery, Ye Olde College Diner, The Waffle Shop, and Herwig's Austrian Bistro.

John Bruno (1984-86)

Bruno is one of the more compelling characters for Penn State football, not just in the 1980s but all time.

John Bruno

Talk to the guys on the '86 championship team, and they'll tell you that chances are Penn State doesn't win the 1987 Fiesta Bowl without Bruno. In a contest that turned into a defensive slugfest where field possession took on paramount importance, Bruno continually punted Miami deep in its own territory. There's a convincing argument to be made that he was the game's MVP, but punters never receive such awards, so Bruno had to settle for the admiration of his teammates and coaches.

That a punter has such a storied place in the history of a prominent program speaks to how valuable Bruno was on the field. Off of it, he didn't have nearly as much time as he should have. That's because his life ended tragically early. He died of skin cancer at the age of 27 in 1992.

"He was a great kid and an outstanding person and a delight to be around," Joe Paterno said in a *Daily Collegian* article at the time of Bruno's passing. "He was loved by everyone and he was a fun guy. It's a terrible loss."

Bruno cataloged a successful career, averaging 41.7 yards on 204 career punts for teams that finished a combined 29-6. He especially shined in the Fiesta Bowl, booting nine kicks for an average of 43 yards in his final career game.

The St. Louis Cardinals drafted Bruno in the fifth round of the 1987 NFL Draft. He was waived, though he was briefly with the Pittsburgh Steelers that season during the NFL players' strike.

"He was a different style punter," Tom Bradley said in the *Daily Collegian* article. "One thing about his punting was that he was extremely accurate. He was never concerned with average."

Shane Conlan (1983-86)

If one linebacker physically embodied Linebacker U, Conlan might be it. He looked the part, and the fact that he wasn't highly recruited out of high school makes his story even better. Penn State was the only school to offer him a scholarship. Add in a bunch of talent and toughness, and Conlan was an imposing obstacle for offenses.

Shane Conlan

Conlan provided some of his best plays when they were needed most, evident by his eight tackles and two interceptions in the '87 Fiesta Bowl to clinch the program's second national title. His second pick set up the game-winning touchdown run by D.J. Dozier.

Conlan was a two-time All-American at Penn State (1985-86), becoming the sixth Nittany Lion to ever achieve that impressive recognition. As a team captain, he led Penn State in tackles during the team's national title season in 1986, finishing with 79 total and 63 solo. He left the program with 274 tackles, fourth all-time in program history at the time.

Conlan was selected by the Buffalo Bills with the eighth overall pick in the 1987 NFL Draft, and he enjoyed a successful pro career. He played nine years in the NFL, six with Buffalo and three others with the St. Louis Rams, and played in three Pro Bowls. He also was the defensive rookie of the year with the Bills in '87.

D.J. Dozier (1983-86)

Dozier scored one of the most iconic touchdowns in Penn State history, dashing into the end zone from seven yards out for the winning score in the Nittany Lions' 14-10 win in the 1987 Fiesta Bowl that clinched the team's second national title.

More so than any one play, however, Dozier's time at Penn State is best described as consistent production. In his four years, he never rushed for less than 691 yards in a season—actually rushing for a career-high 1,002 yards during his freshman year in '83. Dozier left Penn State second on the all-time list with 3,227 career rushing yards and still ranks seventh all-time.

D.J. Dozier

A two-sport star, Dozier was drafted in the first round of the 1987 NFL Draft by Minnesota. He played five years in the league, scoring seven touchdowns. After leaving the NFL following the 1991 season with Detroit, he appeared in 25 games for the New York Mets in 1992. In 47 at-bats, he finished with nine hits and four runs scored, also smacking two doubles.

Gregg Garrity (1979-82)

Gregg Garrity

Garrity wanted to play for Penn State. He must've, because he started his career with the Nittany Lions as a walk-on, with Paterno telling him he would eventually earn a scholarship if he proved he could play at the Division I level. He did, continuing a family tradition. Garrity's father also played for the Nittany Lions and was Paterno's first recruit as an assistant.

Garrity battled his way up the depth chart, playing a key role as an undersized but dependable receiver for Blackledge. The two connected on what's still one of the most iconic plays in Penn State history—a fly route that turned into a touchdown in the '83 Sugar Bowl, providing the winning margin for the program's first national title in a 27-23 victory over Georgia. Garrity still receives copies of the *Sports Illustrated* that captured his score, and once joked that he thought he'd signed every available copy by now.

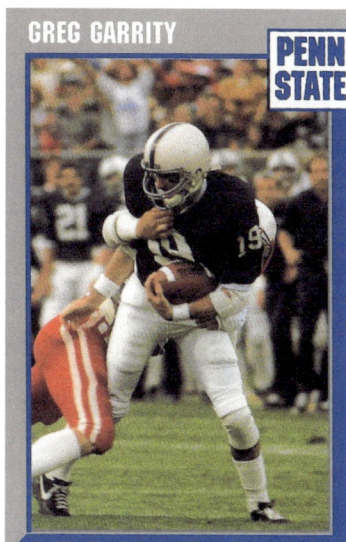

Kenny Jackson

Kenny Jackson (1980-83)

Jackson was the featured receiver for the Nittany Lions in the early '80s, catching two passes in the 1981 upset over No. 1 Pitt and helping fuel the offense during the '82 championship season. He finished that year with 41 catches for 697 yards and seven touchdowns, impressive numbers for a traditionally run-heavy offense.

One reason why Paterno finally relented and started to turn the offense loose is the influx of offensive firepower that the program assembled in the '80s, and Jackson was as big a reason for the change in philosophy as any other teammates. Jackson still ranks ninth all-time at Penn State with 2,006 receiving yards, and his 25 receiving touchdowns are second-best ever for the Nittany Lions. He also added two rushing scores in his collegiate career.

The Philadelphia Eagles drafted Jackson with the fourth overall pick in the 1984 NFL Draft. He played eight years in the league (seven with the Eagles, one with the Houston Oilers), totaling 126 catches for 2,170 yards.

Mike Munchak (1978-79, 81)

Upon arriving at Penn State, coaches continually shifted Munchak along both the offensive and defensive lines. Eventually, he ended up at offensive guard, and it's difficult to imagine the situation working out better for Munchak, a native of Scranton, Pennsylvania, who's now enshrined in the NFL Hall of Fame in Canton, Ohio.

Munchak helped lead the way for the Nittany Lions and Curt Warner in their win over USC in the 1982 Fiesta Bowl. The 26-10 victory capped off an impressive end to the 1981 season—Penn State beat Notre Dame, No. 1-ranked Pitt, and the Trojans—catapulting the Nittany Lions into the '82 championship season. Munchak had a year of eligibility remaining and could have returned since he redshirted a previous year due to an injury, but he felt a sense of loyalty to his recruiting class.

Mike Munchak

In Jordan Hyman's book, *Game of My Life*, Munchak talked about watching Penn State win the national title in '82: "I would have loved to have been there. I would be lying to say I wouldn't have wanted to win it or been there for that. … But that was their time and that was for them, and I felt like I was still part of it."

After being selected eighth overall in the 1982 NFL Draft

by the Houston Oilers, Munchak embarked on a legendary career. His No. 63 was retired by the Oilers after making first- or second-team All-Pro 10 times and being elected to the Pro Bowl nine times. He was then voted into the NFL Hall of Fame with the Class of 2001.

Currently, Munchak is the offensive line coach for the Denver Broncos, continuing his lifelong love affair with football, one buoyed by his time at Penn State.

Mark Robinson (1981-83)

Robinson starred as a free safety, earning All-American honors during his junior year and playing a critical role during Penn State's national title season of 1982. A story from *The Daily Collegian* in '83 describes Robinson's relentless energy on the field.

Mark Robinson

"Mark Robinson went in hard—like he always does," a reporter wrote in describing a play that Robinson was injured in during his senior year as he went after Alabama's quarterback. The same article mentioned that Robinson was often compared to all-time Penn State legend Jack Ham, who's in both the College Football and NFL Hall of Fame, for his tackling prowess.

Robinson also authored two of the longest plays in program history: a 92-yard punt return against Rutgers in 1982 and a 91-yard interception return against No. 1 Pitt in 1981. He scored a touchdown on each play.

Robinson has stayed connected to the game over the years. For 21 seasons, he served as the color analyst for South Florida, before stepping down in 2018 to spend more time with his family.

John Shaffer (1983-86)

Fans who watched Penn State throughout the '80s are familiar with John Shaffer's place in the history of Penn State football. Of course, they are. More recent graduates might've heard the name once or twice. It sounds familiar, like a friend of a friend who you met one time.

Shaffer quarterbacked Penn State to the program's second national title in 1986, including a win over Miami in the '87 Fiesta Bowl. In other words, Shaffer is a Penn State legend. One of the best descriptions of Shaffer you'll hear appears in Penn State alumnus and college football author Michael Weinreb's article ti-

John Shaffer

tled, *The night college football went to hell*, which is a compelling summary of the '87 Fiesta Bowl:

"When he graduated from Penn State as an academic All-American in the spring of 1987, he had a national championship ring and a reputation as a solid citizen who had no legitimate shot of making it in the National Football League. He went to training camp with the Dallas Cowboys as an undrafted free agent. By the end of August, he did something that many football players could never muster the courage to do: He asked to be cut. He had a degree in finance, with an internship waiting on Wall Street. He had another life to start."

That type of confidence speaks to how Shaffer seemingly was never rattled on the field, losing only one game in his Penn State career: the 1985 national championship in the Orange Bowl. He knew he was, and perhaps more than anything, Shaffer was (and is) a winner. Going back to the seventh grade, Shaffer amassed an extraordinary record of 66-1 as a starting quarterback.

And his last victory ever will forever stand as perhaps the most memorable win in the history of Penn State football.

Blair Thomas (1985-89)

Blair Thomas

Thomas was one of Penn State's bright spots toward the end of the decade, running for a combined 2,756 yards in '87 and '89. The standout back was selected by the Jets with the second overall pick in the NFL Draft. In seven seasons, he rushed for more than 2,200 yards and seven touchdowns for four teams.

At Penn State, he still ranks fifth all-time with 3,301 yards and left the program second on the list, trailing only fellow Nittany Lion great Curt Warner. Thomas' decision to return in 1989 helped the Nittany Lions rebound from a rare losing season in '88, which he missed because of a knee injury. Thomas also contributed for the '86 championship team, rushing for 504 yards and scoring five touchdowns in his sophomore campaign.

For his Penn State career, Thomas scored 23 touchdowns (21 rush, 2 receiving), and also caught 48 passes for 477 yards. He was the first Penn State running back to total two seasons with at least 1,300 rushing yards, and he was chosen for the All-American second-team as a senior.

1981: Players Who Epitomized Paterno's Grand Experiment

Thomas sometimes gets overlooked in the long line of great Penn State running backs, partly because the teams he was on as an upperclassman struggled late in the decade. However, he firmly belongs on the list, and his willingness to return for his senior season helped Penn State start to turn things around as they entered the 1990s.

Curt Warner (1979-82)

"Selfless" is one of the first words that comes to mind when thinking about Curt Warner. Warner was slowed down by injuries, at times, during his Penn State career, and he still left the program as the Nittany Lions' all-time leading rusher with 3,398 yards. Perhaps more than anything else, that speaks to how resilient and dedicated Warner was at Penn State.

Curt Warner

Warner was a legitimate Heisman Trophy candidate entering the 1982 season, though because of a variety of factors—a revamped offensive line and more emphasis on the passing game, for example—he struggled through the first month of the season. More attention was paid to Blackledge, who in addition to being Warner's roommate, called Warner his best friend and the best player he ever played with, either in college or the NFL.

In Bill Contz's book, *When the Lion Roared*, which details the '82 season, Todd Blackledge shared insight into why "selfless" is a perfect description for Warner, who rebounded to score 13 touchdowns that season and still finish in the top 10 in Heisman voting:

"He was a tremendous leader in the weight room, on the field, and in the locker room. He was in terrific shape when the season started, but unfortunately for him, our running game was behind our passing game when September rolled around."

Warner, who rushed for 117 yards and scored two touchdowns in the '83 Sugar Bowl, earned plenty more success and accolades after his Nittany Lion career ended. He was a three-time Pro Bowler with the Seattle Seahawks in the NFL, helping the team advance to the AFC Championship during his rookie season. Seattle chose Warner with the third overall pick, with the Penn State great going after future Hall of Famers John Elway and Eric Dickerson.

1982

In 1982:

The Nittany Lions cap off the 1981 season with a January 1982 26-10 Fiesta Bowl victory over Southern California. Both Joe Paterno and Southern Cal coach John Robinson are said to be in the running to coach the New England Patriots. Both later turn down the job. After the bowl game, JoePa steps down as athletic director to spend more time coaching and more time with his family.

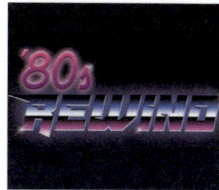

"E.T." hits theatres and quickly became the highest-grossing movie of its time.

Tuition is raised 12 percent to $1,848 per year for in-state residents.

By 1982, one in every thousand college graduates in the United States had earned his or her degree from The Pennsylvania State University.

This is a year for headlines—the Tylenol killer, the first artificial heart, the debut of Diet Coke, the introduction of the Timex-Sinclair 12 ounce computer. But this year will be memorable for Penn Staters as the season when Penn State would go on to beat top-ranked Georgia in the 1983 Sugar Bowl.

Former president Jimmy Carter visits University Park to attend a Barbara Mandel concert. *The Collegian* runs a photo of the singer leaning over for a kiss from the leader, saying that he calls her an 'old friend.'

Princess Grace of Monaco dies in a car accident.

The Vietnam Wall Memorial opens to visitors in Washington, D.C. *The Collegian* reports first time visitor, veteran Dennis D'Andrea saying, "They got it right. They got it just right. They didn't glorify it."

The Israeli-Pakistan conflict continues, with Ronald Reagan proposing self rule for the West Bank and Gaza, but under Jordanian sovereignty.

Top movies this year included "E.T. the Extra-Terrestrial," "Rocky III," "Tron," "Annie," "Poltergeist," "The Dark Crystal," "Blade Runner," and "Star Trek II: The Wrath of Khan."

Top songs included "Billie Jean" by Michael Jackson, "Heat of the Moment" by Asia, "Empty Garden" by Elton John, "Abracadabra" by Steve Miller Band, "Eye of the Tiger" by Survivor, and "I Ran" by A Flock Of Seagulls.

PENN STATE'S *WHY*

Penn State's win over Nebraska remains one of the most memorable nights in Penn State history, and it cast its magic over the remaining season, setting Penn State up for its historic first National Championship.

Philippians 4:13 September 25, 1982, Lions 27, Huskers 24

Reprinted from 1982 National Championship Collector's Edition

UNIVERSITY PARK - Evening was approaching and darkness had already descended upon Beaver Stadium.

Nebraska had just completed its second consecutive 80-yard scoring drive when quarterback Turner Gill dove into the Penn State end zone for a touchdown. The Cornhuskers, down twice by as many as 14, now led for the first time, 24-21.

The Nittany Lions only had the final 78 seconds of the fourth quarter to come back for one of their greatest wins ever.

They did. Here's how:

One minute, 18 seconds left—Nebraska placekicker Kevin Seibel kicks off deep into the Penn State end zone. The kick is not run out and no time expires. It looks as if the Nittany Lions are going to start the drive on their own 20-yard line.

But Dave Ridder, a defensive end when not on the Husker special teams, makes the mistake of pushing a Penn State player to the ground after the whistle has blown. A 15-yard personal foul moves the ball to the Penn State 35.

"The penalty helped," Joe Paterno said. "Anytime you start at your 35, it helps."

1:18 - Already 18 of 31 for 235 yards with two touchdown passes, quarterback Todd Blackledge must somehow pull his team together and lead it downfield once again.

"I wasn't nervous and I wasn't worried," Blackledge said. "I didn't know if we could take it all the way for a touchdown, but I knew we could get in field-goal range.

"I just reminded everybody in the huddle that we practiced this [two-minute offense] every day. We had to keep our poise, not get rattled and do it."

> *"I just reminded everybody in the huddle that we practiced this [two-minute offense] every day. We had to keep our poise, not get rattled and do it."*

On first-and-10 at the Lions' 35, Blackledge drops back to pass. Penn State goes with three wide-outs—Kenny Jackson, Gregg Garrity and Kevin Baugh—leaving Skeeter Nichols, who was subbing for Curt Warner (out with cramps) as the lone setback.

The first of two plays called in the Lion huddle, a screen pass from Blackledge to Nichols, is good for 16 yards.

1:02 - On a first-and-10 at the Nebraska 49, Blackledge throws an incomplete pass in Baugh's direction, stopping the clock.

:57 - Blackledge completes another 16-yard pass, this time to Jackson, who catches the ball and quickly puts his feet down before running out of bounds. It's the fourth catch of the day for Jackson, whose 18-yard TD catch in the third quarter had given Penn State a 21-7 cushion.

:52 - Another first down, this time at the Nebraska 33. Blackledge thought he could catch Nebraska off-guard and on the only play he called off the drive, sent fullback Jon Williams on a draw. A one-yard loss.

"The fans were probably grumbling at the coaches," Blackledge said, "but it was my decision."

:42 - Second down. Blackledge throws deep to Garrity, who has already caught five passes (six if you count one of the two touchdowns called back against the Lions in the first quarter).

The pass is incomplete as Blackledge throws the pass away, safely over the end line.

:36 - Third down, still 11 yards from a first down to the Nebraska 23. Sure that Penn State won't call another draw, the Cornhuskers rush only three men and blanket the secondary with backs and linebackers. They're right, no draw, just another incomplete pass, this one intended for Nichols.

:32 - Fourth-and-11 at the Nebraska 34. "The only time I thought about a tie was when it was fourth-and-11," Paterno later admitted.

A tie would have meant a field goal attempt from 51 yards and freshman Massimo Manca had already missed field goals from 50, 47 and 33 yards in a shaky first half.

Harry Hamilton (17) and state were off to a flying 14-0 start but Gill (12) stood firm.

At halftime, the coaches had decided to let sophomore Nick Gancitano kick any field goals the Lions might try in the second half. But Gancitano had yet to attempt a field goal in his college career and this wasn't the time for his first one.

So Penn State went for it. Blackledge hit Jackson on a curl pattern over the middle for 11 yards. Although Paterno thought "he had that baby by a good two yards," it takes a measurement to confirm that the Lions had their third first down of the drive.

"Once we hit the fourth-and-11 pass to Kenny, I knew we had it," Blackledge said matter-of-factly.

:27 - First-and-10 at the Nebraska 23. It is now standing room only on the sidelines. Many of the record 85,304 who came to see the first game played under the lights in Beaver Stadium were now creating a human fence around the playing field.

Blackledge didn't even notice. "Personally, I just remained calm and kept repeating a Biblical verse in my mind: 'I can do all things through Christ who strengthens me,'" said Blackledge, repeating a slightly altered Philippians 4:13. "That allowed me to stay calm and get the job done."

Blackledge goes back to pass, and as has been the case throughout the day, has plenty of time. The Huskers, with eight men playing defense, have all Lion receivers covered, forcing Blackledge to run out of bounds after gaining six yards. The clock stops.

:13 - Second-and-four at the Nebraska 17. A short out pass to tight end Mike McCloskey is called. It is up to McCloskey as to how deep he will run the pattern. Therefore, it is up to Blackledge to adjust, and he does, hitting McCloskey for a 15-yard gain.

McCloskey catches the ball right before going out of bounds, or does he?

"The ref said I was in," McCloskey calmly explained after the game. "I saw some Nebraska players and they looked pretty confident that I was out. I was worried, but the ref came over and made the call.

"For a second I thought I was out, but it's in the record books now, right?"

:09 - On first-and-goal from the two, Penn State comes out with its foal-like offense of three running backs and two tight ends—McCloskey and junior Kirk Bowman, whose first career reception went for a touchdown in the first quarter.

Nicknamed "Stonehands" because he had dropped a pass the previous week against the Rutgers, Bowman played seven positions in three years. After the next play, Penn State history would record him as a tight end.

1982: Philippians 4:13. September 25, 1982, Lions 27, Huskers 24

The Lions call for a pass with Blackledge faking to the tailback. McCloskey, who lines up at tight end on the left side, is the primary receiver, but he is tied up at the line of scrimmage.

"We only have two guys going out on that pattern, so if one guy is covered, I automatically look to the other tight end dragging across," Blackledge explained.

That leaves just Bowman, who has lined up on the right and is cutting across the middle at the back of the end zone.

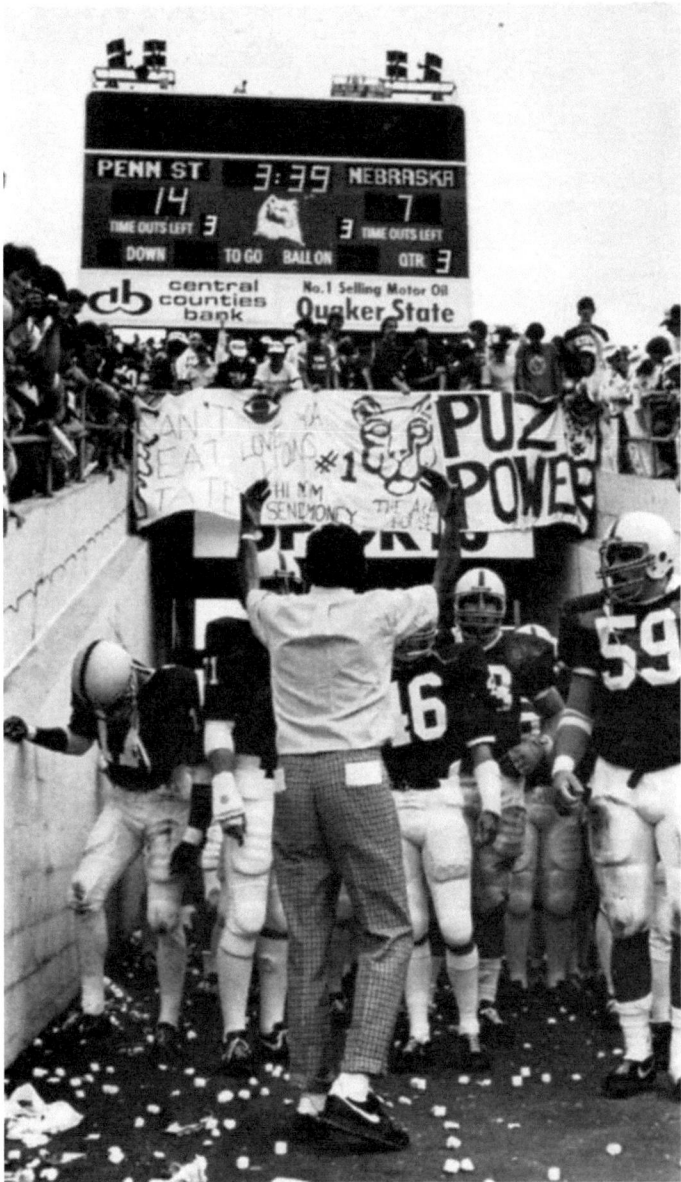

All rise for Paterno to start the second half.

Bowman catch sealed.

> I was hoping, Blackledge said, I didn't see the ball shoot out from underneath him or anything. I was just making sure Kirk had it. But as soon as I saw the guy's arms go up, I was delirious.

"I was just supposed to get off the ball and find an open spot behind the linebacker," Bowman said. "I gave the defensive end a counter step, faking my head like I was going to go to the [right] flat and he took it.

"I was thinking Todd would throw it to Mike, and I just got open and turned around and started waving my arms and yelling."

Blackledge sees him. He throws the ball. The pass travels slowly and a bit short. "I was coaxing the ball. I was saying, 'Come on.' The linebacker just about tipped it," Bowman said.

Then "Stonehands" dives, cradling the ball six inches from the ground. "I was just concerned the officials weren't going to call it," Bowman said. "I just got up as quick as I could and showed them the ball and said: 'I caught it.'"

"I was hoping," Blackledge said, "I didn't see the ball shoot out from underneath him or anything. I was just making sure Kirk had it. But as soon as I saw the guy's arms go up, I was delirious."

So were the fans. They stormed the field. "I was afraid I was going to get killed," Bowman laughed. "I ran out of the mob of players and fans."

The drive covered 65 yards in 10 plays. Just four seconds remained on the clock when the scoreboard registered Penn State 27, Nebraska 24. Manca missed the extra point and Nebraska's

1982: Philippians 4:13. September 25, 1982, Lions 27, Huskers 24

kickoff return fell short as the time ran out.

"We felt that all along we were better than Nebraska," said Blackledge, whose final statistics read 23 of 39 for 295 yards and three TD passes. "That wasn't going to be proved wrong to me or proved wrong to anybody else until there were double zeros up on the board."

The victory complete, the fans returned to the field, tearing down the goal post at the south end. They carried their $1,800 prize out of Beaver Stadium via Gate One and headed west to Locust Lane. From there, they went down College Avenue and up The Mall, depositing the goal post at the steps of Old Main.

"The Miracle of Mount Nittany," as *Sports Illustrated* called it, was over.

> *The Miracle of Mount Nittany," as* Sports Illustrated *called it, was over.*

After listening to Paterno earlier in the week, Penn State fans must have thought it would take a miracle for the Nittany Lions to beat the Cornhuskers.

CBS-TV was televising the game nationally and wanted a late kickoff time. Therefore, the game started at 3:45 p.m. and was the first game Penn State would ever play under the lights at Beaver Stadium. And because of Nebraska's high-powered offense, Paterno was worried the portable lights would not be enough.

"Don't bring flashlights," he warned on his public television show, TV Quarterbacks. "Bring candles to light to St. Jude."

St. Jude is the patron saint of lost causes.

Penn State knew Nebraska would be a challenge. The Cornhuskers entered the game 2-0, ranked second in the nation and had compiled 883 yards of total offense and 43 first downs in a 68-0 win over New Mexico State the previous week.

But against the Huskers, the Nittany Lions rolled up more yards offensively, 505-472, and scored first. In fact, they scored three times before one touchdown even counted.

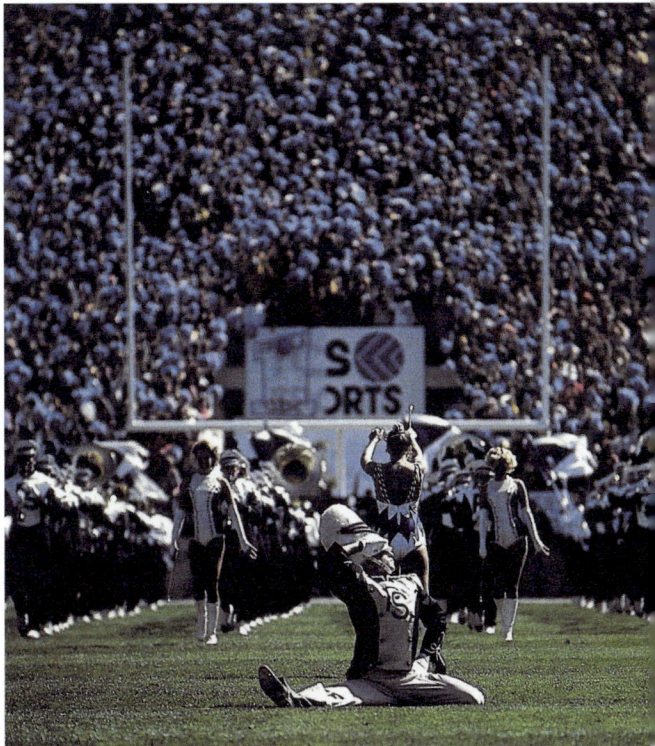

Early in the first quarter, Blackledge connected with Jackson and then Garrity on touchdown passes, only to have motion penalties against the Lions to nullify them both.

A 50-yard field goal attempt by Manca was wide left, but it took Penn State's defense just 1:46 to get the ball back for the offense. An over-the-shoulder catch by Warner for 43 yards set up Penn State's first touchdown, a 14-yard pass from Blackledge to Bowman that put State ahead, 7-0.

"Maybe I found a home," Bowman said after the game. "I was recruited as a linebacker and was there for a day. Then I moved to defensive end." Bowman also played defensive tackle, middle guard and offensive guard before moving back to tight end, his old high school position.

The Lion defense held Nebraska to just 52 yards in 13 plays in the first quarter and set up Penn State's second touchdown when defensive end Al Harris recovered a bad pitch by Nebraska quarterback Turner Gill.

Starting from their own 29, the Nittany Lions went 71 yards in six plays to take a 14-0 lead. Outside of a 21-yard catch by Garrity and an incomplete pass, the drive was all Warner, whose runs of 15, 31, two and finally two yards for the touchdown showed he was back in form.

Warner finished the first half with 69 yards on 12 carries, but saw little action in the final two quarters due to bad leg cramps. "I kept saying, 'Are you all right, are you all right?'" Paterno said.

He wasn't, but still led the Lion rushers with 78 yards and caught three passes for 47 yards. Penn State finished with 210 yards rushing, its highest in four games. Williams gained 65 yards on 10 carries, while Skeeter Nichols (seven carries, 32 yards) and Joel Coles (four carries, 20 yards) came through in the second half.

In the final 32 seconds of the first half, Gill attempted seven passes—and completed four—to take Nebraska 80 yards for a touchdown. The last two passes were to Fryar, and covered 18 and 30 yards. On the 30-yarder, Fryar caught the ball over the middle and then easily shed safety Mark Robinson and defensive back Roger Jackson on his way to the end zone and a very deceiving 14-7 halftime score.

"We probably should have thrown more, earlier," said Gill, who attempted nine passes in the first half before that drive. Gill had a point. In the first two quarters, the Cornhuskers managed just 61 yards rushing, and Roger Craig, hampered by a thigh injury that sidelined him the second half, was responsible for 27 of those.

Penn State scored first in the second half, driving 83 yards in

1982: Philippians 4:13. September 25, 1982, Lions 27, Huskers 24

seven plays to take a 21-7 lead on Blackledge's 18-yard pass to Jackson, who split a pair of defenders.

Gill and running back Mike Rozier combined to take Nebraska on another 80-yard drive, with Gill passing the final two yards to Rozier, making the score 21-14. In that drive, Rozier carried seven times for 27 yards, while Gill ran three times for 37 yards, and completed two passes for 19 yards.

"We mixed up our game plan in the second half," Gill said. "We threw the ball well, but made too many mistakes, too many turnovers."

In the next 35 seconds, the ball was turned over twice by State on fumbles by Williams and Nichols, and once by the Huskers when Gill was intercepted by Al Harris. But Nebraska got the better of the exchange, because Siebel hit a 37-yard field goal that pulled Nebraska to within four, 21-17.

Seconds before the field goal, portable lights atop the press box flickered and then died. Perhaps it was an omen, because shortly thereafter Blackledge underthrew Garrity and was intercepted.

That's when both the lights and Nebraska's offense went to work again. Again alternating the pass and run, Gill directed the Huskers 80 yards downfield for the goalhead touchdown. The 13-play drive, which consumed 5:34, gave Nebraska a 24-21 lead and left just 78 seconds for the Nittany Lions to come back.

And they did.

Seconds before the field goal, the set of portable lights atop the press box flickered and then died. Perhaps it was an omen, because shortly thereafter Blackledge underthrew Garrity and was intercepted.

Greatest Moments at Beaver Stadium:
Sept. 25, 1982 - Penn State 27, Nebraska 24

Fans call this the greatest game ever played at Beaver Stadium. With just 1 minute and 14 seconds left on the clock and no time outs, quarterback Todd Blackledge led a come-from-behind 65-yard drive in 10 plays to beat No. 3 Nebraska. His 15-yard sideline pass to Mike McCloskey at the two-yard-line with nine seconds remaining was controversial, and the subsequent touchdown pass to Kirk Bowman had the record crowd of 85,304 celebrating inside and outside the lighted stadium for hours.

1983

In 1983:

In January, the Nittany Lions upset the top-ranked Georgia Bulldogs 27-23 at the Sugar Bowl in New Orleans. This victory—the first national championship—was a long time coming. Paterno said, "It feels pretty good. It's like all those things—it doesn't set in until you've had a chance to think about it. I have a great squad and a great group of young people. They just seem to have that little chemistry. I think this is the best football team I've ever had."

Celebrations go on for days. On January 4, 15,000 students fill Old Main Lawn to celebrate. Pennsylvania Governor Dick Thornbrough proclaims the first week of January "Penn State National Football Championship Week."

After the retirement of University President John W. Oswald this year, 58-year-old Vice Chancellor Bryce Jordan, steps into the role. "The challenge of this presidency is to sustain the Penn State tradition and even expand its superb reputation as one of the country's top institutions," he said.

Joe Paterno parlays the energy from the win into a monumental speech to the University Trustees, where he urged the university to be number one in more than just football. This watershed moment sees the football paragon become a champion for excellence in higher education. "What are we? Who are we?" he asked.

In fall of 1983, the university finally did away with the system that required students to camp out—sometimes for three days—to get a dorm room. The students now only need to send in a card stating preferences and a room will be assigned to them. This year, students also adjust from quarters to trimesters and computerized registration.

Ray-Ban sales skyrocketed after Tom Cruise wore them in the blockbuster, "Risky Business."

Todd Blackledge

The Phi Psi 500 has its 15th anniversary, sponsored by Stroh's, and features students drinking 50 cent beer at various bars along the 1.1 mile route. "Students will be carded at the beginning and end of the race," an ad reads. It will be one of the last Phi Psi 500s, as tensions continue to rise between "town and gown" over noise and alcohol at student events. See the Phi Psi 500 in its glory days here: **youtu.be/1KQO7i2DHLw.**

In gymnastics, British Terry Bartlett leads the Nittany Lions to a second place team finish in NCAA competition. His skill lands him on the British Olympic team in the 1984 Olympics in Los Angeles.

Top movies in 1983 included "Never Say Never Again," "National Lampoon's Vacation," "The Outsiders," "A Christmas Story," "Return of the Jedi," "Superman III," "Scarface," "The Big Chill," and "Psycho II."

Top songs include "Every Breath You Take" by The Police, "Flashdance... What a Feeling" by Irene Cara, "Mr. Roboto" by Styx, and "Total Eclipse of the Heart" by Bonnie Tyler.

Pi Kappa Alpha calendar girls. *Photo courtesy Chuck Fong*

PENN STATE

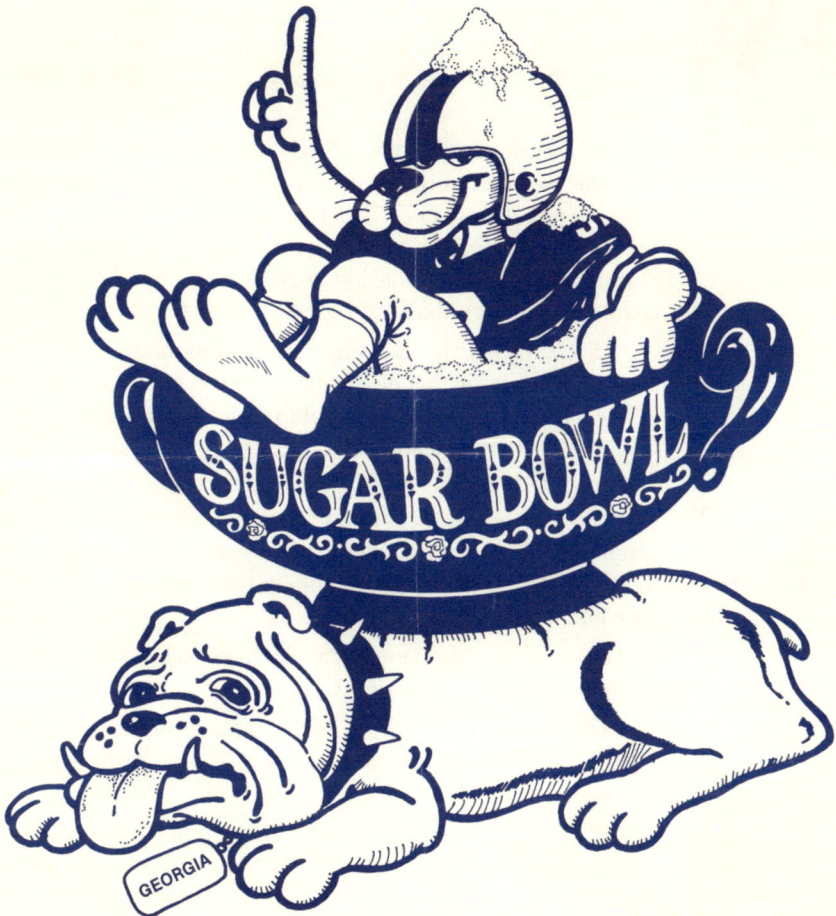

JANUARY 1, 1983

1983: Sugar Bowl

Penn State finally broke through and won their first national championship despite having many undefeated seasons.

Kenny Jackson gets a hug from Gregg Garrity.

Number One, January 1, 1983
Lions 27, Bulldogs 23

Reprinted from 1982 National Champions Collector's Edition

NEW ORLEANS - The last time the Nittany Lions played in the Sugar Bowl—against Alabama in 1979—Joe Paterno admitted he made a mistake. And it wasn't calling two fourth-quarter dive plays up the middle from the one-yard line either.

Although he had been there twice before (a 14-0 loss to Oklahoma in '72 and a 13-6 loss to Alabama in '75), in 1979 Paterno incorrectly assumed the Sugar Bowl was like any other bowl game. It was not.

New Orleans had Bourbon Street and distractions galore. Further, the Sugar Bowl is also the bowl game for the winner of the Southeastern Conference and therefore has a built-in partisan Southern following. In 1979, Paterno and Penn State were not able to cope and Penn State lost its No. 1 ranking and the national championship to Alabama, 14-7.

"I felt bad about the Alabama game last time down here because I wasn't ready for it—all the hoopla and everything," Paterno said before facing Georgia. "You've got to realize when you play down here, you're the away team and you've got to treat it like that. It's not like the other places.

"With all the distractions and a game that big, I never got a couple of things together, never had some time to myself to get them together. This year we did most of our work at home before we came."

Penn State practiced for 10 days in State College before leaving for New Orleans the day after Christmas.

"The coaches kept us in the right frame of mind," guard Pete Speros said. "We worked really hard at school, really hard. Joe pushed us to the fullest extent that he could."

For a number of reasons, many of the practices were held in the Indoor Sports Complex. The complex, with its artificial turf, not only mirrored the indoor conditions of the Superdome, but also allowed the team to become accustomed to the crowd noise it could expect New Year's night. Paterno had placed 10 blaring loudspeakers along the practice field to simulate crowd noise.

"It would give you a headache when you walked out of practices," said split end Gregg Garrity. "But I think it really helped us out because we were used to the distractions."

The Nittany Lions faced plenty of distractions once in New

Orleans, beginning in their own hotel, where nearly all of the 1,500 guests were Penn State fans.

The Hilton's general manager, Joe Frederick, was a Penn State graduate and took extra steps to make the hotel a very special headquarters for both the team and its fans. A Penn State souvenir shop was set up, a message board was erected, a continuous tailgate went on in the lobby and the hotel's cable television system offered a channel of 1982 Penn State football highlights.

Blue and white was everywhere, forcing Paterno to once again draw upon his experiences at the Sugar Bowl.

"We were even smarter getting out of the hotel. We went down the service elevator," he said. "Last time we couldn't get out of the elevators and couldn't get out of the lobby."

Outside, up five blocks on Canal Street and then a left down St. Peter Street, was Bourbon Street, the biggest distraction of them all. Monday through Wednesday, when curfew was midnight or later, the players could spend their free time there, among the bars and restaurants and strip joints and shops. Many of them did.

"A lot of people I would meet I'd tell I was Walker,"said Penn State's Walker Lee Ashley. "They'd say, 'No, you're kidding me.'

"I'd say, 'I'm Walker Lee Ashley and I'm the defensive co-captain for Penn State.' And they'd say, 'Oh,' like I'm a nobody."

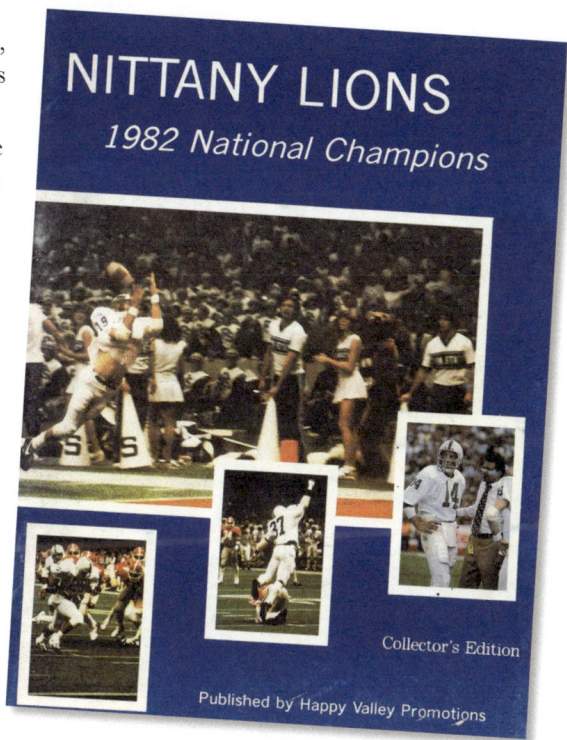

NITTANY LIONS
1982 National Champions

Collector's Edition

Published by Happy Valley Promotions

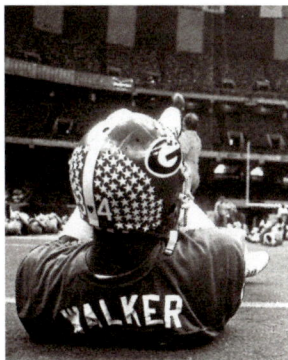

L - R: Bulldogs game, Paterno talks to the team, Herschel lying down.

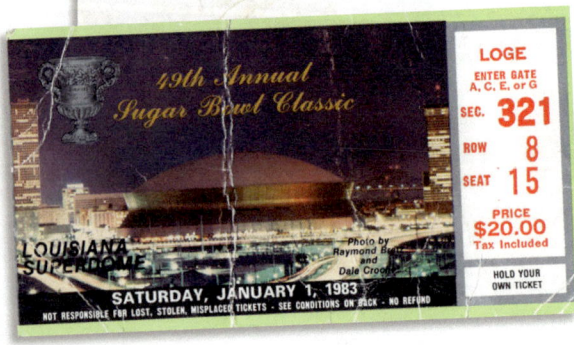

Sugar Bowl ticket,
front and back.

That's because most of the people along Bourbon Street were dressed in red and black. Georgia fans outnumbered Penn State fans three to one. As a result, the Dawgs' cheer was everywhere:

Go Dawgs!

Sic 'em!

Woof-woof-woof-woof-woof-woof!

Penn State fans were found mostly in two places, Fritzel's and Pat O'Brien's. Pat O'Brien's featured three bars, an outdoor patio and waiting lines that extended for almost a block.

Fritzels was renamed Fritzels' Lions' Den for Sugar Bowl week by its owner, Dutch Fritzel. Penn State sports schedules, Love Ya Lions placards and Nittany Lion posters were plastered all over the small tavern, which also featured loud and continuous recordings of the Penn State fight song.

For the past 11 years Fritzel had designated his bar at 733 Bourbon Street as the "home" tavern for the fans of the Sugar Bowl team he thought he would win. And for the past 10 years, he had been right. In 1983, the streak would go to 11.

"Herschel Who?" asked the buttons and the Penn State players in New Orleans. Everyone else knew.

Herschel was Herschel Walker, the 1982 Heisman Trophy winner and the holder of 30 Georgia team records, 15 Southeastern Conference records and 10 NCAA records.

The three seasons before Herschel went to Georgia, the Bulldogs were 20-13-2. The last three seasons with him, they were 32-3, had won three SEC titles, one national title and were on the verge of another.

Herschel was popular; so popular that three times during the week of the Sugar Bowl, he was forced to switch rooms at the New Orleans Marriott, the Georgia team headquarters. Herschel could not go to a team party at a local restaurant, either. He had to settle instead for some fast food to go from Popeye's, a take-out place a block from the Marriott down Canal Street. And he also skipped a team trip to the zoo the day before the game.

Georgia, 11-0 and ranked No. 1 in the country entering the Sugar Bowl, depended heavily upon Walker, who averaged 159

1983: *Number One*

yards per game rushing in the regular season. Georgia Coach Cince Dooley agreed when his offense was called one-dimensional.

"Last year we had three big cannons in Walker, [quarterback Buck] Belue and [split end Scott] Lindsay," said Dooley, unhappy to see the latter two graduate. "We are reduced to one cannon and several pea-shooters, maybe a rifle shot or two."

The cannon was Herschel.

Robinson had two interceptions and three deflections, including this one versus Kay.

It's not a bad name, Hershel," Lion safety Mark Robinson said the Thursday before the game. "I don't mind it. But Mark's better. I want to see how good Herschel is for myself. Maybe after the game they'll come out with a button that says 'Mark Who?' I'd like that."

Robinson's teammate, Walker Lee Ashley, the "other" Walker, said prior to the game he knew exactly who Herschel was.

"Herschel is like any other back, he can go down," Ashley said. "He can, and will be, stopped on January 1. He'll be mighty sore from the punishment we're going to give him."

"Talk is cheap," Herschel rebutted at a news conference two days before the game. "If people got paid for talking, there would be a lot of rich people in the world.

"Everybody we've played this year has said they're looking forward to tackling me. I know the position I'm in. If I was on defense, I'd want to tackle me, too. I understand what they say and I accept it."

Herschel Walker was the second consecutive Heisman Trophy winner that Penn State tailback Curt Warner would face in a bowl game. In Penn State's 26-10 victory over Southern Cal in the 1982 Fiesta Bowl, Warner rushed for 145 yards on 26 carries and two touchdowns; USC's Marcus Allen was held to 85 yards on 30 carries.

"It seems like I'm always getting in those situations," Warner had said after the Pitt game. Two weeks later, at the start of the Sugar Bowl drills in State College, he added, "I've heard and I've heard and I've heard that Herschel Walker is coming.

"I feel no personal rivalry," Warner added. "I feel it's built up in the media as a personal rivalry, Warner vs. Walker. I'm not going to worry about those things."

Warner and Walker knew and respected each other, having been roommates at an All-American function the year before. In the weeks leading up to the Sugar Bowl, Warner guarded his words when asked about Walker.

"Mr. Walker," Warner called him. "I wouldn't threaten the man," Warner joked, when told of Ashley's promise to make Walker sore.

He played off the matchup between the two backs, although he did promise in a *Sports Illustrated* article that he would comment further after the Sugar Bowl.

Friday morning, at a news conference at the Dixie Brewery, Joe Paterno had seen enough. He was ready for the game.

"I'm tired of seeing you people," Paterno kidded. "I'm tired of eating, I'm tired of people and I'm tired of fighting crowds in the lobby. Let's get this damn thing over with."

That afternoon, while Georgia took the day off and visited the Audubon Zoological Garden, Penn State went through a light half-hour workout in the Superdome. After practice, when the coaches went into the locker room the Penn State players held an informal team meeting on the playing field.

"We were just laying out on the field," co-captain Pete Speros said. "Ken [Kelley], Walker and I felt that we should just talk. Basically, it was the captains and Joel Coles, who always does a lot of talking out there. We all just sat right at midfield and everybody gathered in.

"I said 'Hey, look, the key to this game is us jumping on them right from the start. Let them know they're in the toughest game they've been in all year.

"And that's exactly what we did."

(Left) Ashley put the clamps on Walker, who gained 103 yards. (Right) Warner's nine-yard touchdown run was a piece of art.

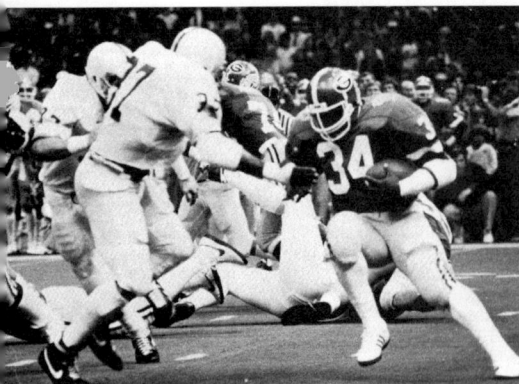

It was New Year's night and outside the fog rolling off the Mississippi River was so thick only half of the 91-yard high Superdome could be seen from the street. Inside, most of the 78,124 fans—a record crowd—were already in their seats when the captains met at midfield for the coin toss.

Penn State won the toss and elected to receive. Georgia opted to defend the south goal, an area populated exclusively by Bulldog fans, meaning that in the first quarter Penn State would be driving toward an end zone full of red.

Kevin Butler's kick went eight yards deep in the end zone, and Tony Mumford wisely chose not to run it out. Penn State took over at its own 20-yard line, and if Nittany Lion bowl history was any indicator, the first play from scrimmage would be a run by Curt Warner for a touchdown.

In Penn State's last two bowl games, Warner had run for a touchdown the first time he touched the football. Against Ohio State in the 1980 Fiesta Bowl, it was a 64-yard run and against Southern Cal in the 1982 Fiesta Bowl, it was a 17-yard run.

The first play was a run by Warner, a quick opener up the middle for four yards, but not for a touchdown. On the next play, the Lions again went to Warner, on a seven-yard pass from quarterback Todd Blackledge. A run by fullback Jon Williams failed to gain a yard on first-and-10 at the 31, but after just three plays, the Lion offense already had a different look to it.

First, Dave Laube was in at long guard for Dick Maginnis, who had pulled a hamstring in team drills on Monday. And second, Penn State was going with some odd offensive formations to take advantage of Georgia's eight-man defensive front.

"Going into the ballgame we put in a couple of sets to throw the football," Paterno said. "We felt Georgia's three-deep arrangement might give them some trouble. So we went with two tight ends and a double flanker.

"We worked hard on it. We knew we couldn't make a living out of it, but we wanted to make sure we got a good start in the ball game."

In essence, what the Lions planned to do was attack Georgia at its strongest point—in the secondary. In 1982, the Bulldogs led the nation in interceptions with 35. Junior roverback Terry Hoage had 12 of those, also tops in the nation, and California junior

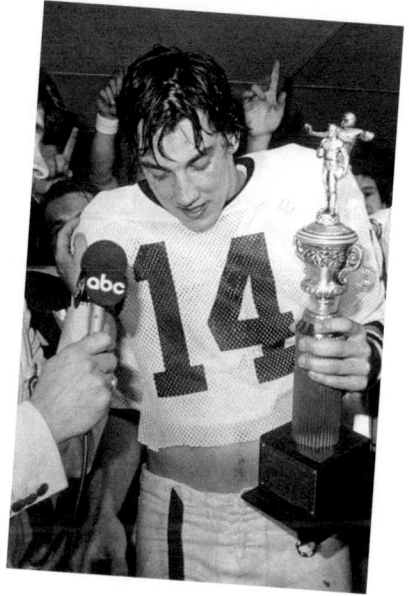

Todd Blackledge with the Miller Digby Award for Most Outstanding Player in the Sugar Bowl. Photo credit Allstate Sugar Bowl

college transfer Jeff Sanchez intercepted nine. Only 10 Division I-A teams intercepted more than the two of them combined.

Paterno was prepared to match strengths. "I told Todd going into the ballgame: 'Hey, baby, we're not going to start screwing around with this thing now. We've come too far. We're going to throw it and throw it and throw it. So get the arm ready.'"

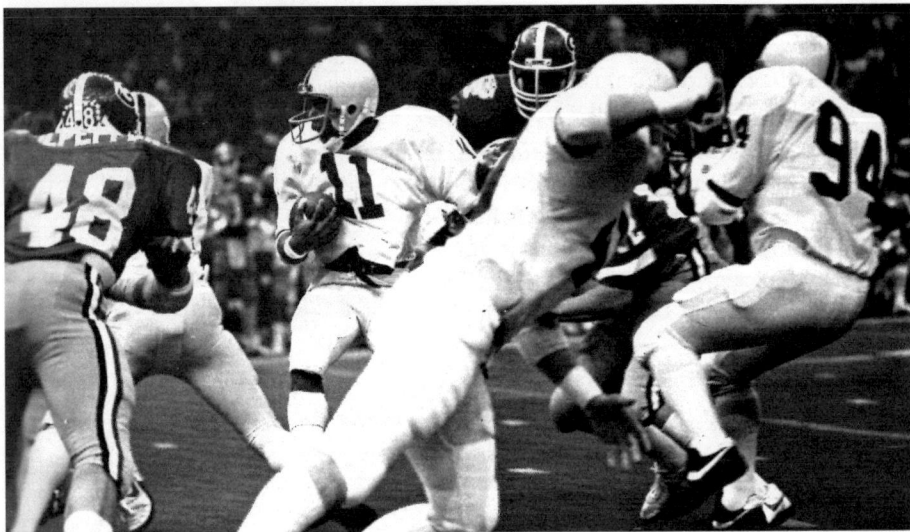

Baugh and the Lions' punt return were the center of attention.

On the Lions' fourth play of the drive, Blackledge's second pass found tight end Mike McCloskey across the middle for a 33-yard gain. Blackledge passed again, completing a 27-yard pass to Gregg Garrity, who had lined up split right with Kenny Jackson. Blackledge then went back to McCloskey and completed his fourth pass of the drive, for seven yards.

That put the Lions on the two-yard line, where they lined up with a power I backfield. Warner swept left, and from behind a good block from Joel Coles, he scored on his second carry of the game. The touchdown was only the second by Penn State in four Sugar Bowl appearances.

Nick Gancitano kicked the extra point and after just 2:51, the Nittany Lions led, 7-0. The scoring drive covered 80 yards in seven plays, with Blackledge completing four of four passes for 74 yards. Blackledge had sensed that Penn State would get off to a good start.

"I think we were hungrier for the national championship," he said.

Georgia came right back. The Bulldogs controlled the ball for more than six minutes and covered 70 yards in 16 plays to set

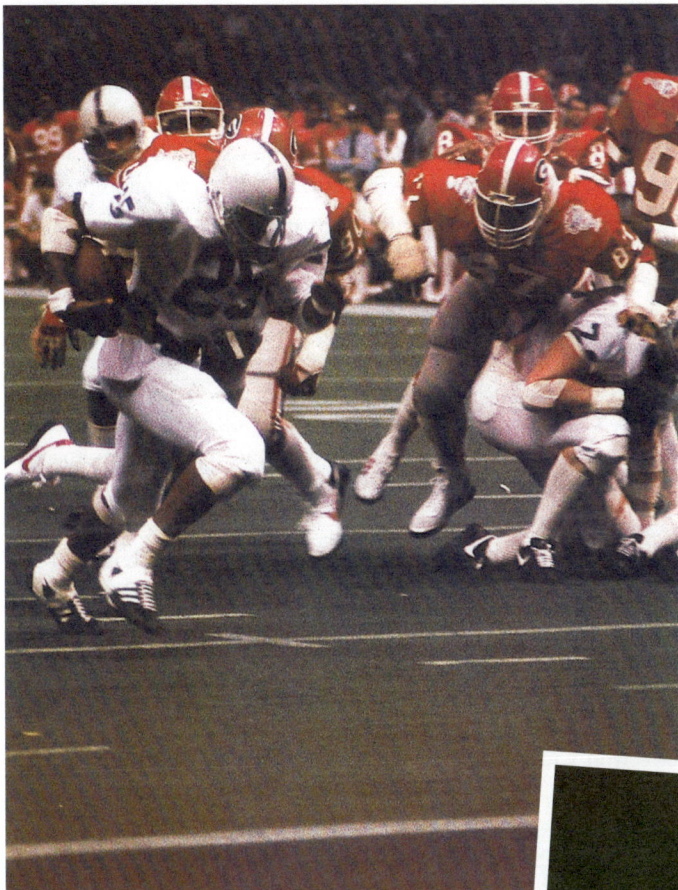

L - R: Curt Warner dances to nine-yard Sugar Bowl touchdown., Ashley celebrates.

up a 27-yard field goal by Butler that made the score 7-3. Herschel Walker carried six times in the drive for 40 yards—including a 12-yarder, his longest of the day—and on two of those carries safety Mark Robinson stopped Walker with a solo tackle.

The Nittany Lions took awhile to adjust to their defensive strategy of stringing out any running play involving Walker, forcing him to run sideline and not upfield. But on his last carry of the drive, Walker gained just two yards and the Lions had their defenses straightened out.

"When Walker cut back, we were waiting for him. And when he went outside, we forced him to give a little ground. [Walker Lee] Ashley kept pushing him back so he couldn't take the corner and accelerate up," Paterno said. "And then when it looked like Walker was going to break a big one, Robinson came through with the great play. We were counting on Robinson being good enough to do that."

Midway through the drive Georgia quarterback John Lastinger completed a key pass—a 16-yarder to tight end Clarence Kay for a first down on a third-and-eight play—but he also overthrew Kay on another play when he was wide open in the end zone.

No one was quite sure what to expect from Lastinger. He entered the game with very unimpressive statistics. In 1982, the junior completed only 41 percent of his passes and averaged only 5.6 completions per game.

"He's a lot like a kid we had in '68 and '69," Paterno said. "He was a lousy passer, a lousy runner and had trouble handling the ball. The kid's name? Chuck Burkhart. We were 22-0 with him and he was 33-0 in high school."

Lastinger, who followed in the footsteps of Buck Belue at both Valdosta (Ga.) High school and Georgia, also never lost a game he started at quarterback. He was 14-0 in his senior year of high school and 11-0 in his first season as the Dawgs' starting quarterback.

Georgia Coach Vince Dooley knew the bottom line: "We have won with John Lastinger, although he hasn't been a classic

Before the game, Paterno told Blackledge: "We're going to throw and throw it and throw it. So get your arm ready."

1983: Number One

quarterback."

On Penn State's next two possessions, Blackledge was sacked twice, first by defensive guard Tim Crowe and then by defensive tackle Jimmy Payne.

"They were better individual pass rushers than anybody we faced all year," Paterno said. "They beat us one-on-one a couple of times and that hasn't happened to us very often. When they blitzed, they blitzed effectively."

Payne and fellow tackle Jack Lindsey entered the game troubled by injuries and, as Dooley put it, "How much pain Payne could absorb determined how much Payne would play. He played more than we thought he would."

After two Lion punts and one by the Dawgs, the first quarter ended with Penn State ahead, 7-3. After one quarter, both teams went with what had gotten them in the Sugar Bowl: Walker carried the ball eight times for 48 yards and Blackledge completed five of seven passes for 93 yards.

On the Lions' first possession of the second quarter, Gancitano kicked a 38-yard field goal to give Penn State a 10-3 lead. Only two plays in the seven play, 47-yard drive gained yardage—a 23-yard Blackledge pass to Jackson and a 26-yard run by Warner off a block by Pete Speros.

Georgia returned the kickoff to its own 17-yard line and after two first downs, its offense sputtered. Walker carried three times for seven yards on the drive, forcing Lastinger to the air four times; he completed one.

"We had a good game plan. Jerry Sandusky [the defensive coordinator] was monumental in planning that," Robinson said. "We pushed Herschel off to the side and made some great plays on him. I think that frustrated Georgia's offense when we stopped Herschel. They didn't know what to go to, so they tried to pass."

Georgia punted and Penn State's Kevin Baugh returned the kick 66 yards. Three plays netted minus two yards and Gancitano attempted a 47-yard field goal that was wide left. Georgia got the ball back, but was forced to punt again and Baugh returned the punt 24 yards.

In less than two quarters, Baugh had returned three punts for 96 yards and all three punts were up the middle, a rarity for Penn State. All year, the Lions had returned punts either to the left or right, but Assistant Coach John Rosenberg noticed a weakness in the center of Georgia's punt coverage and Penn State changed its return to exploit it.

"I was surprised that it was there," Baugh said. "It just so happened everyone was hitting their blocks at the right time and the middle opened up."

Five plays and 65 yards after Baugh's 24-yard return, Warner scored on a nine-yard run to increase the Lions' lead to 17-3. The 17 points surpassed the total of 13 Penn State had scored in the three previous Sugar Bowls.

A 36-yard Blackledge pass to Garrity on a streak was the longest play of the drive, but Warner's run was the most artistic.

His touchdown came on a simple off-tackle play where he ran to the right, only to find a pack of Dawgs. So Warner took a stutter step back to his left, switched directions mid-air and upon landing, accelerated into the end zone behind blocks by Coles and tackled Ron Heller.

"I don't know where that one came from, to tell you the truth," Warner grinned. "It's just something that happened. I was blocked outside so I stopped for a second to take a look at it. They overshot the play and I just cut up the middle."

A 10-yard punt return by Baugh and a 13-yard pass from Blackledge to McCloskey set up a 45-yard field goal by Gancitano and Penn State led, 20-3, with 30 seconds remaining in the first half.

Georgia, desperate to get back in the game, put Walker back deep for the kickoff return for only the third time all year. Penn

1983: Number One

State's Massimo Manca kicked away from him, but the ball went out of bounds. Manca kicked again from the 35 and this time Walker switched sides of the field and got the ball, returning it 23 yards to the Georgia 34.

The first play from scrimmage Lastinger completed a 17-yard pass to Kay for a first down on the Penn State 49. After an incomplete pass to Kay, Lastinger connected with flanker Herman Archie on a 13-yard pass and a first down on the Penn State 36.

Georgia called its last timeout of the half with 23 seconds remaining to plan its next play. It was a play Dooley had his teams toy-around with in practice every year, but had only used once before, 18 years ago. The time to use it again had come.

Wide receiver Kevin Harris lined up wide right and ran a curl pattern, catching a pass from Lastinger at the 20. Harris then turned and lateraled the ball to Walker, who had raced downfield, trailing the play. Walker ran to the 10, where he was knocked out of bounds by Robinson.

"We figured if we could get the ball there," Walker said, "there wouldn't be anybody who could keep up with me. They had someone [Robinson] come over there with great pursuit."

> **We figured if we could get the ball there, there wouldn't be anybody who could keep up with me.**

Only nine seconds remained and Lastinger threw again, listing the ball across field to Archie, who was two yards deep in the left corner of the end zone. The play matched the experience of 5-foot-8-inch senior defensive back Dan Biondi and the leap of 6-foot-5-inch Archie, a freshman. Archie won, grabbing the ball over top of Biondi for a touchdown. The drive covered 66 yards in just five plays and put Georgia within striking distance, 20-10, at halftime.

"You guys kept telling me Lastinger couldn't throw," Paterno told a few reporters after the game. "And I kept saying, 'It looks to me as if he can throw.' He was really a clutch player."

In the first half, other than the 26-yard run by Warner, Penn State had moved primarily by the pass. Blackledge completed nine of the 16 passes for 160 yards and no interceptions, but the Bulldogs blamed much of his success on themselves.

"We let some guys get outside of us early," Sanchez said. "We made a lot of mental errors. I don't want to take anything away from Penn State, but we took a lot away from ourselves."

Walker had 75 yards on 17 carries in the first half, but on his last 11 carries he gained just 35 yards, a little more than three yards per carry. The second half wouldn't get any better.

Paterno's halftime message was simple. "I told the squad the biggest part of the game is going to be the first four or five minutes of the second half," he said.

Georgia received the kickoff to start the second half and drove 69 yards in 11 plays, the final play was a one-yard run by Walker for a touchdown that cut Penn State's lead to 20-17. Walker carried five times for just 18 yards on the drive, so the big plays had to come through the air—and they did, on two passes by Lastinger to Harris for 11 and 24 yards.

"Lastinger is not one who normally exerts himself in situations like that," Dooley said. "He played well and kept us in the game."

The next three times the Nittany Lions got the ball, their drives ended when Georgia dumped Blackledge, who was sacked a season-high of five times. He completed just one pass in the third quarter.

"I kind of lost my poise," Blackledge said. "I knew they were going to come tough with the rush. I wasn't picking up the blitzes and throwing the ball when I should have. I didn't want to throw a careless pass or an interception."

While Blackledge was too cautious, Lastinger wasn't careful enough. As a result, Robinson intercepted him twice in the third quarter. In addition, Robinson finished the game with three pass deflections and nine tackles, prompting praise from both coaches:

Paterno: "He's the greatest secondary player we've ever had."

Dooley: "That Robinson is no safety—he's a linebacker playing safety."

Students (standing) Greg Woodman, Wayne Dillahey, (kneeling) Scott Stampahar, Jack Dandrea, Mark Pulos wear authentic jerseys in their New Orleans hotel room as they prepare to go to the Sugar Bowl.

1983: Number One

Robinson also had quite a bit to do with holding Walker to 19 yards on nine carries in the fourth quarter. "Mark ended up making five or six tackles against Herschel that might have made the difference in the game," Paterno said.

Robinson was just the final man in the Lions' chain, really. Ashley and hero linebacker Harry Hamilton fought off Georgia fullback Chris McCarthy and forced Walker to run wide, allowing players like Robinson said, Greg Gattuso and Ken Kelley to tackle the Georgia tailback at an angle, not head-on.

"Our line did a great job of stringing him out," Robinson said. "A lot of times all I had to do was come up and push him over."

While Walker was getting stopped on the field, Warner was being helped off it. He suffered a deep bruise in his left thigh and also from cramps, a recurrence of his midseason nemesis. But he kept on coming back.

"When you're playing for the national championship, you forget about those things," Warner said. "I was in pain during the fourth quarter, but it's a one-shot deal and you only get to play in the national championship once."

Warner's first run of the fourth quarter gained 11 yards, but cramps again forced him to the sidelines. Two plays later he was back and his seven-yard run gave Penn State a first-and-10 at the Georgia 47.

In came pass play 6-43, the 11th time that day the Penn State coaches called for a pass on first down. The play was designed to flood Georgia's two-deep secondary with four Lion receivers and force the Bulldogs to make a choice. In this case, right cornerback Tony Flack initially chose to cover Warner, circling out of the Penn State backfield.

"I guessed it was going to be to Curt or I," said Garrity, whose pattern called for a streak down the left sideline. "We had a two-

Penn State players, coaches and fans celebrate their first national championship after defeating Georgia in the 1983 Sugar Bowl.

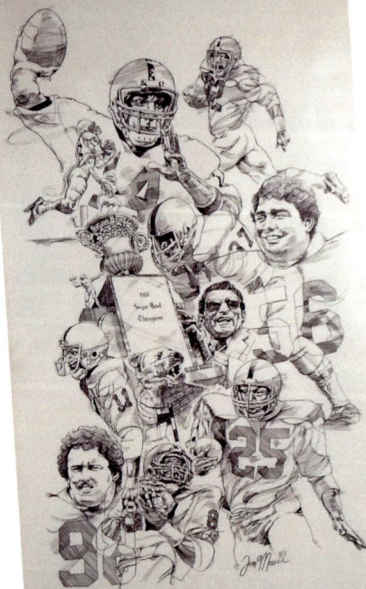

PENN STATE NITTANY LIONS

'82 NATIONAL CHAMPIONS

> "
>
> *It was a clutch play that gave us some breathing room.*
>
> "

on-one situation there and Curt just held the defensive back [Flack] on the hash mark and Todd just lifted it up and it was a perfect pass."

Blackledge: "I don't think Georgia realized what kind of speed Gregg had as far as running the straight pass. We got a great play-action fake on it and it just ended up being a foot race."

A race Garrity won.

"Georgia's secondary has great ball reaction, but they weren't that fast, though," Garrity said. "Hoage ran a 4.8 [40-yard dash] and we were very aware of that. So we figured if we were going to beat them, it was going to be our speed."

Garrity was the first to the football, leaving his feet. He caught the ball in the air while above the two and landed in the end zone for a 47-yard touchdown and a 27-17 Penn State lead.

"There wasn't much to the catch," Garrity said. "It's your basic streak."

"It was a clutch play that gave us some breathing room," Paterno said.

Said Dooley: "I think that was the most important play of the game."

The Lions forced Georgia to punt on its next possession and Penn State's offense then ate up five minutes before reaching a fourth-and-one at the Georgia 31. Ahead by 10 points with seven minutes remaining and confident of State's defense, Paterno sent Giacomarro in to punt.

"I wasn't going to gamble the football game on a long yard in a short yardage situation against a team that plays short yardage as well as they do," Paterno said.

So Giacomarro punted—into the end zone. Georgia took over at its own 20, but the Lion defense stiffened as Ashley sacked Lastinger for an 11-yard loss on a third-and-five.

Georgia punted with 5:38 left in the game, setting up Penn State's first and only turnover when Baugh fumbled the kick at his own 43. Six plays later the Bulldogs cashed in the fumble when Lastinger connected with Kay on a nine-yard touchdown pass and Georgia trailed, 27-23. An extra point and a field goal would only tie the game; Dooley wanted the win and decided to go for two points, with, who else but Herschel, on a quick inside pitch to the right.

"Herschel was supposed to go wide on the play, but he saw

something and he cut back inside," explained Dooley, hinting that Walker may have been a bit rattled. "I don't know why he did. I think if he had continued outside, he could have used his strength to go in. But by that point in the game, Penn State had already done a heck of a job on our running game."

Walker was stopped short of the two points by Ashley and Scott Radecic, among others. "I just thought going for two was the thing to do," Dooley said the next morning. "I still do."

On the ensuing kickoff, Penn State expected an onside kick but Butler, Georgia's kicker, lofted the kick deep and Baugh caught it over his shoulder after the ball bounced once. With 3:53 left in the game, Penn State took possession at its own 14-yard line and after five running plays was faced with a third-and-three from the 32.

Georgia called timeout and Blackledge trotted to the sidelines to talk with Paterno. Blackledge thought the Bulldogs were expecting a run and wanted to surprise them.

"Let's give them the same set and if they play it the same way, I'll check out [change the play at the line of scrimmage] to Garrity for the first down," Blackledge said to Paterno.

"Make sure you throw it far enough," Paterno answered back.

Blackledge did, connecting with Garrity on an out pattern for six yards and a first down.

"It was Todd's idea and it was a gutty call," Paterno said. "He made it and had the confidence he could do it. So, I let him."

The Nittany Lions ran off three more plays and then, with six seconds remaining, Giacomarro punted the ball into the end zone. Penn State won, 27-23, and was the national champion of college football in 1982.

There were many stars in the victory over Georgia, beginning with Todd Blackledge, voted the game's most valuable player after finishing with 13 completions in 23 attempts for 228 yards with one touchdown pass and no interceptions.

"It was a typical Blackledge day," Paterno said. "He fights and struggles, he takes a lot of adversity, but in the clutch he makes the big plays."

A junior on the playing field although a senior in the classroom, Blackledge next faced the decision of whether to make himself eligible for the National Football League draft and turn professional.

"He could be the next Heisman Trophy winner," Paterno said.

There was Curt Warner, who for the second straight year outrushed the Heisman Trophy winner, this time by 14 yards (117-103) on 10 fewer carries (18-28). And, as promised, he made some comments about comparisons between himself and Walker.

It was a typical Blackledge day," Paterno said. "He fights and struggles, he takes a lot of adversity, but in the clutch he makes the big plays.

"I think Herschel Walker is a great running back, but I'm not going to count myself any lower than him or [SMU's] Eric Dickerson or anyone else," Warner said.

"I'm not going to put myself down in any way. I think I'm just as good as anybody else in the country and I think you have to have that type of attitude, although at times you have to keep it to yourself."

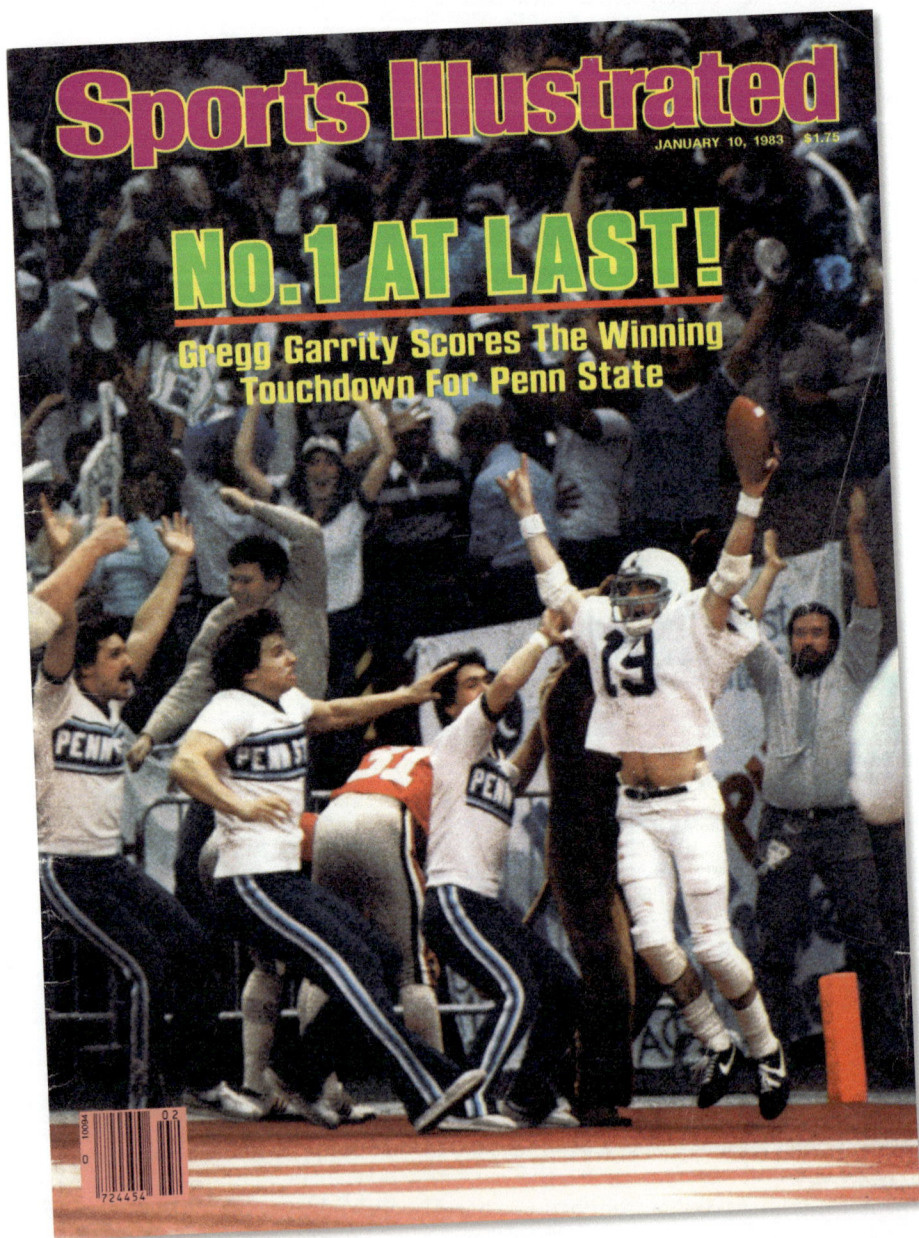

Sports Illustrated

JANUARY 10, 1983 $1.75

No.1 AT LAST!

Gregg Garrity Scores The Winning
Touchdown For Penn State

There was also Gregg Garrity, a walk-on with four receptions for 116 yards—two in the fourth quarter when Penn State needed them most.

"And Garrity's the other receiver," Dooley said. "Some other receiver."

In fact, Dooley was impressed with the entire Lion squad. "They are one of the three best teams I've seen in 19 years of coaching," said Dooley, including Nebraska in 1970 and Pitt in 1976, both national champions.

And then there was the defensive effort of players like Mark Robinson, Walker Lee Ashley, Harry Hamilton, Scott Radecic (who had a game-high 14 tackles despite playing with a bad ankle) and Greg Gattuso.

But Paterno attributed much of the team's success to the team's closeness and cohesiveness.

"They may not have been my most talented team across the board," Paterno said. "But in the sense of talent at skill positions, leadership and poise and the other things that make up a great football team—I think they have those things a little bit more than the other teams have had."

Those attributes allowed the Nittany Lions to rebound from their 42-21 loss to Alabama—admittedly the worst loss ever by a national champion.

"We're the closest team I've ever been on," said senior co-captain Pete Speros. "It didn't matter what class you were in, it didn't matter what color you were, it didn't matter nothing.

"Everyone was in this together. We believed in ourselves; that's half the battle. When you have a lot of great athletes, there's a difference when the team is close, there really is.

"We've always had great teams at Penn State, but this year we were able to win the big one because of all that closeness. We all had character, we all believed in ourselves and we did it."

Winning the national championship did little to slow down Joe Paterno.

The first evening of the new year had passed quickly, and despite Penn State's victory over Georgia, relatively quietly. Shortly after the game, when Paterno arrived back at his suite in the Hilton Hotel with his wife, Sue, he found it crowded with more than 100 people, "a lot of whom I didn't even know were my friends," he joked.

Many of the Penn State players stopped by, as did numerous well-wishers. Paterno, said flanker Kenny Jackson, "was having

"
Winning the National Championship did little to slow down Joe Paterno.
"

Lastinger didn't play like a 'pea shooter.'

the time of his life. We all were." But not too much later the Lion coach, weary from the game and a nagging cold that arrived each time he visited the Sugar Bowl, excused himself in the midst of the celebration and went to his bedroom.

"I left 'em at 2 a.m., got to sleep maybe a half-hour later and was up again at 5," Paterno said.

Just 10 hours after he left the Superdome, Paterno made the short 15-block drive back up Poydras Street to the Hyatt Regency Hotel, adjacent to the dome where Penn State had beaten Georgia. The Sunday morning fog was thick and increased the lazy feeling of the morning after.

Bleary-eyed and drained after just three hours of sleep, Paterno met with the news media for one final time in New Orleans. His walk to the podium was slow and had a tired sway to it. He stood stiffly, grabbing the podium with both hands.

"I feel pretty good about today," he began, flashing his half-cocked grin. "I think we wear No. 1. I think this is the best football team I ever had."

He went on, discussing Georgia and Herschel Walker and the polls. Then Georgia Coach Vince Dooley, Curt Warner and Todd Blackledge spoke. The conference was over in an hour.

Late that afternoon, the Nittany Lions left on a flight from New Orleans to Harrisburg. Mid-air, they learned that both The Associated Press and United Press International had voted Penn State as the top college football team in the country for 1982. The Nittany Lions, 11-1, received 33 of 37 first-place votes in the AP writers' poll. Southern Methodist—11-0-1 and a 7-3 victor over Pitt in the Cotton Bowl—was second, followed by Nebraska, Georgia and UCLA.

SMU, the only major college team to go undefeated in 1982, complained that it should have been No. 1, and Paterno, whose undefeated teams in '68, '69 and '73 were denied a national title, empathized.

"I've been in that position myself, so I can understand it," Paterno said. "But with the schedule we had, we beat three or four of the top teams in the country, so I think there's no question we should be No. 1."

The Nittany Lions' schedule was the toughest in the nation for the second straight season. Their opponents finished with a combined 87-39-2 record; SMU had seven opponents who finished with losing records for a combined record of only 56-66-2.

After the plane landed at Harrisburg International Airport, the team made a brief stop at Penn State's Capitol Campus in Middletown, where they were greeted at a rally attended by Gov. Dick Thornburgh and 5,000 fans.

The Lions then returned to State College, a 90-mile bus ride.

"We rode the buses up here and there was a caravan behind us the whole way," Paterno said at another news conference Sunday night. "All along the highway, there were people standing, waving and holding up signs."

Just outside of State College, the team stopped at another rally and, finally, at the Indoor Sports Complex.

"It's been a great night," Paterno told the thousands of fans gathered there. "We want to thank you for coming out. We hope we can bring you back here a couple more times. We're No. 1."

At 4 p.m. the next day, a Monday, a rally was held at the steps of Old Main on campus. That night Paterno was in New York, and was interviewed on the halftime show of Monday Night Football. And Tuesday morning, he appeared on ABC TV's Good Morning America show with Blackledge and Warner, guests of host David Hartman, who had been on the Penn State sidelines for the Sugar Bowl.

Tuesday afternoon, Joe Paterno was on the road recruiting for 1983 and 1984 and 1985...

And in the next few weeks there was the National Collegiate Athletic Association conference in San Diego, a "Love Ya Lions" parade in State College and banquets honoring him as Dapper Dan's Man of the Year and Kodak's Coach of the Year.

Winning the National Championship did little to slow down Joe Paterno.

Board of Trustees Speech

"I very much appreciate those words. You know this is the first Board meeting I have ever been to in 33 years so if I look a little shocked and scared, bear with me, I really do appreciate this. I would hope maybe on this occasion since I've never addressed a Board meeting, to maybe share some thoughts with you as to where we are and what I hope we can get done here at the University. It pleases me, obviously, to happen to be part of the Number One football team. I am pleased also that it happened at this time in Dr. Oswald's career that he could leave feeling that he finally got it done. Having been a former coach, he knows how tough it is to get on top of the pile and everything else. It pleases me in a lot of ways. But after having said that, and I'm going to be very frank with you, and I may say some things here that maybe I should not, but it does give me an opportunity to tell you how I feel and what I want to do and what kind of contributions I'd like to make to this institution as I stay on. You know, obviously, all of us are disappointed in the newspaper reports that some of our academic departments are not rated very high. That bothers me. It bothers me to see Penn State football be Number One and then to pick up a newspaper several weeks later and we find we don't have many of our disciplines rated up there with the other institutions in the country. I want to share just a couple of things with you and I hope you'll understand where I'm coming from.

"I think this is a magic time for Penn State. Dr. Oswald has said this, and I have felt it, and I think he is probably more attuned to it than anybody. There has never been a

time when Penn State has been more united or proud. Now maybe it's unfortunate that it takes a Number One football team to do that. I don't think we can lose the opportunities that this moment presents to us, and I don't mean in athletics. I'm not even concerned about the athletic aspects of where we are, I think we can handle that and make sure that we can maintain the kind of teams that you people like to see and you can be proud of and identify with the type of students and the type of football players we get. But I think we have got somehow to start right now. I think Dr. Oswald came to us at a time that we absolutely had to retrench in some areas and he has done a magnificent job for us. I for one want to thank him for what he has done for intercollegiate athletics. We would not be Number One in athletics if it had not been for his cooperation. Every time I ever went to him he never said no to me. I'd like to be on record as having said that. Maybe once in a while there has been somebody in between us that has not presented my case accurately, but anytime I have had an opportunity to sit with him and discuss some things that we needed, he's never said no to me. I don't think we'd be where we are if it hadn't happened that way. But I go back to a fact that we are in a national situation that I have never felt as I have felt now.

"I have been all over the country in the last few weeks. I have been in Florida, been in California, I've been in airports in Chicago and Atlanta, you name it, and I've been there recruiting and doing some other things trying to capitalize on the position that you have when you've had success and trying to make some corrections in what we have and the abuses of the intercollegiate program. Some of the thoughts that I have expressed—and I don't mean to make this a testimonial of Dr. Oswald—but he was part of the people that came up with the ideas that we had to raise the level for scholarship. He was part of the Council of the American Council of Education, one of the select committee, that came up with the standards that we proposed out on the Coast and I've gotten a lot of publicity for having made some speeches out there, but it was Dr. Oswald and some other college Presidents who got together and proposed those standards. But everywhere I've gone I've heard nothing but, 'boy, Penn State, Penn State, what a great bunch of people, what a great institution,' and all of those things.

"So we do have a magic moment and we have a great opportunity, and I think we have got to start right now to put our energies together to make Penn State not only Number One, but I think we've got to start to put our energies together to make this a Number One institution by 1990. I don't think that's an unfounded or a way-out objective. I think we need some things. I talk to you now as a faculty member. I talk to you as somebody who

> **"**
> *I think we've got to start to put our energies together to make this a Number One institution by 1990.*
> **"**

has spent 33 years at Penn State, who has two daughters at Penn State, who probably will have three sons at Penn State, who has a wife that graduated from Penn State, who has two brothers-in-law that graduated from Penn State, and I talk to you as somebody I think who knows a little bit about what's going on. Who has recruited against Michigan, Stanford, UCLA, who has recruited against Notre Dame, Princeton, Yale, and Harvard and who has had to identify some things that they have that are better than we have and has had to identify some of our problems. I talk to you as somebody that I think knows a little bit about what's going on in the other guys, and I think a little bit about what's going on here. We need chairs. We need money so that we can get some stars. We need scholarship money. We need scholarship money to get scholars who can be with the stars so that the stars will come in and have some people around that can stimulate them and they can be stimulated by the stars. We need a better library—better libraries would be a better way to put it—so that the stars and the scholars have the tools to realize their potential. We need an environment of dissent and freedom of speech and freedom to express new and controversial ideas. Basically, this Board is in a lot of ways reactionary because you are more conservative than anything else. That is not a criticism of you as individuals, but I think that's a fair criticism of The Pennsylvania State University Board of Trustees for the 33 years that I have known them going back to Jim Milholland who was acting Chairman and President

> " We need an environment of dissent and freedom of speech and freedom to express new and controversial ideas. "

PENN STATE NEW LOGO

One of the Nittany Lions' newest looks in 1983 came off the field, when Penn State athletic department unveiled a specially-designed Nittany Lion logo.

The new logo, which includes both the lion profile and the single word, "PennState," was the brainchild of the New York City firm of Dixon and Parcells, which was commissioned to design a symbol in the spring of 1983. The lion head is an updated version of many designs, while research by Dixon and Parcells found that most people across the country perceive "Penn State" as a single entity.

Registered and copyrighted as a University trademark, the new logo joins a plethora of other symbols and words used to symbolize Penn State.

"Happened to think that since we had such a proliferation of marks it would be in our best interest to establish one mark," Assistant Athletic Director Fran Fisher told *The Centre Daily Times*. "Now we have a distinctive mark and we're the ones introducing it.

PennState

© PENN STATE MCMLXXXIII

when I first came. We need more controversy, we need more freedom, we need more people to come to us with different ideas, we need more minorities. I am constantly fighting the battle, 'we don't have enough blacks; we don't have enough minorities' everywhere I go, and I don't have the answers to it, but I'm giving you some impressions. We can't be afraid, too reactionary to new and disturbing ideas; however, we can't do some of the things all at once. I think that Dr. Oswald and the new President and Ted Eddy, our Provost, have got to sit down–I'm probably not speaking in turn, I'm probably way out of whack, I'm probably on a page that I probably shouldn't be on but I feel so strongly about it I want to say it–to sit down and put down some priorities. We have some excellent departments. And I know because when I get out in the field we have some excellent departments that can be absolutely outstanding in a relatively short time. We also have some departments that are absolutely lousy and we have lazy professors who are only concerned with tenure and only concerned with getting tenure for some of their mediocre colleagues.

"Alright, now I'm telling you how I feel about it and I may be all wet. But I've dealt with all of them, and a lot of these latter groups. Some of these people in the latter group would make Happy Valley Sleepy Hollow if we let them. It's certainly not invigorating. We've got a new President and I think that he and Dr. Oswald need to sit down and have to probably make some tough decisions.

"Pirandello, the brilliant Italian playwright–I suppose brilliant and Italian is redundant–wrote a play 'Six Characters in Search of an Author', in which the characters of an unfinished play come to life and then they try to finish the play. Well, I believe that Penn State has not necessarily all of a sudden come to life. That would be an unfair criticism of all of the great things that have been

> ❝
> *We need more controversy, we need more freedom, we need more people to come to us with different ideas, we need more minorities.*
> ❞

1983: Board of Trustees Speech

done here in the 33 years that I have been here. But I think it's more alive today than at any time in 33 years that I've been here. I think it's well organized, and I think it's got thrust and wants to pursue. It's alive but it's looking. I think we are not looking for bricks and mortar–and most of you people are businessmen–and we are not looking for GSA money. I think we are looking for the soul of this institution. The soul may be an overstatement, but I'm not sure I'm overstating the case. I think we're literally looking for a soul. Who we are, what we are, and I think that basically comes down to soul. We need to find our soul. We need vibrant, aggressive, brilliant teachers and scholars. We have some, but we don't have enough of them and that's why we need chairs. We need to give them the resources to grow and the freedom to challenge some of the old ideas and old conceptions that have made this country backward in a lot of ways, and have made this state the one with the highest unemployment of any state in the northeast part of the country.

"I'm a football coach. I sit down with my staff and I look at our schedule and our squad and we say this is what we want to do and this is what we can do. And then we set priorities and make decisions as to how we can achieve our objectives. We put a plan together and we stick with it. We don't jump from one plan to the other and we bust our butt to get it done. And that's what has to be done with Penn State in the '80s. We can't wait. It would be nice to say we can wait and in three years put together a major fundraising campaign. We can't wait. I am only telling you that as somebody who's in the field. We can only hold up our finger as Number One for six more months and then we have to play the game again and we may not be Number One. Six short months to capture this magic moment. We have got to raise $7 to $10 million

1983: Board of Trustees Speech

bucks as far as I'm concerned in the next six months or we are going to lose some things and an opportunity we have. How do you go about raising $7 to $10 million is somebody else's concern? I'm willing to help in any way I can. We need $7 to $10 million in the next six months to get us the impetus that we need because we don't want to lose it. I think we've got to take this magic moment and stick it in a jar and we've got to preserve it until we open it up in 1990.

"Dr. Eddy, the other day at an alumni meeting down at Pittsburgh where we had over a thousand people in Allegheny County. Stan was there and some of the others were there and the next night we went to Westmoreland County where we had over 580 people and they turned away 300 people. There is a great group out there right now wanting to get involved in it. Dr. Eddy said it the other night better than I can. He said, and he almost sounded like a football coach, we have a great chance and challenge to make our University Number One in many areas and in coming together to do it we may find out we will have as much fun doing it as we had fun doing it in New Orleans. It was a very moving speech and it hit home. I have had a lot of people come to me wanting to know how they can help. I said to you I have given 33 years, two daughters, and probably three sons to Penn State. I am ready to help where I can to make "Number One" mean more than when we stick that finger up; it's only football. We are losing a great President; we're starting a new era. As Jim Tarman said the other night, we are fortunate that where we are that we've been able to get there our way. We've not cheated, I mean not deliberately, you never know with that thick rule book. We've done it with people who legitimately belong in college. We've set a standard in one area that I think created a challenge for us to reach in all of our areas. You are the people who are going to have to help us do it. There are a lot of us that want to get on with it.

"So, thank you very much for this wonderful resolution. I'm moved. I think you know how much I love this institution and how much I appreciate what it has meant to me and my family for 33 glorious years. 33 years of a great love affair that I have had with this place in this town. I have no regrets. I'm only anxious to get on with some other things to make it even bigger and better, not in a sense of size, but in the context of quality and influence in this country and in some of the things that I think it's important for a major institution of this size to do. So, thank you very much. I hope I didn't bore you with it too long."

1984

In 1984:

The IFC proposes an ordinance to outlaw open containers of alcohol in public spaces, gaining criticism, but after an unruly crowd at 1984's Phi Psi 500, this helps clear the way for the council to approve the 1985 race.

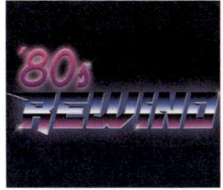

As computers start to make an appearance on campus, Penn State negotiates discounts for students, faculty and staff from Apple, Radio Shack and Zenith—much needed savings as the 'revolutionary' Tandy TRS-80 computer retails for $3,000.

Pay phone calls increase from 10 cents to 25 cents. Tuition rises to $2,312 for PA residents.

In 1984, the Penn State Alumni Association ranked near the top among alumni organizations of all land-grant schools and state universities in both size (70,000 dues-paying members) and percentage of living graduates it included (about 26 percent).

The 1984 election is big news on campus. The USG registers 13,760 students to vote, more than any other university in the country. More than 2,500 people gather in Eisenhower Auditorium for a "Get-out-the-vote" event headlining Reverend Jesse Jackson. Ronald Reagan wins the student vote handily, even more than in non-student dominated precincts.

1984: Timeline

WDFM becomes WPSU and changes formats, eliminating "University of Jam."

The football team finished 6-5, the poorest since JoePa's inaugural year in 1966. In the last game of the season, losing to Pitt at 31-11, Paterno calls his team 'babies.' For the first time in 14 years, the team doesn't play in a bowl game. On the bright side, lifesize cardboard replicas of the beloved coach, dubbed Stand Up Joe debuts this year, and becomes a staple at every tailgate at Beaver Stadium.

The first Ebony & Ivory weekend, a three day event focused on improved race relations, happens on campus.

Happy Valley Promotions unveils Stand Up Joe for the very first time (note the rented RV at the Meadowlands).

The Collegian reports on how to be a yuppie: carry a Wall Street Journal in your backpack, drink imported wine, and only admit to watching public television.

Top movies this year included "Indiana Jones and the Temple of Doom," "Ghostbusters," "Beverly Hills Cop," "Gremlins," "The Karate Kid," "Footloose," and "The Terminator."

Top songs included "When Doves Cry" by Prince, "What's Love Got to Do with It" by Tina Turner, "Footloose" by Kenny Loggins, "Born In The U.S.A." by Bruce Springsteen, and "Against All Odds (Take a Look at Me Now)" by Phil Collins.

Beaver Stadium.
Photo courtesy Chuck Fong

1984: Timeline

Paterno: On Home Night Games, Frosh and Being 0-3

Reprinted from 1984 Football Preview

Tracking down Joe Paterno for a personal interview is a full-time job. For while a D.J. Dozier may come and a Curt Warner may go, for 34 years one thing has remained constant in Penn State football: Joe Paterno. Paterno *is* Penn State football, and, in a broader sense, college football. With the one man who seemed to hold a spell over him on the football field, Paul "Bear" Bryant, now gone, Paterno has become the elder statesman of the game.

Paterno's 18-year record as head coach of the Nittany Lions (he was an assistant to Rip Engle for 16 before that) ranks him first among active major coaches with at least 10 seasons as head coach. Paterno, 57, has compiled a record of 170 wins, 38 losses and two ties. His teams have had three undefeated seasons, but he won his first national championship in 1982 with a squad that went 11-1 following a 27-23 win over Georgia in the Sugar Bowl.

His teams are 11-4-1 in 16 bowl games, including appearances following the last 13 regular seasons.

Off the field, everybody wants to know his secret to success, the results of his widely publicized "Grand Experiment" and his feelings on the sometimes incompatible worlds of college academics and athletics. It is no surprise to find Paterno on television with Phil Donahue, in the pages of *Success* magazine and on a radio sports talk show all in the same week. And as long as Penn State keeps on winning, Paterno's word on football—and just about everything else—will continue to be in constant demand.

All of which makes him a very tough man to get a hold of. The initial process of setting up this interview began in early December, before the Aloha Bowl. It extended through the bowl season and into January, only to be put off until the recruiting season ended with the national letter of intent signing date, February 8.

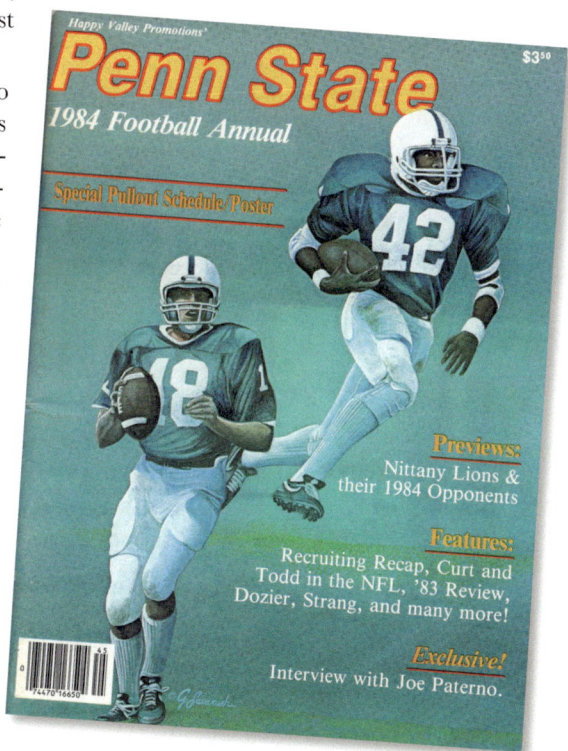

Finally, on what turns out to be an unreasonably warm day in late February, a spare 30 minutes is found in Paterno's schedule. The conversation between Paterno and Mike Poorman of the Football Annual takes place in Paterno's office, a surprisingly small room in the Indoor Sports Complex. On the wall behind Paterno's desk are a few framed pictures, including a photo taken on the Nittany Lion statue. Across from his desk is a plush sofa, and on the wall above that is some pop-out art, a three-quarters life-size montage of Paterno and his football players that jumps out at you. Blue and white predominates.

It is late Friday afternoon and the Nittany Lion coach is trying to squeeze the last bit out of the day before the weekend arrives. After juggling a number of phone calls and some quick meetings with a few of his assistants, Paterno quickly welcomes his visitor and takes a seat on the sofa. With a "Let's go," the interview begins.

FOOTBALL ANNUAL: You've just finished recruiting a new class of freshmen. It seems that recruiting has taken on more importance, year after year, at least from the viewpoint of the fans and media. Will it ever stop?

PATERNO: I think recruiting has gotten out of whack completely. I think that it's almost become another season. And the only problem is, nobody really knows who won. People are constantly saying, "Well, so-and-so had a better year than so-and-so." And nobody really knows until the kids are juniors. That's when you know whether you had a great recruiting year or not.

I think that the newspapers and fans and those talk shows and everybody else is making it much tougher for the kids, and I don't like it. I think it's tough enough to keep things in perspective without all this other hoopla.

FOOTBALL ANNUAL: While we're talking about freshmen, you've said a lot in the past about freshmen eligibility, especially in the past season. Do you see the rule being changed in the future, or will you ever go along with your viewpoint on it and go against the grain and not play freshmen?

PATERNO: I believe it would be better for the kid coming in if he was not eligible to play as a freshman. And nobody will ever convince me that we are right, bringing them and putting them under that kind of pressure and playing them.

But whether we get to that or not, I don't know. I think we probably would have if we had not passed Proposition 48 [of the NCAA by-laws]. But if we make freshmen ineligible now, we take some of the bite out of 48, because the next one, 49-B, says that you can bring them in if they don't have 750 on the college boards, but they can't play us as freshmen, they can't practice as freshmen. We would have taken some of the bite out of that.

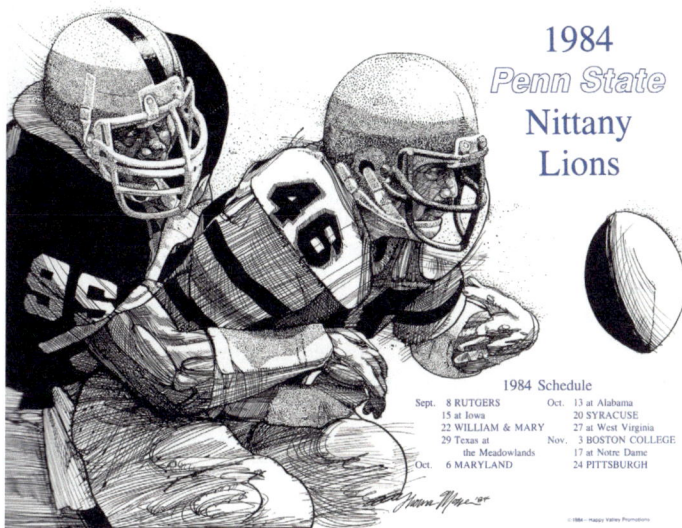

1984
Penn State
Nittany
Lions

1984 Schedule

Sept. 8 RUTGERS   Oct. 13 at Alabama
     15 at Iowa   20 SYRACUSE
     22 WILLIAM & MARY   27 at West Virginia
     29 Texas at   Nov. 3 BOSTON COLLEGE
       the Meadowlands   17 at Notre Dame
Oct. 6 MARYLAND   24 PITTSBURGH

So I think we're probably going to have to wait a little bit before we decide when and if we want freshmen to be ineligible, but I really believe it'll happen.

FOOTBALL ANNUAL: Do you play freshmen because you see your hand being forced to play freshmen because everyone does?

PATERNO: Yeah, well, I don't think you can be fair to a kid. As I've said to kids when we recruit them, even though I'm for the rule being changed, that doesn't mean I'm against freshmen playing if they're good enough. We can't play with one hand tied behind our back. And it's not fair to a freshman or fair to the squad if he's the best player on the team, because as long as you invite him back to preseason practice and he's got to do everything else everybody else does…

If freshmen were ineligible, they'd have a whole different existence. But as long as the rule is what it is, I think you have to play a kid if he's good enough.

FOOTBALL ANNUAL: Turning to last season. Did you learn anything from the past season in terms of waiting to name your starting quarterback? It hasn't changed your philosophy on the subject?

PATERNO: No. You just do what you've got to do each year. My philosophy has never been a philosophy, except that I've always been a one-quarterback man. And I'm not sure that it will always remain that way. I think certain factors will dictate the situation. No, I don't think I would do anything differently than I did last year.

FOOTBALL ANNUAL: You said after the Boston College game last year that in the off-season you're going to re-evaluate the defense. I guess the off-season has really just started, but—

PATERNO: We really haven't had a chance to do much talking, except for a couple of hours. But we've had a lot of pictures in here and the defensive coaches have looked at some pictures.

From now on in, it's going to be all football for me until we start spring practice. And then we'll do some experimenting in spring practice, and see if we can't come up with some different ideas and techniques that might be helpful.

FOOTBALL ANNUAL: In the final seconds of last season's Pitt game, the television cameras focused on you laughing. Were you having fun? And was it anything like the past season in the challenge it presented?

PATERNO: Well, you know anytime things are really going well, there's a tendency to get the job done right. And when things started to go badly, partly because of my doings in the Cincinnati game, and we were 0-3, then it really did become a challenge. It became a question of pride, for the team, for the staff and for me, particularly, on a personal basis. We were determined to get it turned around and when the kids stick with you and they do what they did, there's a great deal of satisfaction.

And it was fun. I enjoyed it. I didn't for one minute mind being 0-3. I know a lot of fans did, and everybody was looking at a lot of different things, but in some ways I enjoyed it. I thought it was a question of now we'll find out, and people out there will find out, that we've got a little something to ourselves. Our kids have got some character and the program has meaning to it and we do have some tradition. And that we're able to overcome a bad start and have a good year. I felt very comfortable that we were going to do it, and when we did it, of course there's going to be some satisfaction.

FOOTBALL ANNUAL: Kenny Jackson is now gone. You two seemed to have a special relationship. You've said a lot of nice things about each other through the years. Can you shed some light on that relationship?

PATERNO: Kenny was one of those people who could have a good relationship with anybody. He was very mature and understood the problems of being a head coach. He was one of those guys who completely believed in the things I believed in, in the sense that you had to hustle every play and what it took to be a winner. Kenny's a real big-leaguer. Anybody who gets him in the pros is getting more than a football player; they're getting a guy who can show some people how to win.

> *Well, you know anytime things are really going well, there's a tendency to get the job done right.*

1984: Paterno: On Home Night Games, Frosh and Being 0-3

He's also an emotional kind of kid, he liked to talk and it was an easy situation. Kenny's one of the finest people I've ever coached. I've coached other people the same caliber as Kenny. I go back to guys like Steve Smear and Denny Onkotz and guys like that, going way back. And then we've had some truly good football players who I never really had a great relationship with, not because they weren't great people, but our personality styles were a little different.

FOOTBALL ANNUAL: At the pep rally the night before last year's Notre Dame game, you twirled your whale pants around your head. Do you really get into things like that—the whale pants, the insignia pants. The big talk of the Aloha Bowl was your outfit.

PATERNO: The Aloha Bowl wasn't planned at all, that was ridiculous. I packed in a hurry and threw anything in that looked like it was colorful and I might want to wear out there. I had to borrow a shirt from my son, Dave. I ordinarily coach with a tie and a shirt, but I didn't have a clean shirt. And I stuck on a pair of pants with it, never even realizing how flashy they were. I don't think a lot of people would've noticed it if the commentator on television hadn't made reference to it so often.

FOOTBALL ANNUAL: But with the whale pants, people really started looking for them—

PATERNO: I don't know. *[Sighs]* The first time I wore those pants, it was kind of like a new beginning. It was the start of the '82 season and in its own kind of way maybe added a little zip. And that's all fine. I get dressed and wear what I have

1984: Paterno: On Home Night Games, Frosh and Being 0-3   91

that's clean.

FOOTBALL ANNUAL: What has changed the most about football since you started coaching?

PATERNO: The publicity being given to college football, and especially our program, about recruiting year-round and everything has changed. We used to get a lot of attention during the season, but then nobody would bug you until spring practice. And maybe even then just a story at the end of spring practice. Now there are publications and newspapers that zero in on you year-round... All the hoopla, the television, the exposure—all those things have changed the game.

I think basically the kids are better. They're more mature, maybe that's because of the exposure. They're obviously better coached, they're better physically, they're better athletes than they've ever been. That part of it has changed.

As far as coaching them, I don't see any difference there. I think on a one-on-one basis it's a little tougher to keep control over the whole squad as it relates to newspaper people, fans and alumni taking time away from their studies and getting them off-beat a little bit. That's a little tougher. You have to constantly talk to them about things you never used to—the agents, the media, you name it. All those distractions. Drugs. I think you have to spend more and more time on things that can cause some problems.

FOOTBALL ANNUAL: Speaking of drugs, everybody from the pro sports teams to the U.S. Olympic Committee is now starting monitoring programs, help sessions, etc. Have you started any such things in your program at all, or is there anything in college football in general?

PATERNO: I think you want to monitor as a deterrent. I think it shows kids how responsible people feel in the sense that drug abuse can ruin them as people and as athletes. I think that monitoring is a good idea because kids understand that it's important, that the peer pressure of smoking a few joints doesn't mean anything.

I just wish there was some way to monitor alcohol, which is very difficult to test unless you get them right away. I think all of that would be good until we get better education for these kids and there's better understanding for the dangers of drug abuse, and then I think we'll work our way out of it.

FOOTBALL ANNUAL: As far as your team goes, if a player had a problem, would he know where to turn within the team structure?

PATERNO: Well, yeah. I don't think you want to monitor or find people to eliminate them. The problem is getting anybody to own up to it one-on-one. Very few of them will do that. But if a kid

does have a problem and you can detect it, now you have a chance to help him. If he doesn't want to be helped, and can't be helped, then you have to eliminate him.

But to think that if a kid—because of some test—shows up that he's been using drugs, to then eliminate him is not fair. Once you find a kid has a problem, you have to try to help him. If you can't help him, you have to get rid of him.

FOOTBALL ANNUAL: Do you find it unsettling that as a coach you have to worry about such things?

PATERNO: That's life, what are you going to do? Too bad if it's unsettling, that's part of your responsibility of being a coach. Too bad it's there, but it's there.

As I said in a speech I made last year in California, you have to have your head in the sand to think that if it's prevalent in the pros, you don't have problems in college. Because those guys come back on campus. A guy like George Rovers leaves South Carolina, then the first year he's with New Orleans he admits to using cocaine. He goes back to the campus to see his buddies, I'm sure he exposes them to it.

And if you're fortunate enough to not have a problem, that's great, that's going to be a plus. But that's not going to be the case. Very few squads in the country do not have kids who are using

drugs. You can't take a group of 100 kids in any group on this campus or any place, and not find a couple. Maybe it's more detrimental to the athlete because of his performance and his ability to develop his potential. In that case, it's more catastrophic.

But I'm sure there are a couple of kids who are using it. I'd be naive to think we don't have a couple such kids on the squad.

FOOTBALL ANNUAL: Looking ahead to your future, when you eventually retire, do you plan to stay in State College? Stay active in the athletic department?

PATERNO: I don't know whether I'd stay active in the athletic department, unless there was a need for me. I'd like to coach another five, six years. I've got a youngster and there's no sense my retiring until he gets into college because you're not going to want to travel around the country when you have a kid in high school; that's not fair to leave him that much.

When I retire, I'd like to do some traveling and maybe get into another career. Whether the other career would involve working at the University or not, I don't really know. I haven't looked that far down the line. I would doubt very much that we would leave State College completely. Maybe go someplace in the wintertime and come back. I will have been here for 40 years. My wife went to school here, all my kids probably will have gone to school here. So I would say I'd be here, but who knows.

FOOTBALL ANNUAL: As for the future of Beaver Stadium, does it look like it'll soon get permanent lights?

PATERNO: I think eventually we're going to have to be thinking about night football. What kind of lights they would be, I don't know. I think the new TV situation, where they allow you to televise some games at night without any restrictions, you've got to be able to have night football. So I would think it'll probably have lights. When, I don't know. I have to talk with [Athletic Director] Jim Tarman and some people in the administration and see what their thoughts are.

FOOTBALL ANNUAL: Then you're anticipating some big changes with television—

PATERNO: The minute they give us some freedom to do things at night, or any time, you've got to have the flexibility of being able to get a prime-time night football game on and that takes lights.

FOOTBALL ANNUAL: So, now you're for the ruling to allow teams to freely negotiate?

PATERNO: No, I don't think each team should freely negotiate. There ought to be some kind of constriction on the teams, whether it's 80 schools or 100 schools or by areas or what. I think there has to be some kind of control.

It's conceivable that the court can come down and say there cannot be any groupings, it's illegal anti-trust. They may say you cannot enter into an agreement with seven other schools as to how you're going to televise. That's one end of the spectrum. The other end, of course, is that they can say the NCAA can continue to do what it's been doing. Someplace in-between is what we think is going to happen.

FOOTBALL ANNUAL: If it goes to the far extreme of a school being able to negotiate totally on its own, a Penn State Pitt game where they're both undefeated at the season's end could conceivably go to the highest bidder for $10 million or more.

PATERNO: Maybe on pay-TV, but again, everybody is speculating on that. Four, five years ago everybody thought cable-TV would be the answer, and then Ted Turner [owner of WTBS in Atlanta] got out of telecasting college football this year. It takes more foresight than I have, but I don't think there's any question that Saturday football is on us. That's not down the road, you're probably going to see some next year.

FOOTBALL ANNUAL: The 1984 schedule includes *eight* teams that went to bowls at the end of the season. Are you ready?

PATERNO: I don't think there's any way you can keep the other guy from getting good. I think the 30 and 95 rules [limiting teams to 30 new scholarships in any one year and 95 overall] and the fact that people are willing to spend the kind of money necessary to have good facilities so they can compete in recruiting have allowed that.

But hey, tough schedule? You've got to like that or you shouldn't be in a situation such as the one we're in. I think the kids enjoy playing a tough schedule. You can't win them all, but...I think people want to see us play good football games, play good football teams. They want us to *win* all of them, too, unfortunately. But most of the time, if you have a good solid football game people are satisfied.

FOOTBALL ANNUAL: Approaching spring practice, where are your major priorities besides finding replacements for the graduating seniors?

PATERNO: I think we want to develop a team that's going to be very enthusiastic and very aggressive. That's one thing I really want to get across this spring: We want to be a really aggressive team on defense. We realize we're going to be a young team and are going to make mistakes, but we want to make them *all out.*

Offensively, we'll have a new coach, we'll have some new input. He's not on-board yet, so we haven't talked much offensively. But I would think we'll play offense somewhat similar to what we've done. And I think we have good potential offensively, depending on how the wideouts come along. We've got to get a couple of wideouts who can come close to the kind of people we've had. And I think if we do that, we'll be OK.

We're going into spring practice with a lot of enthusiasm. I am. I'm looking forward to it, and I'm looking forward to working with the squad. It's going to be a good squad to be around.

FOOTBALL ANNUAL: Who do you see emerging as the team's leaders?

PATERNO: I think guys like [Doug] Strang and some of the other seniors are going to have come to the front. I think Stan Short, and hopefully a kid like Tony Mumford, who had his last shot at things, will come forth and be that type of leader. Defensively, it's going to have to come from some underclassmen. There are so few seniors. Maybe a John Walter, a Carmen Masciantonio, those kinds of people.

But it'll come. I don't think you can ever really predict who's go-

ing to emerge as a leader until it happens, because a lot of guys who are leaders hang back because they've got respect for the other leaders. And then when there's a vacuum, they step in and produce the type of leadership you need.

FOOTBALL ANNUAL: Heading into the 1984 season, what have the returning players learned from last season and the 0-3 start? You can't take anybody lightly?

PATERNO: It's not that. I think it goes way back before that. It goes way back to what kind of leadership we had in the winter program. It goes back to how much some people worked at being better, stronger, over the summer. Some people just literally let themselves and the team down by not getting to be better football players as seniors than they were as juniors. In fact, in some cases they were poorer. Those kinds of things.

But I think once they got into it, everybody tried really hard. I think some people were fatheaded after the national championship—and that includes coaches as well as players—and didn't pay attention to the day-in and day-out things you have to do all year in order to be a good football team with the schedule we have. I think that was the main thing.

And I think also the fact that I didn't do a very good job of handling the quarterback situation. Uh, we had a shaky start. I don't think we could have beaten Nebraska any which way. I doubt very much we could have, but we should have been able to beat Cincinnati, if we had been a little bit more stable. And probably if we had beaten Cincinnati, we would have been a tougher team against Iowa, even though we came close.

FOOTBALL ANNUAL: Two comments about the recruits. One, a lot of them are supposedly good students.

PATERNO: Most of them are really good students.

FOOTBALL ANNUAL: And many of them attended the high school summer football camps held at Penn State. That's quite a recruiting tool.

PATERNO: The football camp has helped. I think kids come here and get an appreciation for what kind of staff we have, what kind of teachers they are, what kind of facilities we have, and I think they get an appreciation for what kind of tradition we have. And it's bound to help you. We don't get them all. Some kids you have in camp and lose.

FOOTBALL ANNUAL: But State College is tough to beat in the summertime.

PATERNO: It's tough to beat anytime.

Penn State 21, Syracuse 5

Reprinted from 1985 Football Preview

UNIVERSITY PARK (Oct. 20) - A healthy D.J. Dozier returned to the starting lineup and put some much-needed punch back into Penn State's offense.

Quarterback Doug Stang, however, was on the shelf this particular game because of a shoulder injury, so sophomore John Shaffer drew his first varsity start before a Homecoming crowd at Beaver Stadium.

Shaffer responded to the challenge, leading the Lions to three touchdowns in the first half and a 21-3 victory over the Orangemen. Shaffer also led Penn State on an 80-yard scoring drive on its first offensive possession.

Four minutes later, Dozier, who rushed for 159 yards on 22 carries, scored on a scintillating 58-yard run. "I think it was my best run ever," Dozier said.

yards. But Paterno let it be known that Strang was still his No. 1 quarterback.

"John played well," Paterno said. "He showed a lot of poise under pressure. But if he's healthy, Strang will play next week. It wouldn't be fair not to let him play. It was the whole team that showed improvement today.

"I think if Doug was in there, things would have turned out well, too. But thank God we have a kid like Shaffer."

You can also thank Penn State's defense, which for the second straight week didn't allow a touchdown. The Lions held the Orange to just 198 yards total offense and a 47-yard, fourth quarter field goal by Don McAulay.

1984: Penn State 21, Syracuse 5

"The defense had to make things happen today," linebacker Shane Conlan said. "We came up with the big plays this week, plays we didn't get against Alabama. The defense is getting better all the time. We were a little upset about the field goal at the end."

Flanker Eric Hamilton, who caught four passes for 69 yards, said: "We've been playing uptight all season. Our goal today was just to have fun out there."

That they did.

Game #7 / At a Glance

Highs...

Dozier finally breaks loose, gaining 159 yards on 22 carries. He also scored on a 58-yard run.

Shaffer gets first varsity start in place of injured Strang and leads Lions on three first-half scoring drives.

Defense doesn't allow a touchdown for second straight week. Holds Orange to 198 yards total offense.

Hamilton catches 4 passes for 69 yards.

...and Lows

Lions don't score in second half.

Gancitano hasn't kicked a field goal in four games.

Surprises

It's hard to believe the Lion defense has improved so much in a year.

The 100-yard performance was the first of the year for Dozier, who had five as a freshman in '83.

Big Play

Mumford's 7-yard TD run in the first quarter. It's all the scoring Penn State needs.

What Joe said:

"In the first half, we played with determination and did some outstanding things. We couldn't do some things we wanted to do in the second half."

Notes

Penn State has won 22 of its last 24 Homecoming games.

Lions had eight sacks, including three by Ginetti and two by White.

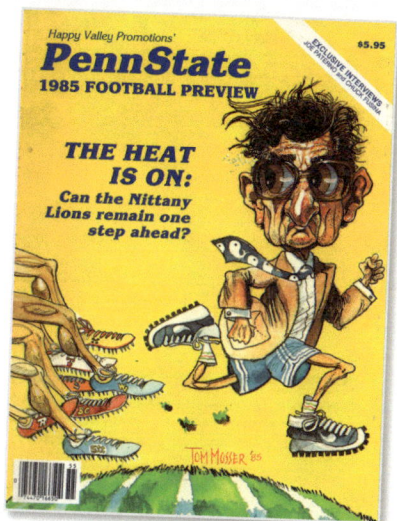

1984: Penn State 21, Syracuse 5

1985

In 1985:

In January, Ronald Reagan took his second oath of office.

On campus, Eddie Murphy brings down the house at Rec Hall. Later on in the year, James Taylor and the Kinks also performed.

Fitness became a craze in the '80s, and brands like Nike and Adidas went from being sportswear to becoming streetwear.

Stricter enforcement of underage drinking makes an impact on campus.

In world news, Ronald Reagan begins summit talks with USSR's Mikhail Gorbachev. Students on campus continue to push administrators to sever relations with companies that do business with the racist government in South Africa. Tensions are rising in Libya and Iran.

This fall Rock Hudson dies of AIDS, and fear of the disease is rampant. The university forms an AIDS policy task force to educate and inform the Penn State community.

In Fall 1985, Penn State pioneers the first total artificial heart. It is implanted into a patient, keeping him alive until his open heart surgery.

At Beaver Stadium, walkways are added around the tops of the end zones and entry ramps at the stadium's corners, lowering the capacity to 83,370.

In football, the team has an unbeaten season, ending the fall at number one. They faced off with the Oklahoma Sooners at the Orange Bowl, losing 25-10 on January 1, 1986.

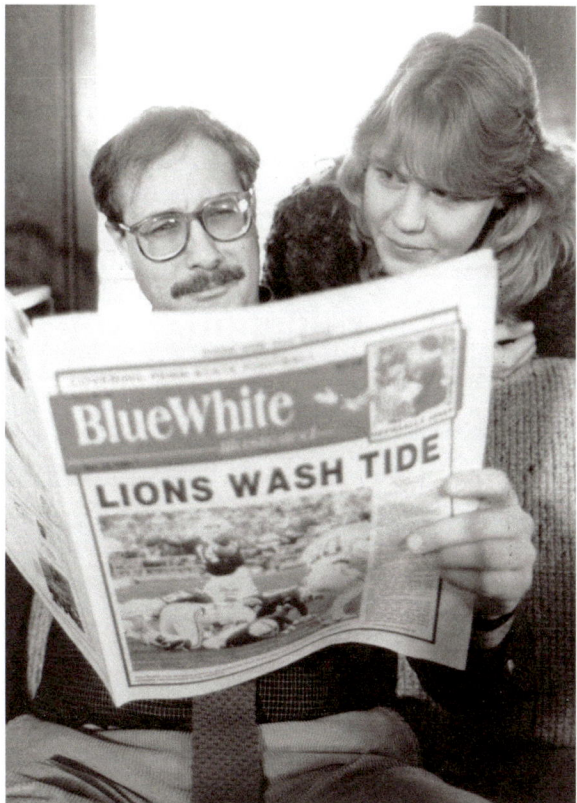

Top movies included "The Breakfast Club," "Back to the Future," "The Goonies," and "Witness."

Top songs included "The Power of Love" by Huey Lewis, "Saving All My Love for You" by Whitney Houston, "Take On Me" by a-ha, and "Some Like It Hot" by The Power Station.

Photo courtesy Sophie Kandler

Greatest Moments at Beaver Stadium:
Nov. 16, 1985 - Penn State 36, Notre Dame 6

Heavy rain started the night before the game and didn't let up until long after Penn State's win. And even though the game was being broadcast on regional TV, 84,000 braved the weather, expecting to watch a close game. Instead, they were treated to the spectacle of No.1-ranked Nittany Lions annihilating Notre Dame en route to an 11-0 regular season and berth in the national championship game vs. Oklahoma in the Orange Bowl.

In the midpoint of the decade, Paterno is hailed as 'larger than life,' but his success didn't change his focus. He made no major endorsements, continued to shun professional coaching offers, and even refused money for the popular "Stand Up Joe" cardboard figures that made their appearance a year before—his percentage went directly into a Paterno Library Scholarship fund.

What remained important for him was giving his staff good leadership, and training his student-athletes for the field, and for life.

Exclusive Interview with Joe Paterno

Reprinted from 1985 Football Preview

There are many ways to paint a picture of who and what Joe Paterno really is.

You can use a wide brush. Crooked nose, shady glasses, white socks, whale pants, parka jacket, cock-eyed grin. Like Champlin's mustache and hat or Groucho's eyebrows or Hope's nose, they are all singularly, and especially together, Joe Paterno.

You can use a fine-toothed comb: Penn State may not really graduate 94 percent of its football players—although its academic record is still one of the best in the country. And didn't he break that NCAA rule this February when he was at the home of Quintus McDonald when the recruit signed a letter of intent.

You can use statistics and numbers. Joe Paterno was born December 21, 1926. He has five children, one wife. His teams have won 176 games, lost 43 and tied just two. His teams are 11-4-1 in bowl appearances. His teams once went 31 games without a loss. Under his guidance, the Nittany Lions have had winning streaks of 23, 19, 15, 12 and 10 straight games. His teams have had three undefeated seasons, but have only been No. 1 once (after an 11-1 season in 1982).

You can take a peek at the awards and honors he has won. National Coach of the Year three times, Eastern Coach of the Year five times. Dapper Dan Man of the Year, Bobby Dodd Coach of the Year, Penn State commencement speaker.

You can look at the financial

picture. It's a very good bet that his yearly salary is in six figures. Each home game grosses $900,000. The revenue from Nittany Lions football pays for the entire varsity sports program at Penn State. That, in itself, is an awesome responsibility.

As is being Joe Paterno.

To many, it seems as if he has been—and always will be—Penn State's football coach. Entering his 20th season as head coach, and his 35th with the Nittany Lions overall, Paterno has become larger than life. Or at least life-size, as the cardboard figures of him attest so well. (Paterno, by the way, makes no money off his cardboard image. His percentage goes directly to a Penn State scholarship fund.)

But he remains a college football coach. He makes no major endorsements, bucks the big-bucks trend by having a weekly in-season TV show on *public television* and has continually shunned offers from professional football to the point where you have to figure they no longer ask.

Save for a brief foray as athletic director, coaching college football has been his life for most of the past four decades. Few can argue that he's done a good—no, great—job of it. Sure, he's cranky with the media sometimes, screeches at his players in practice and preaches loudly to athletic administrators, coaches and college presidents alike. But, in the end, he is simply, morally and honestly the best at what he does.

And he's still having a good time doing it. In an interview with the *Football Preview* in mid-March, Paterno, just back from a vacation in Hawaii, looked fit and was at a great deal of ease. At 58, Joe Paterno looks like he's ready for another trip on the "Road to No. 1."

FOOTBALL PREVIEW: There has been so much talk the past few years about "coach's burn-out," what with Dick Vermeil, Bobby Knight and the like. After nineteen seasons as head coach, aren't you ever worried about that happening to you?

PATERNO: No, because I don't think I get into as many things as they do. It has not been a problem for me. In fact, I just had a week off and took a vacation in Hawaii with my wife.

That's never been a worry. I have a lot of energy and I don't need a lot of sleep; I'm a five or six hours a night kind of guy. And I delegate a

> **"** *Entering his 20th season as head coach, and his 35th with the Nittany Lions overall, Paterno has become larger than life.* **"**

lot of my authority to a good staff. I don't feel like I'm under that much pressure. If I can just get a week off every once in a while, I'm okay.

FOOTBALL PREVIEW: You mention the staff. It seems that just recently people are beginning to understand what an important part it plays in the program. Just how big is its role?

PATERNO: I don't think you can do a good job without a good staff, there's no question about it. The game has gotten so complex that you have to be highly organized in order to get things done effectively. You need not only people who are knowledgeable, but also have the attributes it takes to be efficient—such as discipline and commitment.

The staff is vital to any success we have, but that doesn't mean when things go badly it's the staff's fault. A lot of times it's a question of whether I failed.

FOOTBALL PREVIEW: After a loss you almost always seem to shoulder the blame.

PATERNO: As I should. Heck, I get all the big money [laughs].

I think the really important thing is that I give the staff proper direction and leadership. Sometimes there are decisions that have to be made at my level; sometimes I make good ones and sometimes I make bad ones. But many times people have a tendency to be too critical of the staff in certain situations, particularly when there's a change like last year. We had people leaving and guys moving in, and there was some criticism of those [new] people, feeling that they did not do as good a job as those people who left, which is not fair. The schedule and a lot of things have a big impact on how well you play.

FOOTBALL PREVIEW: In the past five years, it seems like Penn State has forced every Heisman Trophy, every Top Twenty team, every top coach in the nation. Has it reached the point where the quality of the opposition is unappreciated?

PATERNO: That's partly true. The fact that our last two games last season went so poorly, people don't realize what a great job some of our younger kids did early in the

1985: Exclusive Interview with Joe Paterno

year and what a great job our staff did. We were 6-3 at one point, having defeated Maryland, Iowa and Boston College, which were darn good football teams, and came close to beating West Virginia in a tough situation.

I thought our people did really well. I thought I made a couple of tactical errors the last two games in that I was afraid we were getting tired and that we emotionally might have been spent after the Boston College game. So I took it easy on the kids. I think people have a tendency to forget what the staff did for the first nine games. It was an amazing job. The last two games we just had two bad quarters—the second quarter of Pitt, and second quarter of Notre Dame—and didn't have the kind of leadership that could offset that.

FOOTBALL PREVIEW: Is that leadership there now?

PATERNO: There still aren't a lot of seniors on this team, but I think all of us learned a lesson last year. Plus, some of the kids who are going to be juniors played a lot of football as sophomores—the Don Grahams, the Bob Whites—are going to help the seniors give us the kind of leadership we need. We have enough people now who have been in tough football games that they ought to be able to handle anything.

FOOTBALL PREVIEW: Shifting gears here, I've always wondered what you think it is the 84,000 people who fill Beaver Stadium and the thousands more who follow it are really looking for? It's not mere wins and losses, there has to be some psychological explanation for it.

PATERNO: I know. It's gotten to be something that I probably ought to give some thought to, that people identify closely with Penn State football. It's like a vicarious type of existence for them. I don't know where that comes from. You like to have people that are interested in your program, you like them to have that kind of enthusiasm, but sometimes it gets to a point where it almost becomes paranoiac. Their reaction to a couple of losses, their reaction to coaching changes, their reaction to whether you throw the ball enough or don't...well, I look at it as kind of laughable, but it's not laughable to those people. They're very serious about it.

FOOTBALL PREVIEW: And partly because of that, it's gotten to the point where Joe Paterno is Penn State football. Can you even walk down College Avenue? Do you miss that type of thing?

PATERNO: No question about it. The one thing about my job I would like to give up is the notoriety. Basically, I'm a guy who likes people, I like to be around people, but I don't like crowds. I never got into this game because I'm on an ego trip, so I don't particularly like the attention. I would just as soon be another guy in the crowd. It would have been easier for me to bring up my kids, it would have been easier for the family. But that's it, you can't do anything about it, so I don't worry about it.

FOOTBALL PREVIEW: Every coach, it seems, has a particular philosophy he continually preaches. Pittsburgh Steeler Coach Chuck Noll's is "Whatever it takes." You're always saying, "Either you get better or you get worse." Where did that come from and does it apply to both the team and yourself?

PATERNO: I don't know where it came from, but I feel very strongly about it. And I try to apply it to myself. You have to challenge yourself all the time. I try to challenge myself even physically these days, I try to do some things in that direction as well as mentally and discipline-wise. You know, make yourself give up something just to prove that you can do it.

And I do believe you either get better or worse. I think that if you decide you're at a certain level and don't have to get better, you're going to get worse. That's human nature. No matter whether it's physical, what you read, your associations with people, your living habits, I believe very strongly in that and I've tried to preach that to our football team. You go out there and have a bad practice, you're going to be poorer. If you say, "We'll just go out there and maintain this week," you may not even play as well.

FOOTBALL PREVIEW: The three-part *USA Today* recruiting story about top recruit Ned Bolcar had a lot of nice things to say about Penn State and assistant coach Jerry Sandusky. The articles also brought to light all the time and energy that goes into recruiting a single athlete, as well as how attached a player or coach may get to each other—when such a player selects another school, do you feel like a jilted lover?

PATERNO: [laughs] No, no, no. I've never gotten to that stage. Obviously, you're disappointed when you don't get certain kids. And sometimes you do; you get to the point where you genuinely like them, and like their families and like to have them around. You enjoy being around them in addition to the fact that they're good football players. Bolcar was one of them. He was very outgoing and a very easy kid to be around. He would've been fun to have with us.

But a long time ago I came to the conclusion that there isn't one school that's best for everybody. The minute you start thinking that way you get into trouble. That's why we have recruiting. I often tell kids that recruiting is like getting married, that you better not exaggerate too much because when you get married you have to live with each other. And it's the same way with recruiting. What you do is present the best picture you can of what opportunities you offer a kid and then if he doesn't like them, he doesn't like them, you have to forget about him and go on to the next one.

So yes, there are disappointments, but if it's as severe as being jilted, I don't know.

FOOTBALL PREVIEW: In retrospect, it's been two years since Penn State won its first national title. That '82 season is called by many "The year Penn State learned to pass." Is there a hallmark of that squad besides what the public remembers of it?

PATERNO: I think the great thing about the '82 season was that it won the national championship by playing the toughest schedule in the country. Very few teams can do that.

But I'm not so sure the '81 football team, man for man, wasn't a better football team. They didn't play quite as well over the whole year, but '81 and '82 back-to-back with the kind of schedule we had, was a magnificent effort on their part, as were '77 and '78.

I always get a kick out of people trying to say we learned to pass or we learned to do this. If you go back to the '71 team with [quarterback John] Hufnagel and looked at some of the stats to see how much we threw and how much we ran, we didn't throw as much, but our passing game was just as effective.

The '82 team was a team that was in the right spot at the right time. The personnel was just so good. You look at Curt Warner and Kenny Jackson and Todd Blackledge at the skill positions... well, we just had super players. And we had the depth, which you need with our kind of schedule if you're thinking about winning the national championship. That's the hard part for people to appreciate.

We played the toughest schedule in the country last year—I think that came out after just about everybody's evaluation, whether it be the NCAA or *USA Today*. And people don't understand that to handle that kind of schedule and be a national championship contender takes a very, very unusual kind of squad. You can't put that kind of squad together every year when you have good academic standards. Sometimes we cannot find a kid in a certain position who is good enough to come in and handle the academics, so we have to wait maybe a year to fill that position. Therefore

> 66
> *The '82 team was a team that was in the right spot at the right time.*
> 99

it takes maybe two, three years to fit all the pieces together to be a Top Ten squad with our schedule. If we didn't have our schedule it would be different, we could get by with lesser players.

I think people should realistically expect Penn State football to have some problems with the schedule, except for maybe every four or five years when you may have a squad comparable to the '82 squad—if you're lucky.

FOOTBALL PREVIEW: Did last year's squad show the progress necessary to eventually play for the national title in another season or two?

PATERNO: I thought we were making great progress, particularly after the BC game. I felt really good about the squad and that's probably where I made the mistake of thinking the momentum of BC would carry through to Notre Dame and Pitt. I think we had a tendency to not appreciate how good Notre Dame was. I think the coaches did, but I don't think I got it across to the squad.

I've said many times it was almost like a self-fulfilled prophecy. I was scared to death before the season started that we were so young that we wouldn't be able to sustain a certain level of emotion and performance over the whole season. And yet, when we were 6-3, I still worried about it and started to get soft.

I made the statement after the Pitt game that we played like babies—and we did. A lot of people didn't follow up on the second part of what I said; I said, "And I have to blame myself for that." We were not a tough football team, not against Notre Dame and not against Pitt. They weren't tough enough, because I kept telling them to watch themselves in practice and I started to baby them. That, after a while, starts to set in.

FOOTBALL PREVIEW: For thirteen consecutive seasons your teams had gone to bowl games and you always said that the extra practice time was essential in building for next year's game. Because you didn't go to a bowl game in '84, you've lost that extra month. How important is that?

PATERNO: It's important, but we were fortunate last year that we lost so few upperclassmen in the sense of kids who really made a significant contribution so it may not

have affected us that much. I really believe, everything considered, that not going to the bowl game will be good for Penn State football in the future. I think it gave all of us a chance to relax a little bit, to get a couple of things done in perspective. I'm sure we wouldn't have had as good a year recruiting as we did if we had gone to a bowl game. We were able to do maybe a little better job of evaluating and getting started a little quicker. And I think it gave our kids a chance to get away from football a little bit. They had worked awfully hard; there were sixty-some kids up here last summer and it had been a long year for them.

I think after the BC game everybody kind of sighed and said, "We're 6-3 and we're going to have a winning year." Up until then everybody was concerned whether we were going to have a winning year. We just kind of went "Whew," and let all the air out and then we couldn't regain where we had been.

FOOTBALL PREVIEW: So much has been made of the revitalization of Eastern football—Boston College's success under Doug Flutie, West Virginia under Don Nehlen, Syracuse's upset of Nebraska and Dick Anderson's work at Rutgers. For the past fifteen years, Penn State has been one step ahead of them…

PATERNO: Pitt might argue with that, but that's okay.

FOOTBALL PREVIEW: But consistently, Penn State has held that edge over eastern teams. How do you maintain that edge, how do you remain one step ahead?

PATERNO: Well, I don't think one year necessarily proves that there's parity. We have to wait another year or two to really see.

I have hopes we can be a really good football team, although we're still going to have some problems this upcoming year. But I think the following year we ought to be a very, very fine football squad. I think we just have to see what happens. Whether we can stay on top in the sense that we have been kind of the dominant football team—although, like I said, Pitt may argue with us about that—is something that is still there. I think that was proven by the way we were received when we went out to recruit this year. A lot of people thought we'd have a tough time, but we really ended up a little better than we have done in awhile.

FOOTBALL PREVIEW: How has the switch from trimesters to semesters affected the team and your preparation?

PATERNO: That was part of our problem last year, something I didn't adjust to or foresee. In the old days, we had three modules and if a kid needed a stat course, he could push it off to the winter. Now, because of semesters, it seemed that certain classes were given in the fall and not the spring, so the sequence was much tighter and there wasn't as much flexibility. A lot of our kids had to

> 66
> *I really believe, everything considered, that not going to the bowl game will be good for Penn State football in the future.*
> 99

take classes right up to 3:20 and there wasn't any time for meetings. Practice would start at 4:15 and we couldn't go beyond ten of six or six o'clock, because we had a bunch of guys who had classes at 6:30. And more departments are scheduling tests at night. So we were way out of whack, we never got into a sequence where each week was the same. And that makes it tough. We did not adjust well enough to that. Hopefully, now that we've gone through it, we'll get better handling the semester system.

FOOTBALL PREVIEW: You had mentioned recently that there seemed to be a consensus that one team in the East has been a chronic cheater. Who is that and have you turned them into the NCAA?

PATERNO: It's tough sometimes to prove something. You know it, but you can't do anything to prove it. When you say turn people in, you can say, "So-and-so is doing something," and they say, "Can you document it?" And you can't.

As I said, there were three coaches from our area who got together with coaches from other areas of the country and the talk turned to this. The Pac-10 coaches had felt that their league had really cleaned itself up and they asked about us. And I said I think there's only one team in our league cheating and the other two coaches said I was exactly right. They asked who and all three of us said the same school. So it was kind of a unanimous thing. A fourth school that claims they're cheating is in the process of turning them in I think. There's an awful lot of smoke there. If there's a fire for sure, I'm not quite sure. That's why I'm reluctant to mention the school's name.

Now if we can get them straightened out, we'd have a pretty good situation—with football, not basketball.

FOOTBALL PREVIEW: In talking with the players in the offseason, what have you learned about the last season? And what is their attitude heading into the 1985 season?

PATERNO: I think that everything's fine. After I talked to the seniors following the season, and talked to the entire squad, I felt pretty good about things. They weren't blaming anybody, they felt they were young and didn't quite understand what it was going to take at the end of the season. There was some criticism of the coaching, some criticism of themselves, which is what you're going to get if you lose five games. People are going to do some soul-searching.

Overall, I think that it was a mature attitude, one of "Hey, let's learn from what happened last year, but let's put that behind us, let's get on with next year." And that's what I see right now. I see a bunch of guys anxious to get started again.

"Ya Gotta Regatta!"

The Beta Sigma Beta Sy Barash Regatta – a time for fundraising. In April 1985, the 11th annual Beta Sigma Beta event raised nearly $32,000 to be donated to the Centre County unit of the American Cancer Society. The event was co-sponsored by the Kappa Kappa Gamma sorority, UniMart and radio station WXLR and held in honor of Sy Barash, a former president of Beta Sigma Beta who died of cancer in 1975.

Promotion for the event included a "barathon" that raised approximately $500 including the following establishments: Cafe 210 West, The Gingerbread Man, The Lion's Den, The All-American Rathskeller, and The Saloon.

The event was held at Bald Eagle State Park in Howard. Music from local groups like The Hooters, The Phyrst Phamily and The Social Voyeurs; guest appearances from prominent graduates and past football players; tug of war between fraternities, sororities and residence halls; windsurfing and canoe races (including a blindfolded portion!) made for a fun-filled day raising money for a good cause. And the fun didn't end there! The first place raffle ticket winner received a trip for two to Disney World in Orlando, the second prize winner won a windsurfer and the third prize—a 35-millimeter camera.

With such extensive involvement from the community the Regatta event continued to grow and raise substantial funds for the American Cancer Society. In 1985, the donation was the single largest donation received by the Centre County unit. The money was used for research, which is hosted in the national chapter of the society, and education and patient services that would be used in the State College area. In its day, this event grew to be the largest single-fraternity philanthropy in the country, and ended up raising over $300,000 in 15 years before it was discontinued.

PENN STATE'S WHY

Penn State's fraternities turned weekends into opportunities for fun with a purpose.

Classes didn't end until the end of May with the trimester system, making time for warm weather events like the Sy Barash Regatta.

The Regatta stands out as an epic event featuring canoe races, tug of war and windsurfing ... all to raise money for the American Cancer Society.

Regatta. *Photo courtesy Chuck Fong*

1986

In 1986:

In January, the world watches in shock as the Space Shuttle Challenger explodes on air, with six astronauts and teacher Christa McAuliffe aboard.

Tensions rise in race relations as groups form to protest the trustees' refusal to divest. Students build a 'shantytown' from planks and plywood, adorned with slogans like "Divest Now." After 48 days, they take down the shanties, take them to Old Main and 'dedicate' them to the administration. By the next fall, numbers show that Penn State had fallen 25% short of their goals for admissions for African Americans, with cause pointing to the controversy during this school year.

The average tuition cost for in-state residents enrolled at Penn State's University Park campus in 1986 is $2,760.

Penn State celebrates "A Century of Excellence," celebrating 100 years of Penn State football. Congratulatory letters from Ronald Reagan and Pennsylvania State Governor Dick Thornburgh commemorate the event.

"Magnum P.I." is a top TV show for 1986. Other top TV this year includes "Growing Pains," "MacGyver," "Webster," "The A-Team," "Miami Vice," "Hill Street Blues" and "The Cosby Show."

Letters from the president and governor congratulate Penn State for their Century of Excellence.

THE WHITE HOUSE
WASHINGTON

July 7, 1986

I am pleased to send greetings and congratulations to Penn State University as it commemorates its 100th year of participation in intercollegiate football with its "A Century of Excellence" celebration.

Penn State's winning tradition on the football field has provided countless exciting moments, and that tradition has never been stronger than it is today. I know that friends and fans of the Nittany Lions take great pride in athletic achievement, but it is especially gratifying to know that this pride also extends to the fine record of academic prowess compiled by Penn State players over the years. Your football alumni have made great contributions in the arts, literature, science, entertainment, business, politics, and professional sports.

This commitment to excellence both on and off the field is in keeping with the historic mission of your school, and it is a tribute to your concern for the total well-being of the young people who participate in athletics at Penn State. The values learned on the football field -- discipline, preparation, teamwork, self-sacrifice and good sportsmanship -- make not only for victories and championships in autumn, but for triumphs in all of life's seasons.

I take this occasion to wish the 1986 Penn State squad and Coach Paterno the best of luck this year as they continue the grand tradition of Nittany Lion excellence

Ronald Reagan

COMMONWEALTH OF PENNSYLVANIA
OFFICE OF THE GOVERNOR
HARRISBURG

GREETINGS:

The Pennsylvania State University is one of the Commonwealth's most treasured resources. It has provided quality education for generations of men and women, and it has offered them opportunities to participate in numerous athletic, cultural, community and similar activities.

This year marks the 100th anniversary of intercollegiate football at Penn State, and the university is sponsoring special events to recognize this milestone. With a theme, "A Century of Excellence," these commemorations will provide a fitting opportunity for the entire Penn State family to pay tribute to the Nittany Lions.

Best wishes for an enjoyable celebration and for continued success in the years ahead.

Dick Thornburgh
Governor

President Ronald Reagan congratulates Coach Paterno and the No. 1 Nittany Lions.

The Collegian runs a series exploring mysterious secret societies Skull and Bones, Parmi Nous and Lion's Paws, public societies that had gone underground sometime in the '60s. One critic says, "I get the distinct impression that Penn State has its own working version of the star chamber on campus."

In world news, the Iran-Contra Affair makes headlines when Nicaragua downs a plane containing an illegal arms shipment bound for CIA-backed rebels, and Reagan admits his administration has been secretly selling weapons to Iran with 'up to $30 million of those weapons being diverted to Nicaragua.' Penn State alumnus Clair George, CIA's deputy director of operations, is later convicted for his part in the scandal, before receiving a pardon from George H.W. Bush in 1992.

On campus, undercover police carry out a two month investigation before charging 16 fraternities with serving alcohol to minors.

In football, the Nittany Lions beat Pitt 34-14 and clinched a national championship contest against Miami in the Fiesta Bowl. Fans take the north goalpost down College Avenue before parceling it out into tiny "souvenir-sized" pieces. *The Collegian* reports 68 police citations, with one officer understandably suffering from hyperventilation.

Top movies in 1986 included "Pretty in Pink," "Top Gun," "Ferris Bueller's Day Off," "Stand by Me," "Flight of the Navigator," "Aliens," "Labyrinth," and "Crocodile Dundee."

Top songs included "Sledgehammer" by Peter Gabriel, "Live To Tell" by Madonna, "I Can't Wait" by Nu Shooz, "You Give Love a Bad Name" by Bon Jovi, "Invisible Touch" by Genesis, and "Danger Zone" by Kenny Loggins.

Exclusive Interview with Joe Paterno

Reprinted from 1986 Football Preview

Over Perrier and pasta salad, the Nittany Lion coach kicks off his 21st spring practice as the top man. He says his team could lose four games in 1986. Sure... just pass the salt.

It was less than an hour after the Orange Bowl was over when Joe Paterno hurried from the locker room or the team bus, brushing past inquisitive reporters who had asked only a handful of questions of the Lion coach minutes before. "I have nothing else to say," he said, and was gone. That was the last he would formally address the media until a few days before the start of spring drills.

The winter months had passed quickly, so here he was again, facing the same dozen or so familiar faces who cover Penn State football for a living. The 59-year-old coach looked a bit tired, but otherwise showed none of the effects of that season-ending 25-10 loss to Oklahoma in the national championship game. As he made his way to sit down for a working lunch, he greeted each writer and made a bit of small talk. Clearly, Joe Paterno is looking ahead, not backward (not the case last time he lost on Jan. 1).

And why shouldn't he be optimistic? The Nittany Lions, who entered the Orange Bowl 11-0 and ranked No. 1 in the nation, lost only five starters. Their depth should be unmatchable in 1986, when they face the same set of opponents they defeated in 1985. Thirty-seven of Penn State's top 44 players are back. Nevertheless, he says that his team could lose as many as four games if it remains at the same level. That's not likely to happen.

Penn State begins its 100th season of football in 1986 and Joe Paterno embarks on his third decade as head coach (following 16 years as an assistant to the late Rip Engle). The former Brown University quarterback has compiled a 187-44-2 record. Of Penn State's 604 victories, Paterno has had a hand in nearly half (291).

In all his years, Paterno has rarely—if ever—had a team as experienced as the one that will open the 1986 season Sept. 6 in Beaver Stadium. As such, he tells the press between sips of Perrier that he will go easy on some of the older players. There were a few questions concerning the depth chart, spring drills and the health of D.J. Dozier. But most of the questions centered on the Nittany Lion quarterbacks and an offense that was puzzling despite an

> " *Penn State begins its 100th season of football in 1986 and Joe Paterno embarks on his third decade as head coach.* "

undefeated regular season. Before and after eating his pasta salad, Joe Paterno answered them all.

FOOTBALL PREVIEW: What are your thoughts entering spring drills?

PATERNO: Spring is the best time of the year for coaches. You don't have a game to play and you get to work with kids. You get to do some things you wish you had the chance to do in the fall when it comes to techniques. You can experiment with some things.

If we can maintain the same kind of intensity we had last year, we can have some fun this spring. I didn't see that in the winter program as we did a year ago when we didn't have a bowl game. Then we were very concerned about how young we were.

It will be a little bit of a different environment out there this year. Some of the older kids coming back—Shane Conlan, Donnie Graham, Steve Smith—will have been excused from working out in pads. Nine or 10 will come in sweat clothes for 10, 12, 14 days. They'll be around so we don't lose contact with the squad and so we don't lose their leadership.

We probably should be a little farther along than usual on defense, at least with our first group. We have some younger kids we really want to work with. Offensively, I think we obviously want to do a better job with our passing game.

The goals don't change much each spring: you want to make everyone a better football player, you want to teach some things that have carry-over value and you want to teach.

FOOTBALL PREVIEW: How important is it to have a good spring?

PATERNO: We better have a good spring. People don't realize that if we play as well this coming year as we played last year, we'll lose four games. We were fortunate last year. The schedule's tougher this year. We have to play West Virginia, Boston College, Alabama and Notre Dame away this year. If we play exactly the same as we did last year, we'll lose four games. We have to be better, so we have to have a good spring.

FOOTBALL PREVIEW: Who will be the fifth-year players this season?

PATERNO: Shane Conlan, Don Graham, Duffy Cobbs and Bobby White are coming back on defense. On offense, there's Dave Clark, Brian Siverling, Steve Smith, Keith Radecic, Darrell Giles, Sid Lewis, Eric Hamilton, Massimo Manca, John Bruno (and Dan Morgan).

The ones we lost would be guys like Eddie Boone, Eufard Cooper, Tom Wilk, Don Ginnetti—kids who would have had to strug-

gle to play a great deal. Rob Smith and Bob Ontko had a tough choice. Smitty was married and thought he had enough football; the same with Bobby.

FOOTBALL PREVIEW: What is the rationale for giving some of the players a break in spring practice?

PATERNO: I think there ought to be at least one spring in college where you're not out for spring football. This is the last spring they'll be in college. I would like to just tell them to forget all about it all spring, but I'd hate to lose that leadership. I've asked them to come out, be around the young kids and help coach. They worked with the position coaches about what days they'll come out, but I don't want them in pads.

It won't be everyone. Siverling and Morgan, who made a position switch last spring, will have to come out. The wideouts, Lewis and Giles, I want to get a really good look at them. And we have a new coach there who wants to get to know them.

Spring's a pretty nice time of the year here. Play a little golf, tennis, take a look at the girls—those kind of things I never did.

FOOTBALL PREVIEW: Have there ever been this many players who have received a break from spring drills?

PATERNO: You'd have to go back to the 1960s when we had more red-shirts stick around—guys like Dick Anderson and Pete Liske, who were out for baseball, and Charlie Sieminski.

FOOTBALL PREVIEW: Could you talk a little bit about Jim Caldwell (the new wide receiver coach from Louisville) and what

1986: Exclusive Interview with Joe Paterno

D.J. Dozier

he brings to the program?

PATERNO: A couple of years ago when I was trying to get (current Lion assistant) Ron Dickerson to come here and he turned me down, I then talked to Jim because he had been highly recommended by Ron and some other people who had recommended Ron. So Jim's name kept popping up. Then when I was talking to Jim, Ron changed his mind and decided to come, so I kept Jim in the back of my mind.

I was very, very impressed with Jim, so when an opening came about, he's the guy I went for. He's a young coach, only about 31, but he's had a great deal of experience. I don't know if I've ever had someone come more highly recommended.

FOOTBALL PREVIEW: Do you feel better about the wideouts this season?

PATERNO: In going back over the films to get the big picture, I thought Eric Hamilton was probably the most under-rated football player on our team last year. He was really a big-league weapon. Everybody was talking about (Ray) Roundtree and (Michael) Timpson and their great speed, but Hamilton made some great catches in the clutch and blocked really well. So we're in better shape there.

FOOTBALL PREVIEW: Are you going to do anything about the trouble with the offense?

PATERNO: Well, I don't think we had trouble with the offense. I disagree with you on that. I think we only punted the ball once (actually twice) in the second half of the Orange Bowl against a good Oklahoma football team. We didn't execute well enough in that particular game, but that's like saying Miami's going to get rid of their offense because Tennessee annihilated them. That doesn't make sense.

1986: Exclusive Interview with Joe Paterno

We were starting to play well. We scored 30-some points against both Pitt and Notre Dame. I don't really think we had any problems with the offense. The type of game we play doesn't lend itself to what some people call a "good offense." We don't pull a lot of wild things. We play ball control and we're a safe football team that doesn't want to put its defense under the gun. We think we can play defense and kick the ball well enough to win most games if we don't turn the ball over.

Overall, we played well offensively—as far as what I consider well, if not other people—until we played Oklahoma and turned the ball over five times. I think we obviously have to be more productive in our passing game, but I don't think it's a problem.

FOOTBALL PREVIEW: Will you try many new things on offense?

PATERNO: We'll experiment a bit, a play here, a play there. But we're not going to change much. That's how people get in trouble, that's how people get fired: they do what people think they should do.

FOOTBALL PREVIEW: What are your thoughts on the quarterback situation?

PATERNO: It should be interesting. I have been very, very uptight about the criticism John Shaffer has received. I'm not so sure John should be criticized as badly as he was after that particular ball game (the Orange Bowl). I'm reluctant to criticize anyone who worked as hard as John did and stayed healthy.

Maybe I have to look at myself. We may have asked him to

Curt Warner,
all-time rusher.

do too many things. We're taking a good, hard look at our offense, particularly in the passing game, and seeing if we've had too much, how we approach the teaching of it and if we're fair. But I also look at the films and look at some of the things he's done and the fact we won 11 games... Anyway, I think in all fairness to both John and Matt, it should be a wide-open battle in the spring, as it will be in some other spots.

FOOTBALL PREVIEW: Are you worried that the fans and all the comments may have destroyed Shaffer's confidence?

PATERNO: No, and as you know, I really don't care what the fans think. They're going to have their opinion, no matter what. So there's no sense in worrying about that.

I don't think John's confidence has been destroyed and I don't think it should be. Everyone is entitled to a bad game. Unfortunately, it came at a bad spot. Once again, I'm not so sure I'm ready to blame John Shaffer. I think John played well and there are some things we could have done to help him in that game. It's a situation where we have two good football players and we could win with either one of them. I said that all of last year and I'll say it again.

FOOTBALL PREVIEW: Is this a re-evaluation then, because without naming names after the Orange Bowl it did sound as if you were putting a large part of the blame on Shaffer.

PATERNO: No, I didn't. All I said was that we didn't pass that well. That's what I said. I said our passing game was not good enough to beat a team as strong as Oklahoma was. And I think that was obvious.

We didn't throw the ball well enough. We went into the game figuring we had to throw for a couple of hundred yards in order to score enough points to beat them, but a lot of things figured into our getting licked in that game besides the fact we didn't throw well. And they're things we had control over. The part we didn't do well was have an efficient game. That's not to blame John completely; there are other things we could have done.

FOOTBALL PREVIEW: Looking at it from Matt Knizner's point of view, should he feel he's going into spring practice with a chance to win the starting job?

PATERNO: Absolutely. I told that to both kids. I'm not about to put myself in a situation where I think Shaffer's not good enough to win and I'm not going to put myself in a position where Matt Knizner should have to assume that he's a second-stringer. I think when you have two people who are that close at any position, you have to constantly be evaluating and there has to be some competitive situations where one has the opportunity to move ahead of the other or else you're not going to get any work out of them. We're going into the spring with the idea that Matt's got a chance. And I would say that's true elsewhere.

FOOTBALL PREVIEW: Why is Quintus McDonald moving from tight end to inside linebacker?

PATERNO: He didn't want to play tight end. I'd like to keep him at tight end; he'd be a great tight end eventually. But he didn't have his heart in it. He wants to be a linebacker. He doesn't want to play over there. He's big, he can run, he has a lot of power and could end up with good hands. He could end up being a really good blocker some day. And he had good body control despite being a big linebacker. Most linebackers could play tight end.

FOOTBALL PREVIEW: What is your philosophy on moving players around?

PATERNO: There are a number of things that go into it. You have to make sure that you don't have someone No. 2 at one position when he could be No. 1 at another position, regardless of where that other position is—except maybe at quarterback.

The way we pick our football team is by giving the defense first crack at a player. The defense gets the best football players. The first 11, the best players, fill in the 11 spots on defense. Then we go to the offense. Now, if you have a guy who is a 6-foot-3, 275-pound offensive lineman who may not have the feet to be a

defensive lineman, but the defense needs him, then he goes there. Defense gets first crack, because if you can play defense and kick, you'll at least have a decent year.

Sometimes there's a guy like Todd Moules last year, who could've started on defense. But we felt we had people who could do as well in that spot, so we moved him to offense. And Moules had that certain personality, even if he hadn't been a senior, to help the offense.

As far as making that move with a senior, I wouldn't do it unless I felt that the senior had a chance to be a professional football player. I think you owe that to a kid. I don't think Moules will ever have a chance to be a defensive lineman in pro football; I do think he's a prospect as an offensive lineman. He has a chance to be a pro guard. So you ask a kid to make a move that's going to give us the best team possible—until the last move. The last time you move a kid you have to do what's best for him.

FOOTBALL PREVIEW: The same situation occurred with Jimmy Cefalo when you moved him to wideout.

PATERNO: Absolutely. Jimmy didn't have the power to ever be a big-league running back. But you knew he could be a wideout. He got five, six years out of pro football, put some money in the bank and got started on a good career.

FOOTBALL PREVIEW: Could you comment on the loss of Moules on the offensive line?

PATERNO: It's a big loss, particularly when it comes to leadership. Moules was a great guy. He and I had our differences on TV, unfortunately, but I'm very, very fond of Todd. A great player, very

1986: Exclusive Interview with Joe Paterno

mature. The senior starters were all that way. They'll be tough to replace. They all were leaders and very businesslike out there.

The way we play football, we have to be a dominant offensive line. We have to wear down people to the point where we can do the things we want to do. We have to improve there. You all talk quarterback, but to me that's one area where I'm concerned. When we've been good, we've had a couple of kids who've gone in the first three or four rounds (of the NFL draft). Unless some of those guys suck it up and really go to work, I don't see anybody in that category. They're a concern of mine. They're good, but they're not looking at anybody we play in the eye—the Munchacks, Farrels, Dorneys—and some of them have the capability to do that.

FOOTBALL PREVIEW: How much work do you want to give D.J. Dozier in the spring and preseason?

PATERNO: I think D.J. needs to get the feel of things again. He played awfully hard last year, but I think the out-in-out-back-in-again kept him from getting back in the groove of where he was playing so well. He made a couple of runs, a couple of bad decisions on cuts up front, so I think he needs some work. How much, I don't know.

The way we play football, we have to be a dominant offensive line. We have to wear down people to the point where we can do the things we want to do. We have to improve there.

We'd like to get a look at some other kids. We have to be fair to Dave Clark, too. I'm a little surprised that Dozier's picture is on the (1986 season) schedule. Not that he doesn't deserve it, but I think he has to make sure that he's not playing behind Clark, because Clark had the best average and was probably the best tailback we had last year. That's not because Dozier isn't potentially the best we have, but if I were to evaluate strictly on the pictures and not knowing I would say Clark had the better year. And I think Brian Thomas has an outstanding chance to be a good tailback one day. Whether he can handle all the things he has to learn, I don't know. But he has an awful lot of ability.

FOOTBALL PREVIEW: What kind of senior year are you expecting from D.J.? Last year at this time we were talking about him being a potential Heisman Trophy candidate.

PATERNO: He has to stay healthy, there's no doubt about that. You get into problems, and I've said this many times, unless you practice as well as play. Every time a guy loses a couple of games and comes back, everyone says, "Well, you've got him back." We get him back, but he's not the football player he would have been if he hadn't gotten hurt.

I don't think D.J. had a great year last year, but it was not his fault. When he was in he played as hard you can play. He's a great competitor. I don't think anybody who's ever seen him play has

ever seen him not give everything for every play. He doesn't pace himself or anything on the football field. It's not a question of what he's done; it's a question of his injuries. He has to stay healthy and do things over and over again, so that when he gets those two or three opportunities to make a big play each game, he sees them and does them. That's his style. If he gets in the secondary a couple times a ball game, we'll get those plays out of him. He did that a couple of times last year, but nowhere near as many as we thought he was going to have to do in order to be successful.

FOOTBALL PREVIEW: The last two times Penn State played for the national championship, the season that followed you had four losses. Is there anything you can do to keep this team from looking back?

PATERNO: I didn't even know that happened. I do know why it happened to us in '79 and in '83. In '83 we opened with Nebraska. Temple might be tougher than Nebraska, I don't know. Every squad is different. I would not like to get into the reasons why we had our problems in '79. In '83, it was different.

The team won all its games in '68 and did it again in '69. The team in '72, they lost two games and came back and won them all. And in '77, we lost only one to Kentucky and came back the next year and won them all (in the regular season).

The past year I felt we were better than what I thought we were going to be. I would hope we'll be on the move this year, and I have no reason to think otherwise. Even being better this year, like I said, we could lose four games. And that wouldn't be because we lost the national championship. That's just a matter of fact.

FOOTBALL PREVIEW: Has the Orange Bowl loss had an affect on the mood of the squad?

PATERNO: I don't know, but I'm assuming that there's some pride there or else they wouldn't have gotten as far as they did last year. I hope there's enough pride in their own individual ability and in the football team that they weren't pleased about getting licked in a big game like that. I'm assuming that they're going to come back and be better.

Traditions Abound at Dear Old Penn State

BY G.R. SEVERINE

Reprinted from 1986 Football Preview

PENN STATE'S WHY

Autumn Saturdays were filled with fanatical fans and honored traditions. But more than that, they were filled by thousands of alumni returning to the place they'd come to call home.

From long-forgotten events such as Poverty Day, to newer trends like away games on closed-circuit television, Penn State has developed a rich and envious football tradition among its fanatic following. In its 100 years, some rituals have fallen by the wayside, while others have made the transition from Beaver Field to Beaver Stadium.

College traditions can be defined as the unwritten customs, events, ideals and individuals that influence and create the character of that institution. Fred Lewis Pattee defined traditions as "the body of talk at a gathering of alumni, the stories of old fellows who were graduated long ago; everything combined that has made a college." It is these traditions passed down by word of mouth that has created a colorful past associated with Penn State football.

Poverty Day is one of those traditions which has faded to the yellowed pages of rare scrapbooks in Pattee Library's Penn State Room. In the 1920s, when freshmen were subject to ridicule, upperclassmen selected a group of freshmen to entertain the crowds at one game a season. Dressed in rags, prancing around the field, these "freshies" were the halftime show.

A different, more enduring and popular crowd-pleaser is "Ladies and Gentlemen, the Penn State Blue Band." Taking the field at each game, the 220-member band stirs up the packed stadium with Penn State fight songs.

This contemporary musical tradition was molded and formed over the past 88 years. The band started as a six-member Cadet Bugle Corps founded by George Deike ('03) in 1898. It op-

erated as a small, military-style band until 1901, when increased support and an $800 donation from trustee Andrew Carnegie was available to purchase Diston brand silver instruments and became the College Band.

The band still wore the brown uniforms associated with the Spanish-American War until a 1924 acquisition of navy blue uniforms. Only the best of the band achieved the coveted blue uniforms and hence, the elite members were referred to as the Blue Band of the College Band.

Women were not introduced into the Blue Band until 1973, except during a brief period from 1944 to 1945. The 1973 season opener also saw the first appearance of the Touch of Blue. In 1968, the Blue Band silks first appeared in Beaver Stadium. They originally carried the colors of Penn State's opponent, but today they present the Penn State colors.

While the band has a long and illustrious history, its command is marked by stability. Only four permanent directors have led the band onto the playing field. Wilfred O. "Tommy" Thompson (1914-1938), Hummel "Hum" Fishburn (1939-1947) and James Dunlop (1947-1975) passed the baton down to Dr. Ned Diehl. Under the direction of Dr. Diehl, and with the legacy of these former directors, the Blue Band continues to bring the audience to its feet as an integral part of each football game.

Another long-standing tradition is Penn State's annual Homecoming celebration. Initiated by some influential alumni, they

1986: Traditions Abound at Dear Old Penn State

pressed the University to hold a Homecoming celebration that would encourage past graduates to return to their alma mater. This celebration was held in the fall of 1914 in conjunction with a home football game.

It was in the 1930s that the social fraternities and sororities got involved with the homecoming activities. The first Greek lawn displays which raised the competition of spirit among the undergraduates and alumni was in 1931. Other campus-wide traditions soon emerged like the bonfire (1934) and the Homecoming Queen (1940).

Although student disinterest dulled Homecoming in the 1960s and early '70s, the excitement of Homecoming activities has returned. The Greek influence still dominates in activities such as the vigil at the Lion Shrine, candlelight choir celebrations, the parade, the bonfire and fireworks, and the coronation of the Homecoming Queen and King. Despite the changes in attitudes and years, alumni return faithfully each year to observe the longstanding tradition of Homecoming.

Tailgating is Penn State. This die-hard tradition is almost as important as the game itself. Who can forget those sunny, crisp mornings crowded around the car with sandwiches and cold drinks? Thousands of alumni and football fans trek hundreds of miles to socialize hours before kickoff, crowded around a hot grill and an ice-cold case of beer.

And after the game or tailgating, fans have been going over to the Nittany Lion Inn to listen to the Tarnished Six, a traditional dixieland jazz band that has been entertaining since 1931.

The history of tailgating is not accurate because of its informal nature. However, the stadium relocation prior to the 1960 season stepped up its popularity. Today, tailgating has become such a solid tradition, it has become nearly as important as the game. As one fan alluded to tailgating, "It's the tail that wags the football lion."

Acres and acres of parking enable the fans to enjoy the entire football experience. In the shadow of Mount Nittany and entranced by the roar of the crowd, tailgating at Penn State is a football tradition unrivaled at any other university.

In the '60s, despite student apathy, a group of students identified themselves as Students for State. Their mission was to develop school spirit. They painted paw prints from the shrine to the football locker rooms and then to the stadium. This track was to symbolize the awakening of the lion's spirit and its entrance into the hearts of those about to play. However, the group lost interest and disbanded in 1972.

Another football-related tradition were the "S" block students. These were seniors who participated in a giant card display. Each student had a blue and white card, which he would hold above his head. In unison they would spell words at halftime. This group, too, lost interest and faded into a tradition of the past, although another student group might try again during the coming season.

The game, as well as its customs and side events, constantly changes and evolves. Some recent traditions reflect the widespread enthusiasm of Penn State today.

The demand for promotional and novelty items has created a big business in Happy Valley. Today, local companies produce everything from Penn State T-shirts to a Penn State Master Card emblazoned with the school logo. The fans' demand for items to display their school spirit has produced Penn State underwear, an official Pennsylvania vanity license plate, Blue Band records and tapes, game-day buttons and even a cardboard likeness of Coach Joe Paterno. This phenomenon is growing and will likely produce even more unusual products for proud Penn Staters.

The growth in football fanaticism has necessitated new traditions organized by the Alumni Association. In 1976, the Alumni Association made the radio broadcast of games available to alumni clubs via telephone. This telephone hook-up was limited to the six-line capacity of the Association's phone system. Then in 1984, a new Penn State connection—a 900 number—was initiated for the Penn State-Maryland game. For 50 cents the first minute and 35 cents for each additional minute, alumni groups were able to dial the phone and hear the game. Considering the price of long distance travel, hotel accommodations, game tickets and meals, this is an economical way to tune in. During the last season, the 900 service logged over 17,000 calls and almost 100,000 minutes of use.

Another tradition firmly established is television and radio connections. With TCS radio and television broadcasts of every game, Penn State football is made available to every media market that wishes to carry the Nittany Lions. In conjunction with the Alumni Association, games are also available via closed-circuit TV for club parties. Alumni clubs also hold away-game parties and brunches. This provides a common ground for graduates who live near an away game to meet and celebrate Penn State football.

The Alumni Association provides another valuable tradition, The Football Letter. This publication grew from a one-page mimeographed sheet and maintains tradition as the oldest football newsletter continually published by an alumni office. Ridge Riley started the newsletter in 1938, with John Black taking over after Riley's death in January 1976.

Penn State football and the traditions associated with it create a distinctive individuality for the University. The institution becomes a sum of all its history, customs and evolving traditions. There is no doubt that when you mention the name Penn State, a fine football tradition is immediately envisioned. Now, with the football program's Century of Excellence celebration, we are reminded of all the pieces, both present and forgotten, that make up the sum.

1987

In 1987:

On January 2, the Nittany Lions won their second national championship in a bout that commentators called "The Game of the Century." In the weeks before the game, the teams were touted as a good v. evil—Pennsylvania downhome values against Miami Vice and battle fatigues. Just named "Sportsman of the Year," by *Sports Illustrated*, Joe Paterno has created a signature brand with his Jesuit values, Robert Browning quotes, rolled up pants and strict dress codes for his players off the field. Miami Coach Jimmy Johnson's players, on the other hand, took pride in their bad-boy persona, casual dress code and run-ins with the law. With a winning score of 14-10, Penn State took home the national championship for the second time in five years. Back home, there were victory parades and a near-worship of Joe Paterno as he returned to campus. "Here comes God!" is one familiar cry.

The Bangles had the biggest song of the year with "Walk Like an Egyptian."

During the fall 1987 season, the Nittany Lions played without fifteen starters from the championship game; after an 8-3 season, they lost to Clemson in the Citrus Bowl.

On October 19, 1987— known as Black Monday— the Dow Jones Industrial Average fell by 508 points, or by 22.6%. Up to this point in history, this was the largest percentage drop in one day. The crash sparked fears of extended economic instability around the world.

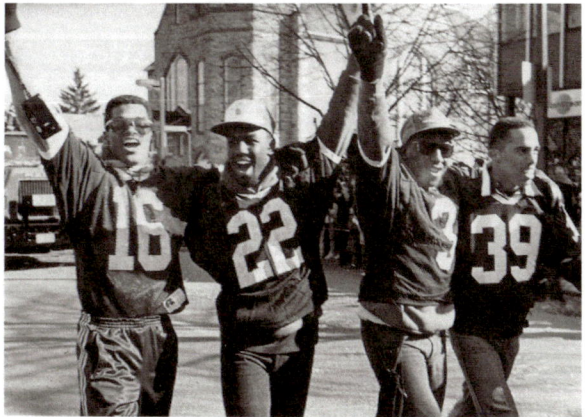

As they walk down College Avenue in State College, the Nittany Lion Smurfs Duffy Cobbs (16), Ray Isom (22), Marques Henderson (3) and Eddie Johnson (39) stand tall.

Top movies this year included "Lethal Weapon," "Predator," "Dirty Dancing," "Wall Street," "The Princess Bride," "The Untouchables," "Spaceballs," "Full Metal Jacket," "Harry and the Hendersons," "3 Men And A Baby," and "Overboard."

Top songs included "Bad" by Michael Jackson, "Always" by Atlantic Starr, "I Still Haven't Found What I'm Looking For" by U2, "(I've Had) The Time of My Life" by Bill Medley and Jennifer Warnes, "Big Love" by Fleetwood Mac, and "Head to Toe" by Lisa Velez.

1986 FOOTBALL REVIEW

$4.95

PENN STATE

*Special
Fiesta
Bowl
Section*

National Champs Again

▶ **How They Did It
Season in Review**

▶ **Exclusive
Paterno/Sandusky
Interview**

1986: Fiesta Bowl

How the No. 1 Team Was Built

BY RON BRACKEN

Reprinted from 1986 National Champions Football Review

The Sunkist Fiesta Bowl victory over Miami and the ensuing No. 1 ranking should come as no surprise to avid Penn State fans. Joe Paterno's veteran team spent a lot of time paying its dues the past few years.

Installment No. 1: Three straight losses in 1983 after winning the 1982 national championship before salvaging an 8-4-1 record.

Installment No. 2: A 6-5 record in 1984.

Installment Nos. 3 and 4: A 44-7 loss to Notre Dame and a 31-11 spanking by Pitt to close that '84 campaign.

Installment No. 5: A 25-10 loss to Oklahoma in the 1986 Orange Bowl, a loss that caused the Lions to lose their No. 1 ranking and gain a new offensive strategy.

Those are big prices to pay for success. But hey, Rome wasn't built in a day. So why should a Penn State football team?

After the 1984 season, it might have been hard to envision that the Lions of Paterno would ever again challenge for No. 1 even once, let alone twice. But in the rubble of that 6-5 season were the building blocks of the team that went 23-1 over the past two years.

It would take some switching, some addition and subtraction, some molding, polishing, refitting and refinishing, but many of the ingredients necessary were already at Paterno's disposal way back in the 1982 season. They were just red-shirts, that's all.

Eleven starters in the 1987 Sunkist Fiesta Bowl, were freshmen in 1982. Ten stood on the sidelines Jan. 1, 1983 in the Superdome, while the 11th, Massimo Manca, served as the backup kicker against Georgia that day. That group formed the nucleus for Paterno's second national championship squad this decade.

Paterno had an inkling how good they were. He wasn't sure, but he had a good feeling about them. So he eased them into the lineup, and after a few growing pains, they responded by winning nine of their final 10 games of 1983. He filled the gaps with two good recruiting years. What followed was a 5-2 start in 1984, marred only by a mismatch against Texas and tough 6-0 loss at Alabama. It was good enough to convince Paterno that his rebuilding project was going to plan.

And why not? He had done it before; he could do it again. Still, the questions about the Lions' "demise" continued. Finally, on Oct. 20, 1984, he had heard enough.

PENN STATE'S WHY

The second national championship was a fable for the ages: "The Game of the Century" that portrayed the game as "good v. evil," Pennsylvania down home values against Miami Vice and battle fatigues. Joe Paterno maintained his signature brand of his Jesuit values, Robert Browning quotes, rolled up pants and strict dress codes for his players off the field, while the players of Jimmy Johnson, former Pitt assistant coach who became Miami's head coach, took pride in their bad-boy persona, casual dress code and run-ins with the law.

With a winning score of 14-10, Penn State took home the national championship for the second time in five years.

"People get so critical," Paterno scolded the press that day. "I'm trying to put together a squad that some day can win the national championship."

The message was out: The Master knew what he had in place. He knew all that was needed was time for the ingredients to mix. And we all now know that he was right.

Consider the list of players who saw action in one capacity or another that day against Syracuse: Mitch Frerotte, Mark Sickler, Chris Conlin, Stephen Davis, Brian Siverling, Pete Giftopoulos, Eric Hamilton, Ray Rountree, Sid Lewis, John Shaffer, Matt Knizner, D.J. Dozier, Dave Clark, Steve Smith, Tim Manoa, Mike Russo, Matt Johnson, Pete Curkendall, Bob White, Dan Morgan, Rich Kuzy, Tim Johnson, Shane Conlan, Don Graham, Trey Bauer, Mike Beckish, Chris Collins, Duffy Cobbs, Ray Isom, Marques Henderson, Dwayne Downing, Drew Bycoskie, Darrel Giles, John Bruno, Massimo Manca, Kurt Bernier, Gregg Johns and Paul Pomfret.

Every one of them was on the squad that defeated Miami in the Sunkist Fiesta Bowl. Frerotte, of course, was a medical red-shirt in 1986, but he started against Oklahoma in the Orange Bowl. And severe knee injuries reduced Collins and Bycoskie to shells of their former selves. But everyone else had a key role in the national championship squad.

Shaffer started in place of the injured Doug Strang against Syracuse that day and Knizner was next in line. It was that way the past two years, a loss to Oklahoma notwithstanding. Shaffer was 23-1 as a starter over the past two seasons. Knizner, the winner in relief against Alabama in 1985, will get his shot next year.

Dozier was already solidly entrenched at tailback, with Clark behind him. The following year Blair Thomas was mixed in for depth. Good planning, that, because he was needed. In 1984, Smith was slightly ahead of Manoa at fullback, but over the past two years it became a dead heat. (Some say even their mothers can't tell them apart on the football field.) The two of them have been equally effective in an offense that has been modified to both take advantage of their abilities and to take some heat off the tailbacks.

Siverling was then a gangly red-shirt sophomore who was biding his time behind incumbent Dean DiMidio. Last year, he took over the starting job; this past season he was one of Shaffer's most dependable receivers. Pomfret, who had special teams time against Syracuse, became the backup tight end. Giftopoulos was a freshman tight end that year, playing behind DiMidio, Siverling and John Walter. This past season he started at inside linebacker (much to Vinny's chagrin) and he may become the next Shane Conlan.

Conlin was already the starter at tackle as a sophomore and

Stan Clayton, this past season's other starter at tackle, was being red-shirted. Davis wound up backing up Conlin, starting when he was hurt. Morgan was switched from defensive end to the offensive line, where he started at guard. The other starting guard was Steve Winiewski, a sophomore who out-dueled Kuzy for the starting job. Frerotte and Sickler were guards as well. Sickler has since moved to tackle; Frerotte will go to defense when he comes back in the spring. Radecic was already being groomed to take over for Nick Haden that year. In 1985 he won the center's job from Rob Smith and was the anchor up front ever since.

A year ago Eric Hamilton stepped into a flanker's job and turned in a superb job. Roundtree has been a longtime starter at split end, providing the offense with a deep threat, especially in the absence of Michael Timpson. Lewis and Giles were backups at split end. Jerry Hug and Jimmy Coates, additions a year later, added quality and quantity.

All but one of the starters on this year's defense saw playing time that day against Syracuse and in virtually the same positions. If you had any questions as to why the '86 defense performed so well, the answer is rooted in that early experience.

The ends against Syracuse in 1984 were White, Morgan, Kuzy and Tim Johnson. In the revamped defense of 1986, White and Johnson were tackles in the three-man front while Russo was the nose guard. Matt Johnson was the backup to both Russo and Tim Johnson, while Curkendall was listed even with White as a starter. Sophomore Rich Schonewolf was behind White and Curkendall, one of only six sophomores who has been able to make a dent in the two-deep chart. (Joe must be saving the other guys for the next run at No. 1).

Graham was an inside linebacker in '84, lining up alongside Carmen Masciantonio. Last year he was moved to an outside

Left, Center: Bob White was on Paterno's five year plan, as was his teammate on the other side of the defensive line, Don Graham, center.

Right: Shaffer completed 55.9 percent of his passes in 1986, 11.2 percent better than the year before.

1987: How the No. 1 Team Was Built

spot where his speed and agility served him well as an outstanding blitzer. Bernier became his backup and was a big hitter on the special teams. Quintus McDonald, one of the country's most heavily recruited athletes two years ago, challenged Bernier for playing time.

Bauer emerged as a fiery leader of the defense from his inside backer spot alongside Giftopoulos. Sophomore Scott Gob backed him up, while Beckish saw action behind Giftopoulos and junior Troy Davis.

After his gutty Fiesta Bowl performance, there's little doubt that Conlan will be remembered as one of the finest linebackers to ever play at Penn State. He's a certified first-round draft pick. That potential was already evident in the '84 Syracuse game when he had five tackles, including two for nine yards in the losses. Junior Keith Karpinski came along the following year and is now the heir apparent.

The hero job in 1984 belonged to Michael Zorduch, who kept it until he graduated after 1985. Henderson stepped into the breach and filled it well. Sophomore Sherrod Range signed on in the spring of 1985 and, with freshman Brian Chizmar, provided depth. Isom took over the safety job from Darrell Giles in the Iowa game in 1984 and has been rock solid ever since. Few safeties have played longer or better for Paterno.

Cobbs was already in the lineup at his cornerback position against Syracuse and gradually developed into one of the better corners in Penn State history. Downing got blooded against the Orangemen and will likely succeed Cobbs. Eddie Johnson, the starter at the other corner, was still in high school the fall of 1984. One of the plums of his recruiting class, he got a chance to show his talent early last year when inserted in the lineup late in the East Carolina game when the Pirates were moving and the Lions went to a man-to-man defense. That is a supreme compliment for a rookie. Johnson has gotten better with every game since that day. Behind him was sophomore Gary Wilkerson, who broke up what would have been a season-destroying touchdown pass.

Manca was sharing time with Nick Gancitano that fall of 1984, handling the kickoffs while Gancitano took care of the placements. Over the last two years, Manca has had the job to himself. Bruno was exactly the kind of punter Paterno likes: He didn't shank the ball and he kicked it out of bounds inside the 20 with some consistency. Although Manca slumped somewhat in '86, Paterno's success at building up the kicking game has gone largely unnoticed.

After the 14-10 win over Miami, it's not likely any building project by Paterno will ever be questioned again. And if it is, all he has to do is point back to that October afternoon in 1984 and say, "There's the blueprint."

Lion linebacker Don Graham shows the nation who's No. 1 after sacking Testaverde.

Sportsman and Coach of the Year Reflects on Century of Excellence Season

Reprinted from 1986 National Champions Football Review

After capturing his second national title in five years, as well as coach of the year and *Sports Illustrated's* Sportsman of the Year honors, one might think Joseph Vincent Paterno, better known as JoePa, would begin a long-deserved vacation.

But January and February also happen to be the height of the recruiting season, and Paterno will not rest until he has signed his share of high school seniors (he can sign 30, the NCAA maximum), who he hopes will represent the university well both on and off the field.

Paterno, in State College for only the second time since leaving for Arizona, gave up 20 minutes of his time to talk with *Football Review's* Chris Lindsley, who asked the 60-year-old Brooklyn native to reflect on the Century of Excellence season.

FOOTBALL REVIEW: With all that's gone on this year, the Century of Excellence, winning the national championship, and all the recognition you've received, could you have imagined a better script?

PATERNO: I guess not. I think everything happened that you hope would happen, particularly since it is our 100th year and we had a bunch of kids that worked hard to make it happen. Sometimes people work hard and it doesn't happen. So for the tradition and the individuals, it's been great.

FOOTBALL REVIEW: What about for you personally, with receiving the coach of the year honors as well as being named the Sportsman of the Year?

PATERNO: Obviously it's one of those years you don't think would ever happen to you, but I've had so many good things happen to me... I just think the timing of everything makes me feel really good. That we did do the big three dinners, that we did talk about our 100th year in football, that people expected us to do well and the kids did well, all those things have been very gratifying to me. The awards themselves, they're only indicative of what the other people have done. So I'm not carried away with the awards. I'm just glad to be part of this whole thing.

FOOTBALL REVIEW: After a game like the Fiesta Bowl, people often say it takes a while for it all to sink in. Has it sunk in yet?

PATERNO: I don't know if it will ever sink in in the sense that

PENN STATE'S WHY

In this interview, Paterno had just led the team to their second national championship, been named Sportsman of the Year, and was commemorating the football program's century of excellence.

But he made sure the success had more to do with Penn State's values of training the whole person than it did with his skill, saying, "I think the Sports Illustrated award was a direct complement to Penn State's belief in the way intercollegiate athletics should be."

maybe people think it will. I haven't got time. I've been out recruiting. This is only the second day I've been in State College since before we left for the bowl trip. I came back a week ago Friday from San Diego, went to Philadelphia then came back here late Friday night, was here Saturday and then Sunday I was on the road. And I just got back last night. I don't really have time to think about it. I'm worried about next year right now.

FOOTBALL REVIEW: Does winning the national championship again plus the exposure you've received this season make recruiting easier?

PATERNO: I don't think recruiting's ever easy. I think a lot of people know about you, obviously it opens up a lot of doors, but you've got people talking about how long it will take to play and a lot of other nonsense, and everybody gets in on it now and they kind of gang up on you. They know they've got to beat Penn State, so you've got to beat down a lot of people who are trying to organize to direct their attack at Penn State.

I don't mean that in a dirty sense, but they know so much about us, and they talk about this kid's coming or that kid's coming, they practically watch your every move. We're going to have to be aggressive. Right now, we're not in very good shape. I think we can get better, but right now we've got a lot of work ahead.

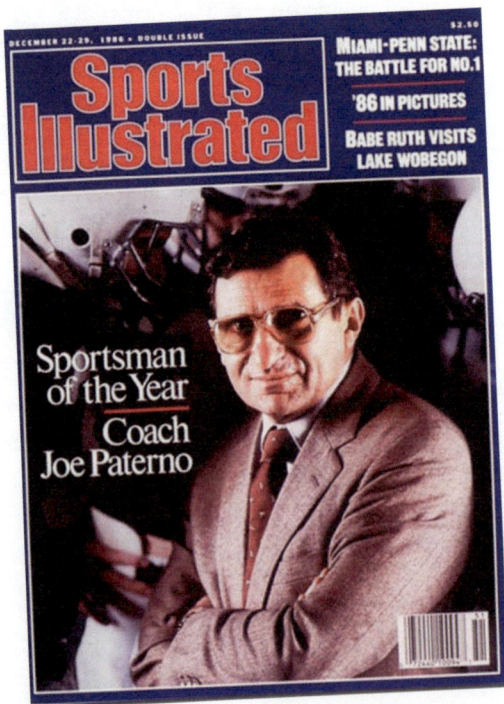

Sports Illustrated

DECEMBER 22-29, 1986 • DOUBLE ISSUE — $2.50

MIAMI-PENN STATE: THE BATTLE FOR NO.1

'86 IN PICTURES

BABE RUTH VISITS LAKE WOBEGON

Sportsman of the Year Coach Joe Paterno

FOOTBALL REVIEW: You said after the '82 season that you were on the road to too much with personal engagements, and that it hurt the football team. Is there a chance of that happening again?

PATERNO: No. I'm going to alienate a lot of people who want me—alumni, sportswriters and things like that, but I'm going to have to say no. We've got a massive regrouping to do.

FOOTBALL REVIEW: After beating Miami, it would seem like you deserve a vacation, yet you push on. Do you ever rest?

PATERNO: After that (national letter of intent day, which is Feb. 11), my wife and I will take a vacation sometime late in February, and then we're talking late May and then a couple weeks in the summer sometime, but to take a week off now would be disastrous.

FOOTBALL REVIEW: Is it hard to

keep going without a break?

PATERNO: That's one of the things I like about the job. I've always been a guy that's fond of rebuilding; the fun is getting there. I'm going to look forward to it; I'll probably have more fun this year than I did last year as far as trying to get the team to be as good as it can be, and it's going to be a tough job.

FOOTBALL REVIEW: What are your thoughts on Penn State's good guy image.

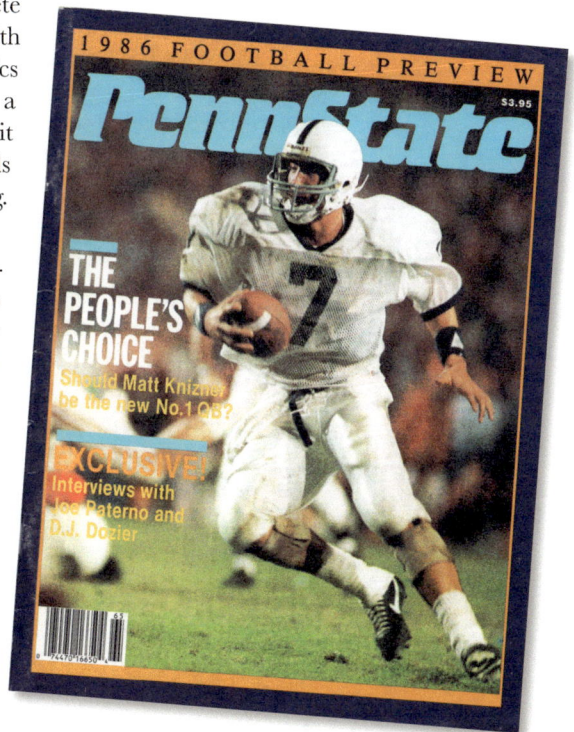

I've always been a guy that's fond of rebuilding; the fun is getting there.

PATERNO: I don't like the word good guy. If somebody said they acted like responsible and mature kids, and knew who they were and what they were, and they were not about to get detracted from that. I think people have a personality. You have a program, and you have a certain method of doing certain things, and I think it's important to be able to keep that and not lose it.

And our kids, regardless of what was said or done by other people, they were themselves. And whether that means they were good or bad I don't think makes much sense. The fact is they had the ingredients, the maturity and the confidence to know who they are, what they are, and how they can get things done and then they didn't get sidetracked.

FOOTBALL REVIEW: Pete Axthelm of *Newsweek* said that with all that's gone on in college athletics recently, with Penn State winning a game of this magnitude, maybe it would be a signal to other schools that they can win without cheating. How do you assess that statement?

PATERNO: I think it's always reassuring when you see somebody who appears to be doing it the right way to be successful, and I hope we will encourage schools who maybe aren't cheating, but debating whether they can be successful with a clean program. I think there are more people doing it the right way than people realize. I think it's unfortunate that the guys who have been breaking some rules are the guys people write about.

That's why the *Sports Illustrated* award meant so much to me. Not because of me but because I really feel this was an award for the university and our intercollegiate

program. Not just football. We have 28 sports, and almost all of them are extremely competitive. So I think the *Sports Illustrated* award was a direct compliment to Penn State's belief in the way intercollegiate athletics should be. And it's not something Joe Paterno averted. I came here 37 years ago and they were doing it the right way.

FOOTBALL REVIEW: What about a player like Oklahoma's Brian Bosworth. Could he play at Penn State?

PATERNO: Bosworth wouldn't come here. Bosworth would have to look at our program and make a decision as to whether he wanted to be a part of this program or not. That's one of the important things about recruiting. You've got to be honest. You can't lead a kid into a situation if he's not going to be happy there.

If Bosworth would have come he would have come here understanding what the rules were. He would know what he was getting into. And there are kids who turn us down because they don't want to be part of this program. That doesn't make them bad guys. It would be an awfully dull world if everybody wanted to do it the way we wanted to do it. I feel bad sometimes because people think I'm trying to be a good example as opposed to somebody else being a bad example.

I couldn't coach any other way. For me to go out there and see kids with earrings and things like that, that would be tough for me at my age, because we've had a lot of success. But that doesn't mean those kids are bad kids. It doesn't mean that at all. It just means that we have a certain style, a certain program, and I can't change.

FOOTBALL REVIEW: You've talked a lot about this year's team as being special. Looking back, how did you get such a group together?

PATERNO: Again, I think when we went out to recruit them, those guys believed in the kind of things Penn State stood for. Shane Conlan only had one scholarship (offer), John Shaffer came here knowing exactly what kind of program we had...Knizer, Dozier came here, and they could have gone any place in the country, they came here knowing what kind of program we had. Once you're up front and people start off together, and we all believe in the same things, I've always been a believer you can do anything if you work at it.

FOOTBALL REVIEW: Being one of the most outspoken advocates for a playoff system in college football, how do you react when D.J. Dozier, for example, says he is against it?

PATERNO: That's fine. That's up to them...If we had a playoff system and our teams said they didn't want to go, we wouldn't

> **"**
> *I've always been a believer you can do anything if you work at it.*
> **"**

1987: Sportsman and Coach of the Year Reflects on Century of Excellence

play, but the ones who wanted to play could play. But I think our guys would have been very upset if they didn't have the chance to play Miami.

If they had been voted No. 2 they would have known the frustration. These guys have had three shots to play for it so they don't know the frustration. I feel for the '68, '69 and '73 teams that were great, but never became national champs because some newspaper people or other coaches didn't think they were good enough.

FOOTBALL REVIEW: During the Fiesta Bowl, NBC commentator Bob Griese said that John Shaffer wouldn't have made Miami's team, and that Vinny Testaverde wouldn't have won the Heisman at Penn State. How do you react to that?

PATERNO: I don't pay any attention to it, because Bob doesn't know what he's talking about. He can make that statement, but I don't agree with it at all.

FOOTBALL REVIEW: Could Testaverde have won the Heisman at Penn State?

PATERNO: Sure. Fusina was a Heisman Trophy candidate who was second as a quarterback and he won the Maxwell Trophy. Richie Lucas was a quarterback here and he was a No. 1 draft pick. Griese doesn't know what he's talking about in that area... Knizner may be a Heisman Trophy candidate next year. We may throw the ball 45 times a game. I don't know what we're going to do. We'll do what we have to do.

My satisfaction comes from knowing we've done the best job we can.

FOOTBALL REVIEW: Is there any way you can top this season?

PATERNO: My satisfaction comes from knowing we've done the best job we can. I think this staff has done a marvelous job with this group of kids, and they probably did a better job last year to get them over the hump after those two disastrous losses. And then to come off those two games and beat a Maryland team down in Maryland on as hot a day as we've ever played, hanging in there was tough...We struggled. There was never an easy game. That's not saying it's not satisfying for this team. I'm just talking about me personally.

FOOTBALL REVIEW: What keeps you going?

PATERNO: I like coaching. I enjoy it. I enjoy the challenge of it, I particularly enjoy college coaching, because right now we've got to rebuild a football team...I'm looking forward to seeing what Matt can do. I'm really excited about Matt having a chance now. I'm anxious to see if we can have a good year recruiting. Those things I enjoy, and that's what keeps me going. To win a national championship is fine; that's what you strive for. But striving is what's fun."

To win a national championship is fine; that's what you strive for. But striving is what's fun."

Happy Valley: Oh, What a Feeling!

BY JOAN KURILLA

Reprinted from 1987 Football Preview

What is this place called Happy Valley? Well, actually it's not a place; it's a frame of mind, a way of life. It means that people like to live here, and others like to visit.

Happy Valley is youth, life, scores of people in pursuit of happiness in downtown State College, the heart of the Centre Region. It's costumed residents celebrating a Victorian Christmas at Bellefonte; a turn-of-the-century Memorial Day at Boalsburg; and scores of farm folk getting together at Grange Fair in Centre Hall. That is the ambiance of this central Pennsylvania area.

Penn State's $20 Million Touchdown

Home games prove a bonanza to the merchants in a college town.

By N. R. KLEINFIELD

STATE COLLEGE, Pa. — THE start of the college football season is always a happy time for Jack Garbrick. Not that the games themselves mean a whole lot to him. He never watches them. He flies over them.

Most of the year, his meal ticket is leasing and operating Ferris wheels and tilt-a-whirls at carnivals and fairs. But piloting planes is his abiding interest. Five years ago, he had a chance to buy some lettering for banners that are dragged behind airplanes. A lightbulb went on. Why not sell time over Beaver Stadium during the home games of the Nittany Lions of Pennsylvania State University?

It was one of those ideas right for its time. The Nittany Lions were a sizzling-hot team; last year, of course, they were the national champions. Every home game, therefore, Jack Garbrick has three Cessna 172's buzzing overhead, towing as many as 15 messages a game ("Marry me Ethel," "Greetings From Pennsylvania Christmas Tree Growers"). The price is $200 an hour during the game, with a bargain rate before and afterward.

"I wouldn't say I'm getting rich off the banners," Mr. Garbrick said. "But it's good work and gives me another excuse to fire up the planes."

The planes were crowding the sky again last weekend, when the 1987 college season opened and the Lions trounced Bowling Green, rewarding the coach, Joe Paterno, with his 200th career victory. Hundreds of other local businesses also cashed in on that contest and again yesterday, when the Lions played host to the University of Alabama. Davidson Florist sold a dozen or so blue and white mum football corsages each Saturday, at $2.95 apiece. The Unimart convenience stores and gas stations in town pumped about 30 percent more gasoline than usual. And the Learning Station child development center took in about 20 kids for its special football Saturday day-care sessions.

Add up the mums and the gasoline and the babysitting fees, and it becomes obvious that college football is big business, and not only to the universities and television networks. A recently-completed study by Penn

Continued on Page 8

A Sales Scoreboard

Estimates of spending in State College region by 54,000 non-resident fans during the seven Penn State home-game football weekends in 1986.

Stadium	$8,283,600
Restaurants	2,693,100
Lodging	2,075,100
Retail shopping	1,793,500
Private auto	984,900
Clothing and equipment for use in stadium	801,700
Bars, nightclubs, lounges	743,200
Food, beverages in retail stores	588,100
Commercial transportation	247,800
Admission fees	103,400
Donations	105,100
Personal and health	41,300
Baby sitter fees	25,100
Equipment rentals	17,900
Other	1,944,900
TOTAL	$20,448,600

Based on a mail survey of 1,974 season ticket holders living at least 25 miles outside of the State College region, 86 percent of whom responded.

Source: Pennsylvania State University

Cheering on the Nittany Lions, an economic force to be reckoned with.

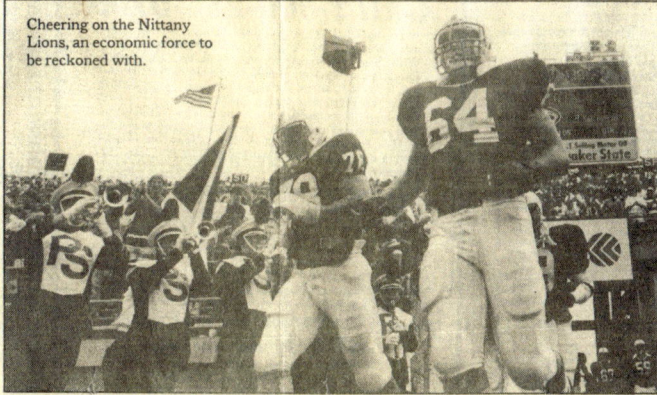

The New York Times/Paul Hosefros

Whether the crowds are roaring with the Nittany Lions in the fall, winding through the Central Pennsylvania Festival of the Arts in the summer, or cheering for Sy Barash Regatta racers in the spring, they are enthusiastic, alive and full of the delights that have been wrought from these rolling hills, once roamed only by the Shawnee and Muncy Indians.

Where else can one attend professional theater, tour historic iron works, golf a championship bent-grass course, hike a part of the Appalachian trail and visit a flock of newborn lambs—all within an hour's drive?

Happy Valley is a kaleidoscope of life as it was and life as it can be. It's a combination of the quality of pastoral family living, the dignity of old towns with descendants of old families, and the more upbeat atmosphere of academe.

The area offers a shopping smorgasbord, ranging from the sophisticated boutiques of State College to the country charm of Lemont and Boalsburg, to the general stores, bake shops, and antique barns in surrounding rural areas. Christmas is transformed

Arts Fest 1988.
*Photo courtesy of
Sophie Kandler*

into a special time in Victorian Bellefonte.

The densely forested mountains that surround the towns must look much the same as they did when Col. James Potter discovered the lush valley in 1759, recognizing the inherent value of its resources—slow-burning hardwood and thick, ruddy veins of iron ore. That discovery marked the beginning of a lucrative smelting business and the start of new settlements, which ultimately formed Centre County. Centre Furnace and the Centre Furnace Mansion which stand on the edge of the Penn State campus just off Route 26, and Curtin Village near Milesburg, are restored memorials to that early era.

Along the way, small communities developed: Milesburg, Bellefonte, Centre Hall, Lemont and Boalsburg among the earliest. By the mid-1800s, with most of the valley cleared of its hardwood, the land was sold off for farming, launching the events that led to the development and growth of Penn State and the State College community.

As early as 1851, members of the Pennsylvania Agricultural Society began discussing the establishment of a state agriculture school and by 1855, the Farmer's High School of the State of Pennsylvania opened its doors. Shortly after, the school was renamed the Agriculture College, and a few years later, it became known as the Pennsylvania State College. The nearby cluster of old farm houses, a few townhouses, and a centrally located roadhouse grew as a support community without any identification or name of its own. It was commonly referred to as State College because people who attended or visited the school were "going to the State College." After 40 years, the no-name town formally adopted the name.

And how the town grew, slowly at first from what is now College Avenue and Allen Street, into a quiet residential community of professors and merchants. The building boom of the '40s never really stopped, but even through the '50s, the burgeoning town had a sleepy, homey atmosphere. Restaurants were few and there was one bar with beer only. The closest liquor store was in Bellefonte. Memory may exaggerate, but it was next to impossible to buy a loaf of bread or a tankful of gasoline after 6 p.m. Private homes and fraternities were the party centers.

Today, it seems, all of Happy Valley is one huge party. Rock music permeates fraternity areas on and off campus as students toss Frisbees or otherwise catch the rays. At night, downtown State College throbs with movie-goers, window shoppers and diners.

What would be the reaction of Col. Potter, who most likely dined on wild game and whatever meager stores he was able to bring in from the east, to the array of fresh seafood, international cuisine, and fast food selections at every turn? And wouldn't he have enjoyed the internationally known performers and musicians brought to Penn State through the Artists Series; the stage and screen stars at Centre Stage; and the famous artists at the Penn State Museum of Art?

The busiest, and wackiest, times in Happy Valley are football weekends through the fall and Arts Festival days in mid-July. People, people everywhere as people from all over Pennsylvania and beyond converge upon the area with one thing in mind: fun.

For six or seven autumn weekends, Happy Valley is transformed into a huge blue-and-white campsite surrounded by "No Vacancy" signs at motels overflowing with blue-and-white people who flood the restaurants, bars, and shops with blue-and-white cheer. The camaraderie, especially after an important win, is unequaled by any event throughout the year.

The Central Pennsylvania Festival of the Arts turns central campus and downtown State College into a living stage of artists

and craftsmen, browsers and buyers, performers and watchers, and just plain fun-lovers for four days in mid-July.

Year-round, life in Happy Valley has a certain kind of charm. Young families and retired folk can enjoy art-in-the-park in State College on Summerfest Saturdays in June; in Bellefonte, it's Sunday afternoons of music in the library, concerts at the gazebo, and community theater in the schools. Boalsburg also offers community theater, two museums, and Music at the Mansion.

> *Year-round, life in Happy Valley has a certain kind of charm.*

It's a delicate madness, this Happy Valley: a kaleidoscopic ambivalence of jeans and black tie, Bach and rock, beer and Brie, raucous sports and serene resorts. It's a place for all seasons, a space for all reasons.

Greatest Moments at Beaver Stadium: Nov. 21, 1987 - Penn State 21, Notre Dame 20

This game might be the coldest on record at Beaver Stadium. With 30-mile-an-hour winds, snow flurries and wind chills of zero to 18 degrees, Penn State's die hard fans were numb and shivering by the time Penn State narrowly won against Notre Dame.

Notre Dame scored with just 30 seconds remaining, and went for the win, but their quarterback Tony Rice was tackled short of the goal by linebacker Pete Curkendall. Paterno later said, "It was a moment that will always be frozen in the history of Penn State football." (Frozen being the operative word)

1987: Happy Valley: Oh, What a Feeling!

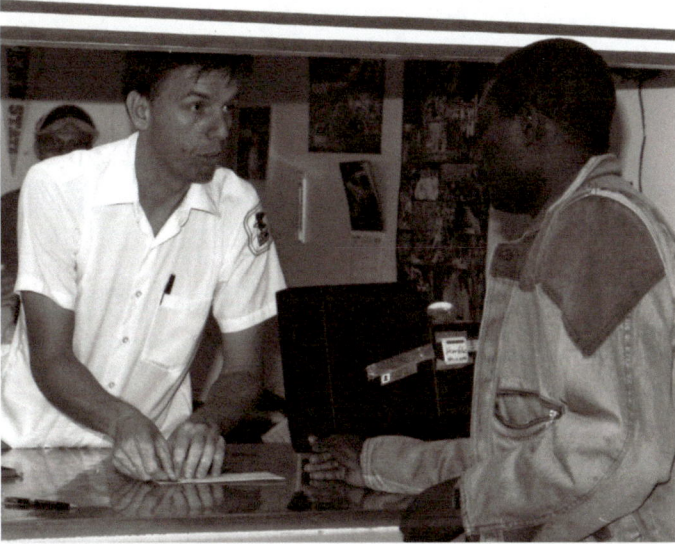

State College's downtown offered year-round fun with familiar faces, favorite places, and a bar and music scene that couldn't be beat.

Top: Mike Herr, AKA Mike the Mailman

Middle left: Sorority Rush. Middle right: The Saloon. *Photo courtesy of Chuck Fong*

Bottom left: Ernie Oelbermann and the Phyrst Phamily. Bottom right: Rinaldo's Barber Shop on Allen Street.

1988

In 1988:

Michael Dukakis and George H.W. Bush ran for the presidency; Joe Paterno publicly endorses George H.W. Bush.

Flo Jo captivates the crowds at the 1988 Olympics.

On campus, the trustees again revisit the divisive South African apartheid issue, and vote to support divestment in what *The Collegian* calls a 'stunning move.' However, by spring, the country would watch as 88 students occupied the Telecommunications Building for 15 hours to protest Bryce Jordan pulling out of race relation talks, bringing 40 state troopers to campus.

Phi Psi 500, now in its 21st year, is mostly dry, with several participating bars serving non-alcoholic drinks to runners. Turnout is markedly lower this year.

Penn State favorites include Crazy Daze playing Grateful Dead covers; The Earth Tones; Queen Bee and the Blue Hornets; and Jr Mangan playing at Champs and Cafe 210 West.

Psychology Today names Happy Valley 'the lowest stress town' out of 286 contenders. Adding to the joy: Penn State basketball player Suzie McConnell wins a gold medal as part of the U.S. women's basketball team at the 1988 Olympics, where Penn State wrestler Ken Chertow also competes for the U.S. Back home, Penn State hosts the Special Olympics for the first time.

Around the world, the U.S. and Canada reached a free trade agreement, Pan Am 747 explodes and crashes in Lockerbie, Scotland, killing all 259 aboard.

In world news, Salman Rushdie publishes Satanic Verses, and Iran sentences him to death.

Top movies included "Willow," "Cocktail," "Moonwalker," "Beetlejuice," "Rain Man," "Big," "Die Hard," "Young Guns," "Dirty Rotten Scoundrels," "Who Framed Roger Rabbit," "Twins," and "Crossing Delancey."

Top songs included "A Groovy Kind of Love" by Phil Collins, "Don't Worry Be Happy" by Bobby McFerrin, "The Flame" by Cheap Trick, "I'll Always Love You" by Taylor Dayne, and "Fast Car" by Tracy Chapman.

Paterno's Convention Speech

Reprinted from 1989 Football Preview

On Aug. 17, 1988, at the Republican National Convention, Joe Paterno seconded the nomination of George Bush as the party's candidate for the President of the United States. Here's the text of that speech:

"This is the fourth time I've been in this dome. The last two visits Penn State was playing for the national championship. In 1982, we were fortunate to beat a great Georgia team and in 1978, right over there in that end zone, a great goal line stand by Bear Bryant's Alabama team beat us. Bear, if you're watching, I hope I don't blow this one.

"I know a lot of people are wondering what an Italian-American football coach from Brooklyn is doing here. So am I.

"However, I hope that after 40 years of trying to help young men and women reach their potential as human beings, I'm here as an educator.

"Obviously, I am here because George Bush invited me, and on behalf of my family and myself and the state of Pennsylvania, I want to thank him for this great honor.

"I'm here for someone and not because I'm against anyone.

"I'm here because I believe George Bush will be one of America's great presidents.

"I'm here because I believe in quality education at all levels and I am convinced George Bush will be an education president.

"I'm here because I have been back to the section of Brooklyn where my immigrant grandparents and mother grew up. I have been to the inner cities of this country to recruit athletes for Penn State, and this country cannot continue to let these people live without hope—hope to dream the dreams my family dreamed.

"George Bush wants a better life for all Americans, especially the ones we left behind.

"I'm here because, like President Ford, I'll be damned if I will sit still when people who can't even carry George Bush's shoes ridicule him!

"After a lifetime of being around great competitors, I know a winner and I know a leader. I know the difference between bravado and the quiet, dignified confidence of a Joe DiMaggio, of a Walter Payton, of a George Bush.

"George Bush will be a great President of the United States, and I humbly second his nomination."

> **"** *After a lifetime of being around great competitors, I know a winner and I know a leader. I know the difference between bravado and the quiet, dignified confidence of a Joe DiMaggio, of a Walter Payton, of a George Bush.* **"**

Stop and Smell the Roses

BY GREG WOODMAN

Reprinted from 1988 Football Preview

What are the distinct geographical boundaries of the area called Happy Valley? Is it just the Penn State campus, Beaver Stadium, College Avenue, and five bars with lots of memories?

If the area is growing as much as it appears, will Happy Valley soon be called "Big Valley" and lose all of its charm?

Is Happy Valley just an ordinary college town? Where did the title Happy Valley come from? Why does the name seem to be spreading? Nittany Valley would seem more catchy.

We've all heard or read the area's common description: "Happy Valley, raw beauty, tranquilly situated amongst mountains equally inaccessible from everywhere—it's bucolic."

There are many college towns in nice places. And many warmer areas in the winter. Why the growing affection? Everyone who knows Happy Valley (and the ranks are swelling) loves to come back to this isolated and insulated womb.

In fact, the only changes that are really happening in Happy Valley are purely to accommodate the masses that are coming back to visit. The actual population in Centre County is surprisingly projected to grow at a rate of only one percent per year

PENN STATE'S
WHY

What is it about Happy Valley, this 'land of Oz,' that draws us back? This article pointed out what Penn State and Happy Valley had become—a place where economic growth and bucolic beauty, sleepy town life and football energy happily coexisted. It wasn't either ... it was both.

HUB lawn, April 1988. *Courtesy Sophie Kandler*

through the year 2000.

I believe the economic growth is coming from the dislocated Penn Staters who return to visit the Land of Oz. The yellow brick road is either Rt. 22, 322, or 80. We all come back to see the wizard. For Penn Staters, Happy Valley is where we develop our courage, heart, and brains.

It's Spring/Summer in the Valley. It's the easiest time to talk about truly experiencing Happy Valley. Winter is now behind us.

Happy Valley is all of Central Pennsylvania. Sure, when I was a student it wasn't more than one street, College Avenue. It took six months before I discovered Allen Street and Beaver Avenue; a year before I ventured across Atherton Street.

The real discoveries were after I graduated. Each year I discovered more; state parks, restaurants like the Old Oak Tavern and the Gamble Mill Tavern, Boalsburg's Memorial Day, Centre Hall, Lemont, and all of the area's lush golf courses! The feeling of discovery recurs each time I take a dislocated, or visiting, Penn Stater to somewhere other than the Tavern for dinner.

To their astonishment there is life beyond the three streets of State College. Most old college friends think I still hang out at the Skellar with my wife three times a week.

"You mean, you don't still do a case of Rocks then hit the 'Gaff for oldies on Thursdays?" an old fraternity brother asked.

I enjoy visits from old fraternity brothers because they are looking for what I affectionately refer to as a "TURN BACK THE CLOCK WEEKEND." And yes. We turn back the clock for us to 1979.

It's the old weekend rituals that all true Penn Staters know, remember, and love. My particular favorite was to stop, as I often did in my six years of college, and "smell the roses." This is done in the area across from College Avenue behind Atherton Hall that has a slight hill to give "stadium-like viewing" of the action of College Avenue at 2:30 in the morning. There used to be a couple of rose bushes up there so we'd say "let's go smell the roses." Great place to go with a couple of slices from "The Cut Pie Shop!" This area grew in popularity for our group only (It's not like climbing Mt. Nittany or sitting on the wall).

Many serious discussions were held there. Yes, the memories of the simpler and more idealistic times. Living among 35,000 17 to 22 year olds. Skipping along with a backpack on one shoulder and looking at all the scenery. Whistling "Sitting on the Dock of the Bay." It was a great time. Living, loving and learning—college life!

It's always fun to turn back the clock, but the locals know you can't do it with your weekend visitors all of the time. And this is where Happy Valley separated itself from everywhere.

The "many-layer theory" comes into play. It's fun to show my old college friends and family how much more there really is. I can't describe it any better than the local writer Joan Kurilla: "Where else can one attend professional theatre, tour historic iron works, golf a championship bentgrass golf course, hike part of the Appalachian trail and visit a flock of newborn lambs.

Happy Valley is a kaleidoscope of life as it was and life as it can be...an ambivalence of jeans and black tie, Bach and rock, beer and Brie, raucous sports and serene resorts. It's a place for all seasons, a space for all reasons."

The name Happy Valley first appeared in print in 1968. This being the 20th anniversary, and with Time magazine dedicating the cover recently to the mystique and nostalgia of 1968, this equally revered publication should also look back.

Summing up 1968, the articles and photos in "Time" illustrate "unresolved conflicts tearing at American life." One college town, as usual, seemed isolated from the action. So in a mocking sort of way the "sleepy town" of State College was referred to as Happy Valley, in a student editorial.

> **"** *So in a mocking sort of way the "sleepy town" of State College was referred to as Happy Valley, in a student editorial.* **"**

"Newsweek" magazine, another of our publication colleagues, recently ran a cover story saying the 1990s are here. Based on *"Newsweek's"* indicators, Happy Valley will be "in" more than ever. Greed is gone, yuppies dead.

To hear it from *"Newsweek,"* it's once again hip to get together with old friends at the Skellar, wear your old letter sweater, picnic in the country with the family, eat big meals. This will be Happy Valley's decade.

In 1968 another important first for Happy Valley occurred. Joe Paterno, in only his third year as head coach, led Penn State to its first undefeated year. Joe and Happy Valley both have grown in prominence and prestige in two decades. No question, Joe's impact has spread the Happy Valley story. Just listen as football announcers Keith Jackson and Brent Musburger sing the praises of the area on a cool, crisp fall afternoon. The cameras pan the valley for the whole country to see.

The author, Greg Woodman, with his parents at his graduation.

Not to imply that the area's growth was based solely on football's success. Mr. Paterno would be the first to say his love for this area was a factor prompting him to turn down millions to move to New England.

Tuscaloosa, South Bend, Norman, and other famous college football towns are not in economic boom periods. You can safely say that Joe Paterno let the cat, or the Nittany Lion, out of the bag. First he told the story to parents of recruits. Then his teams' efforts spread the word to the rest of the world.

Not only is it number one in the hearts of more than 200,000 living Penn State graduates, Happy Valley is also the darling of the state of Pennsylvania.

Black Mondays, grinding poverty, unscrupulous agents and recessions just don't seem to find their way up the winding roads. It's kind of like Switzerland.

Two other anniversaries that point to the late '60s influence. The Arts Festival began in 1966 and the Lion Country Visitors Bureau began in 1963.

The festival draws in more than 300,000 people every July and more than $20 million. As for the tourist bureau, they either have the easiest job in America or should be paid a bonus.

Don't be alarmed with the changes in the valley. At closer look you'll still see an Andy Hardy movie set in the 1930s.

Well, it's springtime and the roses are smelling good. So click your heels three times and keep saying, "There's no place like Happy Valley… There's no place like Happy Valley."

Attend a fraternity formal in the '80s, and sooner or later, you'd find yourself posing for Chuck Fong. He's immortalized his collection of formal photos at the new Scholar Hotel located at 219 W. Beaver Avenue.

Paterno: Back to the Drawing Board

Reprinted from 1988 Football Preview

It is 1:02 p.m. on a spring-like March day when Joe Paterno walks through the front door of the Penn State football office. He is two minutes late.

I forgive him.

As we walk through the foyer and past his assistant coaches' offices, Paterno peels off his famous blue parka—the one he paces the sideline in every chilly November afternoon—and he makes a little bit of small talk. "Sorry I'm late," "How are you doing?," that kind of thing. He is friendly, but his mind is elsewhere.

It's always been that way with Paterno, at least since I can remember. (My first encounter with the coach came as an undergraduate in 1979, when I covered my first Penn State football game.) He seems to be thinking ahead, forever planning not just the next step, but the step beyond that. That is how his teams have won 207 games (with 48 losses and two ties) since he succeeded his mentor, Rip Engle, as head coach in 1966. Joe Paterno must be one helluva chess player.

At the end of the hallway is Paterno's office, certainly not as spacious or overwhelming as one might expect. It's a bit more flashy than his team's uniforms, what with a large oil painting of a Penn State game (the 1982 Sugar Bowl, I believe) on one wall. But the colors are muted, and the wall unit to the right of his desk is surprisingly free of memorabilia. There are a few photographs, certificates and trophies (including the one Paterno received for being named *Sports Illustrated's* 1986 "Sportsman of the Year"), but not many.

When Paterno steps out of his office, I steal a quick look at the bookshelf. Among the titles: "Dianetics," the do-it-yourself guide to mental health and well-being; "Vince," a biography of legendary coach Vince Lombardi; Ridge Riley's "The Road to No. 1," the definitive history of Penn State football; and the "Athlete's Guide to Agents," necessary reading for any college football coach these days.

Somehow, none of the titles surprise me.

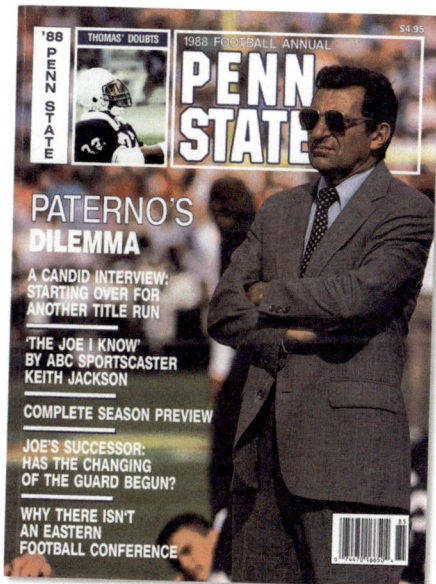

In a minute, Paterno returns. He looks comfortable, tanned and darn dapper. No rolled up pants, no white socks, no goofy whale pants and no blue sweater. His hair remains almost totally jet-black, and, to be honest, he looks younger than his 61 years. Later, as the conversation progresses, I notice that it's easier to look the coach in the eye these days; his trademark dark-tinted glasses aren't so dark.

Quickly, we get down to business. Paterno unbuttons his sports coat and takes a seat on the office sofa. I settle in on a big easy chair. For the next 40 minutes, we cover a wide variety of subjects, from the 1988 Penn State football team to the 1988 presidential race to sports agents to Paterno's work as vice chairman of The Campaign for Penn State, a $200 million fundraising effort. He is short and noncommittal when it comes to talking football; he says he's starting over this season and all positions are open. Beyond that, he offers little about his current football team. Very little. Clearly, though, he has his hands full.

However, when the subject turns in any other direction, he is affable, engaging and interesting. Paterno talks freely about his impending retirement, which he says will come in five years. It's the same answer I've heard since I was a Penn State junior in 1980, but this time I believe him. He appears more comfortable talking about that eventuality, and although he doesn't reveal it, he seems to have started formulating a post-Penn State football game plan. Like I said, he is alway thinking of the step beyond the next step.

Two comments from the interview really strike me. One is Paterno's assertion that—although he says the decision is not his—he would like to see his successor come from the Penn State ranks. "I would prefer that he come from the staff," is what he said.

The second comment is more of a reaction. When I told him that nine of the 22 players he recruited in 1984 (the class of '88) were no longer at Penn State, he seemed genuinely surprised. So am I. It is a high figure, especially for Penn State. Too high. Paterno places part of the blame on the players themselves, saying they came to Penn State for the "wrong reason." Obviously, Paterno must shoulder part of the blame as well. I suspect he knows that, and that is the reason why he spent the time since his team's embarrassing 35-10 Citrus Bowl loss getting his players "back in the groove, as far as attitude, academics" are concerned. When that is done, Penn State should once again return to the Top 20.

FOOTBALL PREVIEW: What is the status of Blair Thomas?

PATERNO: It's a long shot as to whether he'll be ready. But if anybody can do it, he can. I think it's a question for the medical people to handle.

FOOTBALL PREVIEW: If Blair doesn't return next season, is there a chance John Greene will move to tailback?

PATERNO: I haven't thought about it and I haven't talked to the staff about it. I don't like to waste time thinking about something that might happen. When the time comes, I'll make that decision.

FOOTBALL PREVIEW: Here's a definite: Pete Giftopoulos and Trey Bayer are both gone. That's a big void in the linebacking corps; who do you see that is going to step in?

PATERNO: That's why we have spring practice. (Scott) Gob has played well. But Darryl Washington is gone, too. That's one of the things we have to do this spring, find a couple of good players who can play inside.

FOOTBALL PREVIEW: Outside linebacker Quintus McDonald (*USA Today* Defensive Player of the Year in high school) will be a senior next season. Has he developed as you would have liked?

PATERNO: He's had so darn many bumps and bruises and injuries. When he finally started to come around last year and we thought he'd be good, he hurt his knee and wasn't able to do much before a game. This will be a crucial spring practice for him.

Someone has to come through for us out there. Of course, Keith Karpinski is solid, but he has to start healthy. After that, it's up in the air.

FOOTBALL PREVIEW: Have you ever gone into a spring practice with as many question marks?

PATERNO: Well, last year was interesting. Sure, we have a lot of question marks. The only thing I've done much of is try to make sure that we're getting back in the groove, as far as attitude, academics, making sure we had a good winter program. I've not really given much thought to the positions or anything else. I realize we're only two weeks away from spring practice, but I have not zeroed on what the problems are and what have you.

We have a lot of things we have to get done this spring, no question about it. We have to get a quarterback. Without Roundtree, and Timpson not available and Jimmy Coates gone, some young kids are going to have to step in at wideout. We lost some key people on the offensive line. We have a big job ahead of us.

FOOTBALL PREVIEW: As far as "getting things back in the groove," how do you do that, what do you say?

PATERNO: It's a matter of first things first. Obviously, I'm not happy with the way some things worked out academically for our kids. You have to be careful, because that can get to be infectious. We're trying to get that leveled out. I'm disappointed that we didn't have a couple of kids do better in school.

We have to say, "Hey, let's start all over again and get back to

where we're not assuming anything." We have to go back to square one, in everything, starting in the classroom. I'm also talking about personal habits, training methods, those kinds of things.

FOOTBALL PREVIEW: What are you looking forward to about the next season?

PATERNO: There are so many spots to be filled. It's going to be very challenging. I'm going into this thing with the attitude that I'm going to wait and see what happens. I want to see how some people respond to a challenge. I'm not going to go in with any preconceived notion of whether we're good here or not good there. I'm just assuming that I'm literally taking over a new program, and I'm going to find out what we have.

FOOTBALL PREVIEW: Is Tom Bill the leading candidate for quarterback?

PATERNO: Nobody is leading any position. They're all going to have to come out and make the team at every position.

FOOTBALL PREVIEW: Is there a chance of a freshman stepping in during the fall? Will any of them be given a shot?

PATERNO: I don't have the slightest idea.

FOOTBALL PREVIEW: Is there a chance of a game being moved up to Sept. 3 for television?

PATERNO: Nobody's talked it over with me.

FOOTBALL PREVIEW: There have been a couple reports, most recently in *USA Today*, saying that you have four or five more years as coach. Is that true?

> *If I stay healthy, I'm going to coach five more years. I made that commitment to myself and talked it over with my family and they've consented to go along with it. I think that in five years I'll be old enough where I should get out of it.*

PATERNO: I'd like to. I've told people that I'd like to do another five years. I feel good. If I stay healthy, I'm going to coach five more years. I made that commitment to myself and talked it over with my family and they've consented to go along with it. I think that in five years I'll be old enough where I should get out of it. And I think that I won't be too old to get involved in some things that interest me. It's hard to envision myself retiring. I think I'll want to change and maybe not get into something so strenuous and demanding as coaching. If you give yourself a timetable, it gives you a chance to wade into something. It will give me an opportunity to kind of work my way into something new in my life without jeopardizing doing the job that should be done here.

FOOTBALL PREVIEW: I remember that in 1980 you said you'd coach possibly four or five more years. Obviously, it's a tough decision to make. What all goes into it?

PATERNO: It gets tougher all the time. The older you get, the closer you get to where you ought to get out of it.

The way I have looked at it is that I've looked at my family situations. I still have a youngster at home. And in five years, he'll be in the middle of college and somewhat established. I'll be 65. I may not know if I'm doing a good enough job or not doing a good enough job. At that stage you have a tendency to kid yourself.

I think that financially I'll be able to do just about whatever I want to do. Realistically speaking, I don't know if I can maintain the energy needed to do the job much beyond that. I'm a hands-on kind of coach and I wouldn't want to be otherwise. I wouldn't be comfortable any other way. That all fits in the same kind of time frame. I'd like to turn it over to somebody who would have a lot of fun with it. I've had a lot of fun with it. Sixty-Five is still young enough these days to get involved in something else. Whatever that is, I don't know. People want to jump in and say "politics" right away, but I don't know. I have not thought about going into politics in an active way. There's too much involved in running for office. Maybe there will be something developed in politics that would be appropriate and where I wouldn't have to go out and run and all that stuff.

FOOTBALL PREVIEW: When you're talking to recruits next year, or two years down the road, what will you say to them?

PATERNO: I'll tell them when I'm going to retire. That's unless I make a decision to stay three years from now. At that time, I may feel as good as I feel now and I may feel I don't want to get out of it yet. Of course, I can reassess my position. But for now, for the next few years I'll have to tell kids that I'll be here for X number of years and then they'll have to have confidence that the program will be in good hands and that we'll pick a good person. It'll probably be someone who can do a better job…

FOOTBALL PREVIEW: Right.

PATERNO: No, I'm serious about that. A lot of people should be able to do a fine job, and Penn State should be able to get itself a top-notch coach, whether he's on the staff or not.

FOOTBALL PREVIEW: You have said that you don't want to retire until everything in the program, facilities and otherwise, is in place. Does that include having your successor on your staff, making the transition that way?

PATERNO: That depends. If I was going to step out and become the athletic director, I would feel very comfortable saying,

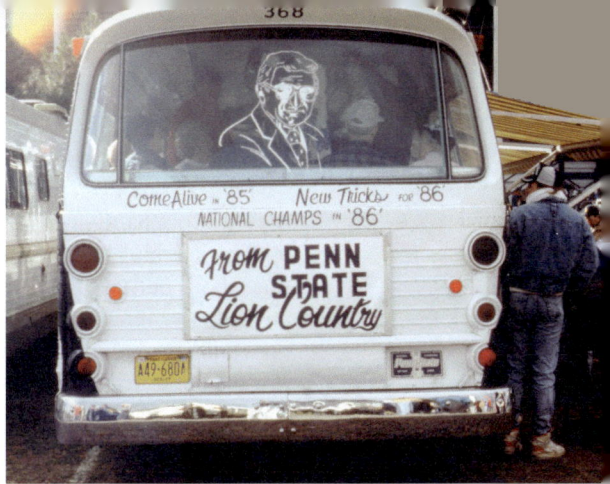

"This is the guy who is going to coach." Then I would be working with him.

I don't think I can make that decision for the athletic director. I have to work hand-in-hand with the athletic director. I'll certainly tell him if I think he's making a mistake. Or, if I think I have someone who is outstanding, I wouldn't hesitate to say that I think this guy is better than anyone else. I would prefer that he come from the staff. Traditionally, that's the way we function around here. But for me to tell you flat-out that it has to be someone from the staff, I can't do that. The athletic director has to work with the guy, so he should be comfortable with him.

So it's not that clear-cut, but I certainly think we have some people on the staff who would be outstanding candidates.

FOOTBALL PREVIEW: When you were athletic director, you fought hard for an Eastern all-sports conference. Is that idea, or one of an Eastern football conference, dead forever?

PATERNO: I don't think it will be dead forever. I think it will happen. When, I don't know. We missed a great opportunity. And I have to blame Syracuse and Pitt and BC, but mostly Syracuse and Pitt, for not having one.

At this stage, I really believe Maryland would be in such a conference by now. We would have had an outstanding basketball conference, as well as a football conference and everything else. We could have had everything we wanted.

It would be a natural for Maryland, coming up instead of going down in the deep South. With them, we'd be in all the major media and TV markets. And Maryland would be in an area where they do much of their recruiting for football and basketball, and lacrosse up on Long Island. Why, we'd have a great lacrosse conference, with Syracuse and Maryland and Penn State as part of it.

I think some day people are going to come to their senses and realize that such a conference is in the best interests of all the sports, not just in the interest of basketball, which all the Big East is right now. For us to get involved in a football conference without basketball doesn't make sense. We'd be giving up too much. And besides, we have a good basketball conference. And it's getting better all the time. There are three or four schools really working hard, including Penn State.

It's a good conference for the other sports as well, swimming and what have you. So there's not as much pressure for Penn State to get involved in another conference for other sports, at least not as much as there used to be. But if I had my preference, I think it would be better for Eastern football and better for all sports if there was an all-sports conference.

FOOTBALL PREVIEW: Still talking basketball, could you comment on the success of Penn State basketball?

PATERNO: I think they're just a couple games away. I think right now it's a mental attitude. Right now I don't think they know how good they are. I was sitting with Jim Tarman at the West Virginia game in Rec Hall, and at halftime I said to him, "Our kids are just as good as theirs." They have a couple of kids who are fine basketball players. They had a good year recruiting, some good kids, and they've already signed three kids in the early period. They only lose two kids off this squad. They could have very easily beaten Temple home and away. They can play anybody tough. Now they have to believe they can beat anybody, not just play with them. Once that happens, they'll be over the hump.

They're very, very close. I think they have a good, solid basketball program. I'd very much like to see it happen. I'm a basketball fan.

FOOTBALL PREVIEW: Syracuse football. Are they for real?

PATERNO: We'll have to see what happens. We had to wait and see after (Doug) Flutie left BC. So it may be and it may not be. We'll just have to wait and see what happens.

FOOTBALL PREVIEW: Every couple years it seems as if someone different rises from the East.

PATERNO: Well, that's good. I think it's good for everybody. I don't think it's a situation where Penn State has to dominate the area.

Pitt and Penn State, for a while there in the 1980s, were playing for the national championship every time they met. And that was great. It certainly wouldn't hurt for Penn State to be at that level, with Syracuse reaching that level, BC capable of being that good, and eventually a Rutgers, a Temple, a West Virginia getting there too.

West Virginia is going to have a great squad next year. They have the big quarterback (Major Harris). And he's going to be a good one.

FOOTBALL PREVIEW: Let's talk about Dick Anderson and Rutgers. He's heading into his fifth year. There have been a couple of bright spots there and almost all the facilities are in place. How's he doing, and do you keep in contact with him at all?

PATERNO: I think he's doing fine. He has to get a little lucky. He's a great player away from being really good. He needs a guy on offense, a Blair Thomas or a quarterback, who is a great player.

He's solid every other way. They play everybody tough. He needs one or two guys who can win the games he's not winning right now. That's the difference between 6-5 and 8-3 and climbing. Their facilities are good, but they still need more things.

FOOTBALL PREVIEW: Are there any feelings about going against George Walsh, your old assistant, when you open against Virginia?

PATERNO: George and I have known each other long enough, and our wives have known each other long enough, that it's no big deal. It's just one of those things where you hope both sides play well, no one gets hurt and you win.

FOOTBALL PREVIEW: What programs across the country do you have the most respect for?

PATERNO: Most of them. Contrary to what you read in the papers, there aren't that many bad programs. There's a lot of good programs; in fact, they're mostly good programs. Most of the schools in the East are good programs. But nobody is going to feature a headline story, "BC had a fine program." But when BC had a basketball player get into a jam going to night school a couple of years ago, that made headlines.

Obviously, there have been some abuses in the Southwest Conference. But even a lot of that stuff is nitpicking: a guy gives a kid $10 dollars or gives him a ride. Or Alabama flies a team to a kid's funeral. Those things make us look bad because they make headlines. But for the most part, the programs that I know are going about things in the right way.

FOOTBALL PREVIEW: Agents notwithstanding, is college football cleaner than it was 10, 20 years ago?

PATERNO: I don't know whether 20 years, since it's hard to remember that far back. But I think it's cleaner now than 10 years ago.

FOOTBALL PREVIEW: Is the issue of agents overblown?

PATERNO: No, no. I think more kids sign with agents than people realize. And maybe some of ours. I don't know. We work awfully hard to make sure our kids get the advice they should get. We do everything the NCAA allows us to do with that three-man panel.

I personally do not have a problem with a kid signing and going pro before his playing time is up, if the kid is good enough. Unfortunately, we've forced the agents into a closet and they're telling kids they're good enough. And because the kids are talking to an agent, they're afraid to come forward and talk to the school, because the fact that they're talking with an agent jeopardizes the player's eligibility.

If a kid is talking to an agent about leaving college early, I'd like it so a kid can come to me and say "What do you think, Coach?" I'd like to tell a kid if he's going to be a sixth- or seventh- or eighth-round pick. And I'd also like to tell him if he's going to be a first-round pick, so he can go sign now. That way he can make up his own mind if the education is more important.

I don't think it's wrong for a kid to do what's best for him. I don't think the NCAA should be poking fingers into people when they only give kids a one-year grant. (Scholarships are renewable each year, at the school's discretion.) Some of the things we ask kids to do, with the summer program or the winter program, and the fact that we don't give them any spending money or even give them all the money they're entitled to from the Pell Grant. I get a big kick out of the Pitt situation. Here's (Athletic Director) Ed Bozik saying that they vote all the time not to give the kids the entire amount of the Pell Grant, and they're in school on one-year grants, and now they're hollering because a kid signs with an agent. It's a little hypocritical.

We're supposed to be in the business of helping young kids develop educationally, emotionally, socially, and that they get what they need and want out of college. They're not here to fill our stadiums for us.

FOOTBALL PREVIEW: Is it more difficult for a kid to do all that than it was when you took over as head coach in the 1960s?

PATERNO: There are more poor kids in college today. There are more blacks in college. It's hard for me to see why anybody gets uptight if a kid who doesn't have beans gets offered a half-million dollars to play pro football before his college time is up.

The only problem I have is that a lot of kids may be talked into playing, like (Pitt's Charles) Gladman. He was not good enough. So he doesn't make it and doesn't get an education either. If a kid could go to a coach and say, "Hey, Coach, how about calling a couple of pro scouts, find out how good they think I am and give me the straight scoop." And if he knew that he was going to get the straight scoop, he might never have gone with an agent. And that's not meant to be critical of Pitt, because nobody gets to that point. Because they won't talk to you.

FOOTBALL PREVIEW: So a kid can't walk in the door and say, "Coach, I'm interested in turning pro?"

PATERNO: He's allowed to say that to you. But he can't come in and say, "My agent told me I'm going to be a first-round draft pick." He has to come in before he gets affiliated with an agent.

FOOTBALL PREVIEW: Shifting gears here. Tomorrow is Super Tuesday. I know you're friends with George Bush. Down the road, either in the Pennsylvania primary or nationally, will you do

> *We're supposed to be in the business of helping young kids develop educationally, emotionally, socially, and that they get what they need and want out of college. They're not here to fill our stadiums for us.*

any stomping for him?

PATERNO: If he asked me to do something, and I can without interfering with my job, I will. I went up to New Hampshire on the day of the debate there, for a rally. I have my fingers crossed for him. I think he'll be an outstanding president. But I can't do certain things in the fall during the national election. I'll be busy.

FOOTBALL PREVIEW: You've always talked about getting into politics.

PATERNO: Well, I've always said the thing I would like the most about politics is to help someone get elected who I have confidence. Bush fits the bill, I'm just not free enough to do as much as I would like to do.

Bush is my kind of guy. He's loyal, he's honest, he's above-board, he's a hard-working guy, and he's prepared himself well for a tough job. He's ready for it.

I think (Robert) Dole is an outstanding guy as well. He's a fine man. I just think the country would be better off with Bush as president and Dole in the Senate.

They'd have a bigger impact that way. I happen to know (Michael) Dukakis. I think he'll make a fine candidate. I know his wife, Kitty. She married one of our former managers. She was a Penn State kid for a couple of years. After the divorce, she remarried Dukakis.

I think it's good for the country that Jesse Jackson is doing so well, particularly when we read in the paper about so much racism occurring on campus. It looks as if people are judging Jackson as a candidate and not necessarily as a black candidate. The more people hear him, the more I think people are impressed by him. He's a very competent candidate.

Despite all that, I happen to think that Bush is the best guy for the job. But I'm not married to being a Republican or a Democrat. Bill Bradley and Mario Cuomo are good men.

FOOTBALL PREVIEW: It had to be a kick visiting the White House with the team last year, and also being invited to a state dinner.

PATERNO: President Reagan is a delightful person. He's a very easy guy to get to know. He makes you feel as if you know him very quickly.

Occasions like that are some trimmings for the turkey, a little extra, that you never expect to get. And that was great for my wife, too.

FOOTBALL PREVIEW: Speaking of Sue. She's finally getting her due for her input into the success of the program. What is her role?

PATERNO: I'll tell you, they aren't going to have much trouble replacing me, but they are going to have a very tough time replacing her. Recruiting parties every Saturday night in our home, entertaining the wives, helping with tutoring kids. She never begrudges me the time I spend at the office or out recruiting. And the moms and the dads will call, and they'll bounce things off to her that don't necessarily get to me.

We also have a listed telephone number, and not many wives would put up with that. She puts up with the cranks. She's unbelievable.

FOOTBALL PREVIEW: What is the convocation center going to do for Penn State and what is it going to do for Penn State basketball?

PATERNO: Well, I've never been one who believed we need that for basketball. I think you have to pack Rec Hall every night first, with 8,000 people. In the long run, of course, it will be better if there's a place for 12,000 or 15,000 people.

I think the university needs a convocation center. Unfortunately, it's going to come out that we need it for sports. I don't think we need it for sports, as much as we need it for concerts, graduation, as a convention center. We need a big league convention area in central Pennsylvania. Our facilities on campus are not adequate any more. It would not only stimulate the economy here, but it would also bring in some brain power that would benefit the entire state.

I think the university is absolutely right in building a convocation center with a 300-room hotel and an alumni center. It will literally be a new component of the campus. It's something we need, but not necessarily for basketball. I'm just speaking for myself. Jim Tarman and Bruce Parkhill may have different thoughts on that.

The area's growing and the roads are getting better. President (Bryce) Jordan is a very progressive guy, very interested in working for the university in terms of economic interests and growth. He's done a great job and shown great leadership.

FOOTBALL PREVIEW: You're helping to spearhead Penn State's massive fund-raising effort. What have you learned by being a part of that?

PATERNO: I've learned just how successful our alumni are, and just how little we've done to blow our own horns. I think it's unbelievable the impact that this university's graduates have had on the country and the world. We have so many people who have done fantastic things. We don't even know about many of them. Most of the people we've been able to contact have been very generous, very loyal, very appreciative of what's gone on at Penn State.

> 66
> *I think it's unbelievable the impact that this university's graduates have had on the country and the world. We have so many people who have done fantastic things.*
> 99

When asked about the quality of a new recruiting class, Joe Paterno almost always replies, "Ask me in four years. I'll let you know then."

So, after four years of waiting, we finally asked about the Class of '88, which has reached the end of its four years at Penn State. At least some of its members have. For many of the 22 recruits who signed in the winter of 1984, the end came sooner than expected.

According to our calculations, nine of the 22 members of the class of '88 left Penn State before four years were up. That's 40.5 percent of the class, not a very high retention figure.

With that in mind, here's how the subject was broached to Paterno, who seemed genuinely surprised that so many of the players from that class didn't make it.

FOOTBALL PREVIEW: A good many players from the senior class didn't make it to this spring. Why is that? Is it a function of having some great classes in front of them, which made it hard for the younger kids to wait their turn?

PATERNO: No, I think it was just the lack of the right kind of people, people who made the wrong choice in coming here to Penn State. They came here for the wrong reasons.

A couple didn't do it academically. They made all kinds of excuses, but they were just outright lazy. As far as academics were concerned, they thought that—for one reason or another—they could get it done on their terms. But they couldn't.

I'm not sure who the nine are who aren't here...

FOOTBALL PREVIEW: Gregg Johnson, Jerry Hug, Craig McCoy, Mike Uhlar, Kevin Woods, George Mrvos...

PATERNO: McCoy?

FOOTBALL PREVIEW: Craig...

PATERNO: Oh, the quarterback.

FOOTBALL PREVIEW: ...Merlin Swartzentruber, Brad Acker and Dave Harper.

PATERNO: I think that was probably our fault. We probably recruited a couple of kids that we didn't evaluate correctly. They weren't good enough. I don't think it was a question of that many great ones ahead of them. The ones you mentioned were not great players regardless. There may have been one great on there...

FOOTBALL PREVIEW: Who is that?

PATERNO: I'm not sure, but even if I remembered I wouldn't tell you.

Over 20 Years and $250,000:
A Look Back at the Phi Psi 500

PENN STATE'S
WHY

Every weekend in Happy Valley was a community event and an opportunity to celebrate. In the '70s and '80s, Phi Psi 500 was one of the most popular 'fun with a purpose' events, a mile long race to raise money for philanthropy.

It was 1988 and the Phi Psi 500 was celebrating 20 years of a tradition. Hosted by the Phi Kappa Psi fraternity and sponsored by Moussy Beer, the Phi Psi 500 was a racing tradition that featured the fun, quirky excitement of Penn State in the '80s.

With 533 registrants consisting of both teams and individual runners, the race was set to raise money for the State College YMCA; Storm Break, an area youth shelter; and the Franklin Firsten Fund, aiding a Phi Kappa Psi brother who suffered from a coma resulting from an aneurysm he suffered in January 1985. The race had a goal to exceed 1987's total of $22,000.

The race was 1.1 miles and began in front of the fraternity house at 403 Locust Lane and took runners on a course through six downtown bars. Participating bars were: Phyrst Inc., The Brickhouse Tavern, The Surf Club Bar and Grill, The All American Rathskeller, The Shandygaff Saloon, and The Brewery.

Participants wore "wacky" costumes as they competed and stopped at the participating bars to chug beer, a big draw for many of the young (though certainly over 21 years old) participants. In 1988, the fraternity and the State College Borough Council agreed on a three-year timetable to eliminate alcohol from the race, which meant that for the 1988 race, at least one bar (The Surf Club

Space Goop at Acacia, 1986.
Photo courtesy B. Hulek

Bar and Grill) would offer only non-alcoholic beverages and each other location would offer a non-alcoholic choice. Runners were required to drink one 10-ounce, 50-cent beverage (either beer or the alternate drink) at each stop before moving on.

The alcohol elimination did end up bringing the race to an end in the early '90s when it lost the interest of participants, but the race had served a meaningful purpose raising over $250,000 over its lifetime.

1989

In 1989:

In their last year before joining the Big Ten, the Nittany Lions went 8-3 and beat Brigham Young 50-39 in the Holiday Bowl.

The Arsenio Hall show begins.

Thousands of Chinese students protest in Tiananmen Square. U.S. troops invade Panama, seeking capture of Manuel Noriega. Tanker Exxon Valdez sends 11 million gallons of crude oil into Alaska's Prince William Sound.

On November 9, the Berlin Wall fell, days after 500,000 protesters gathered in East Berlin.

Signs of the times: Centre County bans smoking in all public buildings and mandatory recycling takes effect on campus. The Interfraternity Council announces that fraternities would no longer sponsor tailgates, and that fraternities would issue wristbands to over-21 party guests.

Penn State reached its first major private fundraising campaign goal when a gift of $10 million took their total to $308 million, starting the Frank and Mary Jean Smeal College of Business Administration. Also, this year, a research and innovation park is announced, complete with a hotel and conference center. The new space is predicted to be home to university researchers as well as corporate tenants.

Top movies include "Indiana Jones and the Last Crusade," "Batman," "Honey, I Shrunk the Kids," "National Lampoon's Christmas Vacation," "Turner & Hooch," "When Harry Met Sally," "Parenthood," and "Dead Poets Society."

Top songs included "Right Here Waiting" by Richard Marx, "Love Shack" by The B-52's, "Lost in Your Eyes" by Debbie Gibson, "Like a Prayer" by Madonna, "When I See You Smile" by Bad English, and "Blame It on the Rain" by Milli Vanilli.

For Paterno, It's Business as Usual

Reprinted from 1989 Football Preview

An exclusive interview with the Penn State coach as he prepares to rebound from his first losing season.

It was three days before the start of spring drills and it was business as usual for Nittany Lion football at the offices in Greenberg Indoor Sports Complex. There was no hint, at least to a visitor, that Penn State was coming off its first losing season in 50 years.

Longtime secretary Mel Capobianco was at the front desk, smiling and answering the telephone with the good cheer usually reserved for national championship seasons at other schools.

Recruiting coordinator John Bove was welcoming a pro scout, who had made the trip to State College to "see some film on Michael" Timpson, the sprinter from Florida who was leaving the Penn State blocks with one year of eligibility unused.

Assistant coach Tom Bradley was walking around in a Penn State grey sweatshirt and blue pants, looking much like he did in the late '70s when he captained the Lion specialty teams with such a ferocity he earned the nickname "Scrap." Bradley was chattering away about "Tag Team Day" in the Penn State weight room. He couldn't wait to see all the players who were going to dress up as their favorite WWF heroes.

In all, the first three people spotted in the office that March day had been associated with Penn State football for 37 years. They all were calm, collected and—dare we say it—even happy. If there were any worries about the effect of a 5-6 season on morale or planning or staffing, their presence assuaged those fears.

As he prepared for the 1989 season, his 24th year as head coach and his 40th on the Penn State staff, Paterno wasn't going to panic. In fact, there wasn't a single change on the Lion staff in the off-season—not that assistants Ron Dickerson and Jerry Sandusky didn't come close to leaving.

Inside the coaches' meeting room, where Paterno was holding a staff meeting of his offensive coaches, it might have been a different story. The Lions, after all, scored all of 10 points in their final two games. Obviously, when a team averages less than 12 points per game over the final half of the season—and drops five of six games—there has to be some room for concern.

Yet, if Paterno was distressed, he certainly didn't show it to this day. He was certainly in a bit of a hurry, but then he always has been. That's one way you get to be a Joe Paterno.

The coach was cordial, friendly and looking very fit. The only hint that he's 62 was a stray grey hair or three. A recent vacation courtesy of Nike left him looking tan and trim.

In some ways, Paterno was more open, more animated than I've ever seen him in the course of over 100 press conferences and interviews. He answered, in-depth, a question about Tom Bill's arrest for underage drinking. He didn't sidestep re-addressing his long ago (and currently very relevant) comment about the ethics of Barry Switzer and Jackie Sherril. He acknowledged that his off-the-field activities affected his coaching—for the "second or third time." And he blamed Syracuse for blowing its series with Penn State.

But most telling, to me, were his comments about State College. Paterno came to town in 1950 with Rip Engle and he never left. It's where he's spent almost four decades, a place one could safely say he put on the map. But State College, and its people, have changed him. "I don't know enough people anymore," said Paterno, adding a bit later that he feels "isolated."

Now, I'm not going to feel sorry for Joe Paterno. But when he says things like that, and cracks up over ESPN's Beano Cook and calls him a nut the same way that Joe Fan does, I see—albeit ever so briefly—a glimpse of the real Joe Paterno.

FOOTBALL PREVIEW: Have there been any encouraging signs in the offseason that bode well for Penn State's football future?

PATERNO: Oh, yeah. But I was encouraged by a lot of the things that happened last year. The kids never quit and they worked hard and they showed a lot of character. And I think that showed.

We have a bunch of kids who are good competitors and have some pride. And I think that's been indicated by the way they've gone through their winter workouts. I'm encouraged from that aspect, but we obviously have got to play better.

FOOTBALL PREVIEW: Not much was made last season of all of the string of injuries along the offense and the fact that Ray Roundtree was denied eligibility. Do you think these people acknowledged all those unforeseen and unavoidable problems that contributed to the 5-6 record?

PATERNO: I think there's a lot of things that went into it. It was a tough year. But really we can't be sitting around feeling sorry

> *Paterno came to town in 1950 with Rip Engle and he never left. It's where he's spent almost four decades, a place one could safely say he put on the map. But State College, and its people, have changed him.*

> *You just have to take a positive attitude that we're going to get better, play better.*

for ourselves. We got to get on with it. And we've kind of put that behind us. I can't do anything about what happened last year in the way of injuries, officiating or bad bounces or anything like that. You just have to take a positive attitude that we're going to get better, play better.

FOOTBALL PREVIEW: With spring drills about to start, what is the status of Blair Thomas? How close is he to 100 percent?

PATERNO: It's tough to tell. We're going to be very careful with him this spring. It's one thing to go through winter workouts and pace yourself a little bit—although he's worked awfully hard—but spring drills are a little different. I'm just going to have to wait and see on him.

FOOTBALL PREVIEW: Before Blair's injury you were pushing him for postseason honors, which is quite uncharacteristic for you. Is that something you're going to pick back up on or would doing that put added pressure on him?

PATERNO: We're just going to take care of one thing at a time. First thing we've got to do is get him where he's back playing the way that he knows how to play and hopefully at 100 percent physically. And then we'll go from there. You know we've got to see how he's playing and what's going on. But I've never given that any thought. I'm just keeping my fingers crossed and hoping he's 100 percent.

FOOTBALL PREVIEW: This is a very young team. Who has been emerging as the leaders of the squad?

PATERNO: It's difficult for me to say, because in the winter program most of the kids have been enthusiastic, and there have been a lot of kids who might fill that role. I've got to see what happens when we get on the practice field and what kind of chemistry develops.

We're still going to be a young team. We don't have a lot of older kids. And it will be interesting to see who does come out of the younger group and which of those kids are going to be leaders, because I don't think we've got enough older people that they can do it themselves.

FOOTBALL PREVIEW: Steve Smith, now with the Raiders, compared this past year's team with the '84 team he was on. Is that a fair comparison?

PATERNO: I don't know, but I hope he's right. There are some indications that might be true. But I don't really know yet until I see them on the practice field.

I have not seen these kids play any football since we lost to Pitt and Notre Dame and what did we get? Did we get a touchdown? I mean, I think we had one touchdown in two games. So for me to say we're comparable to where we were after the '84 season, I don't know. Anything I would say would be a guess, and it might be a lousy guess.

FOOTBALL PREVIEW: Shifting gears here. It's often been said that you have a certain power, or a way or a magic with the media—both locally and nationally—that you can hold them in check. Is that a fair assessment?

PATERNO: [laughing] No, no.

[He laughs heartily again.] I don't think so. I think I take my lumps like everybody else, but I think the media has been fair to me. Every once in a while I get a little perturbed, but I think that's

> " *I think the media has been fair to me.* "

really a little bit of being immature on my part. I think in most cases, in all of my life, the media has been pretty good to me.

But I've tried to be honest, as honest as you can be and still not hurt your football team. There are times where I'd like to say, "We're a lot better football team. We're going to kick their ears in." But instead, I may hem or haw. I don't do that because I want to be dishonest with a newspaper or a media person. I do it because I don't want to hurt the team's chances of winning.

So I think the media has been fair to me, but they've also been critical to me at times. And I think rightly so. But in any case, I don't know about magic spells.

FOOTBALL PREVIEW: One criticism of the media has been its attention to recruiting. There are "recruiting analysts" all over the country and people are buying their word as gospel. Has it gotten out of hand? Should the media police itself in that regard, in at least being more accurate?

PATERNO: Oh, absolutely. I think the media can't have it both ways. They can't be critical of kids who get a false impression as to their importance because the media have helped to build up that image. And they can't feel blameless if some kid believes all of that junk they write about him—because in a lot of cases it is a lot of junk.

They talk about kids being an impact player on this team, an impact player on that team and this guy should start as a fresh- man, and these are the top five quarterbacks in the country and all that kind of nonsense. If you're a young kid or you come from a family where there hasn't been much success, you're liable to get carried away with that. And when a kid does get carried away, the media then crucifies him at times.

So I think there must be some responsibility. I think it's gotten way out of hand. If it were accurate, that would be one thing. But for some guy in Texas to say the best five halfbacks in the coun- try are these five, well, they're dishonest. They claim they've seen them...They couldn't possibly look at all the films of all the kids that they rate. It's impossible.

It's not fair to some kids who maybe don't get the recognition. It's not fair to some kids who, for one reason or another, get the recognition and really don't deserve it and don't understand how far they have to go in order to be able to make it.

And it creates a tremendous problem with some coaches—not for me—but particularly a young coach who's having some prob- lems and does a really good job of recruiting. He recruits solid people that his staff have evaluated to be good. But because the recruits are not Parade All-Americans or because they didn't make somebody else's all-star team or because somebody else hasn't rated them high, their recruiting class doesn't get rated very highly. And then the coach is branded a lousy recruiter. All he hears is, "How come you didn't get so and so?"

Well, the kid may not have been our kind of kid, he may not be a good student or because of a lot of things you don't want to say in the paper. You don't want to say, "Hey, the kid is a bum. He came to our campus and acted like a jerk, he got drunk. I don't want any part of him. Well, he came to our campus and he stole a kid's jacket." You can't say things like that.

There are a lot of reasons you back away from a kid. And I think nobody should evaluate a recruiting class until the kids are in their third year. Then I think you have a pretty good idea of what kind of class you have.

Otherwise, I don't think it does anybody any good. Plus, a lot of what they say is really untrue. Every guy that we recruit is (reported) at least 15 pounds heavier and at least one or two inches taller and runs at least two or three fractions quicker in the 40 than they actually do. It doesn't make news if you recruit a guy who's a 215-pound linebacker, who's 6-foot-1 and runs 5.0. And that's what most of them are. And some of those kids turn out to be great players. But people don't read about that.

FOOTBALL PREVIEW: How do you deal with a recruit who comes in with a bunch of outlandish news clippings?

PATERNO: You've got to try, when you recruit the kid, to keep his feet on the ground. And if you can't, then you've got to make up your mind whether you want to recruit trouble or have him go someplace else. We try to smell that.

If I think a kid is getting out of hand then I'm going to sit him down and tell him, "Hey, look, you're not that good and if you come to Penn State, you're going to have a tough time making it and you better understand that. Not that you can't make it, but you're in the same boat as everybody else. Don't believe all of that nonsense and what have you."

And if he doesn't buy that, then obviously he's going to turn us down. He's going to go someplace where they're going to say, "You're going to start for us right away." And that's happened to us with several kids in the state.

A couple of years ago, we lost a good back—I'm not going to give you his name—because he was promised he would start as a freshman. That's fine, but I think that stuff catches up with you. Plus, the kid expects a little bit more than you can deliver and it becomes a problem... That youngster becomes a problem. Not

> When you talk to a quarterback, my statement is, "Do you want to play on a national championship team? Are you the kind of guy who wants to get in the huddle and say to yourself, 'Hey, this is my team and I'm going to lead them and have 85,000 people up there be critical of it.

> College athletics have a lot of image problems. And Penn State has always been fairly immune to that, and for good reason. Through the years the players have been fairly well-behaved and, for the most part, they're good people.

a problem that they'd eliminate him from the program, but he's been a source of… he's had to be disciplined.

FOOTBALL PREVIEW: You've always said that when you're recruiting a quarterback you want to make sure he can handle playing in front of 80,000 screaming fans. Can you expound upon that and what are the other criteria you look for in a quarterback when you're out there recruiting?

PATERNO: When you talk to a quarterback, my statement is, "Do you want to play on a national championship team? Are you the kind of guy who wants to get in the huddle and say to yourself, 'Hey, this is my team and I'm going to lead them and have 85,000 people up there be critical of it.'"

I try to spell it out right away, try to challenge them. And a lot of kids will back away from that. But the ones who take it—you know, the ones who have it—really respond to that. I don't know any other way to prepare them for it. Obviously, if you're recruiting a quarterback, you look at a kid and see how he performs in big games, whether he can handle some pressure. Or you see if he has taken a team that's losing a championship game and brings them back in the last three minutes.

There are a lot of indications—the way he handles himself when you're around him, the kind of poise he has, his relationship with the kids when you bring him on campus, whether the other kids like him. There are a lot of things that indicated whether a kid has the leadership qualities and the poise necessary to do it. But, we try to make them aware of what it's going to take.

FOOTBALL PREVIEW: So that's something you can sense sitting there in a kid's living room?

PATERNO: Yep. And a lot of kids will back away from it very quickly. A lot of kids turn us down and I'm sure that's the reason.

FOOTBALL PREVIEW: College athletics have a lot of image problems. And Penn State has always been fairly immune to that, and for good reason. Through the years the players have been fairly well-behaved and, for the most part, they're good people. But over the past season one of your players was found guilty of underage drinking for the second time…

PATERNO: Who are you talking about? Tom Bill?

FOOTBALL PREVIEW: Yeah, Tom Bill.

PATERNO: I think Tommy's maturing a little bit. But what were you going to ask me?

FOOTBALL PREVIEW: How do you deal with a situation like that and does it affect your dealings with the player once he crosses the line and is on the field? Do you view that as two separate things?

PATERNO: No, I think you've got to deal with it as one thing and you've got to be fair and not naive. I've never been naive enough to think that everybody on our squad doesn't drink or that it's bad if some of them have a beer.

I come from a home where, when I was in high school, there was a bottle of wine on the table and if I wanted some, I drank it. If I didn't want it, I didn't drink it.

I think Tommy comes from a family where he might have been drinking beer since he was 15, 16 years of age. And he's got to learn that's got to be behind him now, especially now that he's in the limelight. And I think he's coming to grips with that.

He and I have talked extensively about it… We have certain rules and if a kid does embarrass the team, then I'm going to be certain to discipline him in different ways… And I've told him that there's no way he's going to run this football team if he doesn't handle himself in a way that the kids can look up to him. If they can't look up to him, then he can't be their leader if he can't discipline himself. And we're going to see.

But the last offense happened a long time ago. That happened at least six months ago, I think…

FOOTBALL PREVIEW: Has coaching reached the point where it seems like you're spending more time on the administrative duties than the coaching duties?

PATERNO: Well, it has. It had gotten that way. In fact, I think that's one of the problems I've had the last two years. You get a lot of success and all of a sudden you're involved in a lot of things that take time, whether it's fundraising or what have you. Or you get in tremendous demand and you get a little bit careless about the amount of time you spend on the campus. There's more and more interviews and people want to talk about everything.

I hope I've learned a lesson because it's about the second or third time it's happened to me. I just try to eliminate most anything unless it's directly connected with football. Obviously, I've got to do some things with the media; that's part of my responsibility.

But there are some things which I've been doing that I'm going to get out of. And I have gotten out of a lot of things because I do think that you can get pulled away from the football, you can get pulled away from communications with your staff and communications with your players.

You don't talk things out enough and sometimes you're not on the same page with your staff. And the kids sense that and sometimes you go out there to do something, and you think that it's going to be done a certain way, and you really haven't spent enough time with them, going over it with them. So I think that's been a problem for me. But I don't think it will be this year.

FOOTBALL PREVIEW: I hope that doesn't mean your speech at the Republican Convention. That was your right,

1989: For Paterno, It's Business as Usual

it was well-received by the media here and even by the *International Herald-Tribune*, and after all, some things are more important than football.

PATERNO: Oh, there's no question about that. There will be some obligations beyond football, and I obviously intend to keep those, but I've got to be a little bit more careful.

With a thing like that (speech), you spend a lot of time thinking about it, you write it, you have somebody else look at it, you rewrite it. And it's on your mind, whereas I could have been spending that time thinking about how we're going to block our off-tackle play or on personnel or what have you.

FOOTBALL PREVIEW: In line with your speech at the convention… Beano Cook, who authored a piece for The Annual this year, wrote that after you're done with football he sees you in some position in Washington, D.C. Any reaction to that?

PATERNO: Yeah, that guy… He's crazy. I'm going to coach for awhile. I'm having fun. I'm going to stay in it for awhile.

FOOTBALL PREVIEW: Beano also wrote that before Don Canham offered the Michigan job to Bo Schembechler he talked to you about it. Tell me about it.

PATERNO: You see, after the season in 1968 Michigan was looking for a coach. And he called me up, but I said I wasn't interested. If I had been interested, Michigan would have been one of the few places I'd go. I always had a great deal of respect for Michigan because I've known some great Michigan people like Ernie McCoy, who was here, and J.T. White, who was on our staff, and some others. And I was always very impressed with them. It's a quality institution.

Anyway, I went out to Pittsburgh and visited Canham at the Pittsburgh airport. And he said, "Hey, look, I want you to come on out. I really think you'd be great for Michigan and vice versa." And I gave it some thought. Then I thought I don't want to. I didn't want to get into none of the business that "Paterno's going to Michigan." I was just getting started here and I had a young team and I didn't want to leave them.

A couple of days later, Don called me and asked me about some people—about five or six guys—and he mentioned Schembechler. I said, "Well, all I can tell is one night I was with Woody Hayes and he said that Bo Schembechler was the best assistant coach he probably ever had and he would make a good head coach someday." I said that I didn't know Bo very well, but everything I knew about him indicated he was the kind of guy you'd want for your program. I don't know if I had any influence or not, but that's the extent of it.

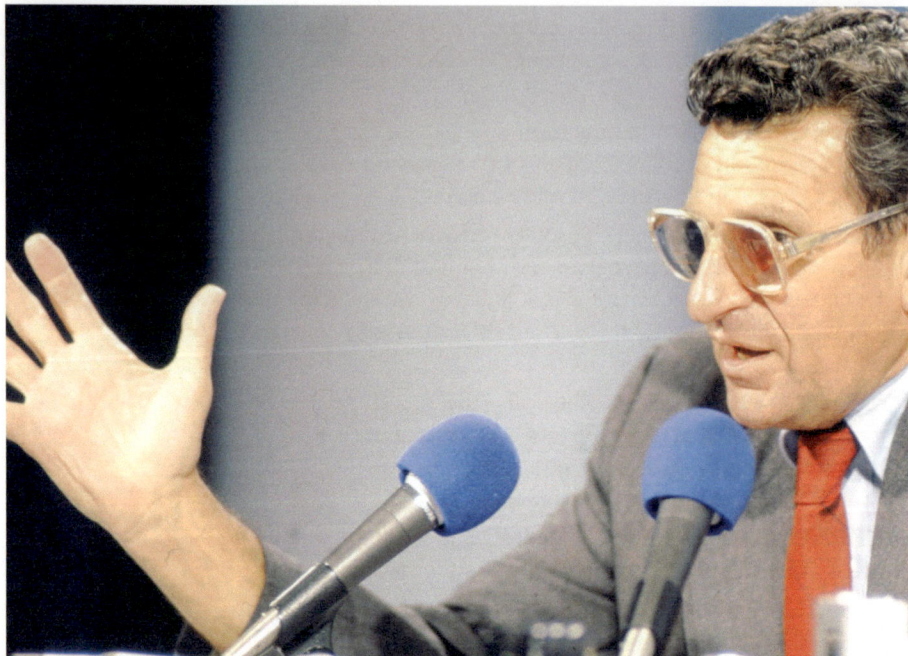

FOOTBALL PREVIEW: As you look to the future, Penn State opens a new era in the '90s, with the schedule and the inclusion of such teams as Southern Cal. What kind of import does it have now that you're really talking a national—east to west, north to south—schedule?

PATERNO: Well, I think it's what we had to work our way to. Again, when I got involved in the university fundraising, I did a lot of travel to California and across the country and I really learned how many alumni we have all over the place.

You have 10-12,000 alumni maybe in California. You got another 4 or 5,000 in Texas, and maybe 6, 7, 8,000 in Florida. You got them in the Midwest… they're all over the place. And they're all dying for us to play a football game there.

I think we have to think about playing a game in the South or Southeast. Miami is a great place to play because it's in a big city with a lot of Penn Staters, it's an easy place for people in the Southeast to get to and right now their program is running high. It's a prestige game for us. It's a television game.

> "
> *We're a national school and I think we have to play a national schedule.*
> "

Southern Cal gets us out on the coast. Notre Dame gets us in the Midwest. We're playing BYU, which is going to get us in the mountain area. We got Texas and then Baylor comes on a little bit later. We're a national school and I think we have to play a national schedule. It's not going to be easy, obviously. But, you know, I hope we'll be deep enough and good enough that every once in a while we can handle most of them. They're not going to be home every year, but I think it's challenging and I think it's something that's right for Penn State at this time.

FOOTBALL PREVIEW: Closer to home, Syracuse Coach Dick MacPherson recently had this to say about the ending of the Penn State-Syracuse series: "There's nobody in the business I respect more. Everyone makes a mistake and I think Joe blew the Syracuse-Penn State series. It's not right. He's too big a man for that." I'm not looking for name-calling, but is there a final word on the series, something that you can put in perspective?

PATERNO: I think I can put it in perspective. All we did is ask Syracuse to help us out with one more home game. Instead of five and five, we wanted six and four (out of ten games), in light of the fact that Syracuse and some other people went into the Big East and devastated our basketball. We're just now recovering. They cut out a home and home (basketball) series. There was no concern whatsoever about the tradition of those games.

I think we have to be practical about this thing. We have to try to get seven home games as frequently as we can. We've got to. We're trying to keep ticket prices down, although they may raise them this year again. (Editor's note: Prices will go up $2 in 1989.) But our game at Texas cost us 25 bucks and Notre Dame charged big bucks for our game last year and somebody else is charging big bucks for our game.

We have a set guarantee. We go to Texas and we're going to get $150,000 or $100,000 but they're upping the price because they're playing us and they're making all that extra dough. The only time Syracuse sells out is when we go up there [laughs]. And yet they don't want to help us with one game.

Now, we got to get seven games and we're going to do it. We're going to play some other people two to one. They're willing to do that. I mean, all we wanted was one game from Syracuse over the next 10 years. So I don't think I'm out of whack. I think Syracuse blew it. We didn't blow it. Syracuse blew it. So that's where I'm coming from. I think Syracuse made a big mistake and I feel bad about it. I would like to play Syracuse. I think it's been a great game.

But I don't think we can continually go along with Syracuse's attitude that, "Hey, we're going to do what we want regardless of how it affects you Penn State when it comes to basketball and this and that. But you've got to do it our way in football. We're not going to give you a break at all in football." That's fine. They're going to have to live with that.

FOOTBALL PREVIEW: Speaking of basketball, you've always been a big fan. It has to feel good to see the success of the program this past season, especially the NIT game against Murray State tomorrow in Rec Hall.

PATERNO: Absolutely. I'm excited about tomorrow night, I hope we get a great crowd. If we don't sell that place out, I'm going to be crushed tomorrow night. These kids are playing well, they're fun to watch. They struggle, those seniors. I'm excited about it. I think Bruce Parkhill has turned the program around now. I really do. I thought they played awfully well against Rutgers. They played well against West Virginia. They're a good basketball team now. They're really good.

FOOTBALL PREVIEW: I understand that you're writing a book. Is it coming out soon?

PATERNO: We're getting close to finishing it up. A fellow on campus, Bernie Asbell, who teaches creative writing, is writing the book with me. In fact, he's doing most of the writing. I get to talk into a tape recorder. He's got most of it done. It will not be an X's and circles type of thing.

FOOTBALL PREVIEW: In your role as an educator, you took an important stand a few weeks ago in front of Old Main when you spoke out against the recent racial incidents on campus (including one where a few black women were slurred by a gang of white males). You've been here so long. What are your feelings about the situation?

PATERNO: Oh, it's tough for me to figure. I mean this town isn't perfect. There's no place that's perfect. I don't care. I've been called Wop and things like that. But it's all different for a black kid here, because there are not a lot of black kids here, and they're bound to feel a little bit isolated.

And I think it's a mere bully that would taunt or abuse a small group like that. And unfortunately, the kids who do it are hurting themselves more than they are hurting the blacks, really. I mean, they are scarring their whole personality. They're not giving themselves a chance to find out what makes somebody else tick who's got a different color to them, who's a little different, who maybe likes different music or has different slang.

The people doing the name-calling are half a person the rest of their lives. And that's what those guys are. They're half people. I think the one good thing that's come out of all this is that, I hope, the black population will see how many people have really genuine concern. I think the university responded and a lot of townspeople responded.

Everybody really feels embarrassed for the kids and feels sorry for them and feel that they have been hurt in a way that they should never have to be hurt. I think that most of the people ral-

lied around them—most of them... This town is not a racist town. This town is a good town that has some racism in it. It is not a racist town. And I would argue that with anybody.

FOOTBALL PREVIEW: State College has changed so much, especially in the past five to 10 years. Is it still the same old town you came here with Rip Engle almost four decades ago?

PATERNO: No. It's still a very livable town. But so many of the people I grew up with are not here anymore. And I've not had a chance to make new friends in this town. Once I got to a certain status, traveling so much, entertaining so much—for the university, for the athletic department, for football—and with recruiting and what have you, it got to a point where I really don't know this town like I used to know it. There are places in this town, people talk about where they live and I don't even know where they are. I've not seen them.

FOOTBALL PREVIEW: Does that sadden you at all?

PATERNO: Oh, sure it saddens me.

FOOTBALL PREVIEW: I bet you can't walk down College Ave. now like you used to.

PATERNO: Well, yes, I do. I do that.

FOOTBALL PREVIEW: You do?

PATERNO: Oh, sure. I do that at odd hours—seven, eight o'clock Sunday night when everyone's not there. I do. I still walk around a great deal. I know the town, "the old town." I know the old State College.

But I don't know enough people anymore. There's a whole bunch of people out there who've been here 12, 15 years that I don't know. They're really becoming leaders in this town and I'm not very familiar with them or don't recognize them. That's where I'm at, that I feel isolated. But I still have places that I go that haven't changed and won't change in my mind—the Corner Room, places like that.

FOOTBALL PREVIEW: Do you feel that way with the coaching profession now, especially given the recent retirement of an old friend, Vince Dooley?

PATERNO: We deal with the Nike shoe people and they have a nice thing they do for guys who are on their staff. They have about 27 or 28 head coaches and we all go away for a week with our wives. We were away over term break. So those guys I've gotten close to. And every once in a while you get a couple of new guys in, and a couple of guys leave.

FOOTBALL PREVIEW: Who's in that group?

PATERNO: Don Nehlen, Pat Dye, Bill Curry, Barry Switzer, he didn't make the trip this year. Bo Schembechler's in there. Jack Bicknell, Larry Smith from Southern Cal. Richard Brooks from Oregon. Earle Bruce. I know I forgot somebody. But there's about 20, 22 coaches on it. So I have those people as friends. And the older guys I know. I know a lot of the older guys.

FOOTBALL PREVIEW: Talking about fellow coaches, you made an off-the-record comment (about not "leaving coaching to the Switzers and Sherrills") a couple years ago for which you took some heat. But given the events of the past year, it made you look like a prophet… and I think you know what I'm saying.

PATERNO: Yeah, I know.

FOOTBALL PREVIEW: Any comment on that? Or are you just going to sit back and not say anything and let that speak for itself?

PATERNO: Well, I'm not one of those guys who like to kick people when they're down. I apologized to Barry. I've gotten to know Barry through the years. I think Barry's obviously not an angel or anything like that, but I don't want to get into that with him. I think he's got enough problems without somebody else getting in there and getting involved.

Jackie Sherrill is different. Sherrill I've never known and never been close to. He's not had much respect for me and I have not had much for him. But there again, I'm just not the kind of guy who likes to see anybody have his career end like that. I wish it would never have happened to him. But it happened, but I don't feel good about that. I really don't.

FOOTBALL PREVIEW: Final question: What's the best thing that happened to you in the off-season?

PATERNO: [laughs] I'm just glad I didn't get fired.

The Paterno Dictionary

BY JIM CARLSON

For those of you who think Joe Paterno is not an extremely intelligent man, just ask yourself how many people have dual vocabularies. Not speak two languages, but own two vocabularies. Not just any old Joe can swing that.

Paterno has shaken the hand of at least two presidents and openly criticized another. He quotes Browning and Frost and can cite the names of composers. And when in that particular arena, he is a true orator.

But he can turn the other cheek and be jocular as well. And it's not your typical coach-ese. It's not like he talks down, just different.

You have to figure that a man through 23 seasons has been through press conference after press conference, from a weekly basis through the season to a daily basis at bowl games. In fact, an extremely rough estimate of press conferences he has been through, and this includes season, bowl, spring and summer estimates, is 1,935. Throw in the telephone calls he receives when something breaks on a national level and we're over 3,000. Thus, it probably is safe to say that if the guy wants to employ two vocabularies, he can do just that.

Let's examine his coaching vocabulary term by term:

"Go by the book and you'll always make the right call."

> **"**
> *Aaah, our defense just got out of whack. Funny thing, though: I've never heard Paterno say "we're in whack.*
> **"**

OUT OF WHACK: This is pretty much self-explanatory. "Their eight-man rush just got us a little out of whack," Paterno has said—a lot of times. "Aaah, our defense just got out of whack."

This term is probably the most contagious. It has appeared in newspaper articles, been heard on countless State College radio shows and has filtered down to Paterno's players. Forget the statements of the modern-day athlete. Many of Penn State's most quotable athletes, such as former quarterback John Shaffer or ex-linebacker Trey Bauer, have put to use the term "out of whack" and never batted a chinstrap while saying it.

Funny thing, though: I've never heard Paterno say "we're *in* whack."

WILLY-NILLY: Not used nearly as much as—or as bad a word as—out of whack; more of a specialized term and probably not even used during the 1988 season. "Aaah, the way that quarterback was scrambling, our defensive play-calling went willy-nilly," Paterno could say, but with more feeling. No players in recent memory have been known to utter "willy-nilly."

LOOSEY-GOOSEY: An eye-opener, used only in certain situations. "Aaah, we were just too loosey-goosey in certain situations," he has said. A player or two has muttered loosey-goosey, but they weren't starters. Never became starters, either.

BIG-LEAGUE: Means something is of high-quality. Certain to be included among every five sentences during press conferences, perhaps every 10 during non-press conference situations. "He's a big-league back. He's a big-league tackle. He's a big-league wideout. He's a big-league coach. This is a big-league tuna fish salad," Paterno has definitely said. Aaah, players use big-league constantly.

NEVER AS GOOD…: "You're never as good as you think you are when you win, and never as bad as you think you are when you lose," Paterno says mainly after a win. And sometimes after a loss. And, aaah, sometimes the players use it, too.

ENOUGH GLORY…: "Aaah, there was enough glory in this game for both teams; neither team deserved to lose," Paterno often says after a close game, usually a win. Players have also.

GOOD, SOLID…: "They're a good, solid team. He's a good, solid linebacker. He's a good, solid coach," Paterno says in his good, solid perfect tone.

AWFULLY: Same as very, but related to big-league as far as frequency is concerned. "They're awfully good; he's awfully good." But you rarely hear him say "We're awfully good." Players say awfully awfully often.

PATERNO: By the Numbers

As of 1990

.460 Percentage of all PSU games as coach (156 as an assistant; 280 as head coach; 957 overall).

.510 Percentage of PSU wins as coach (104 as an assistant; 220 as head coach; 637 overall).

.791 All-time winning percentage (220-57-3).

2 National championships (1982, 1986)

5 Number of children Diana Lynne, Mary Kathryn, David, Joseph Jr. ("Jay"), George Scott.

4 Undefeated seasons (11-0, 1968; 11-0, 1969; 12-0, 1973; 12-0, 1986).

9 Number worn playing football for Brooklyn Tech.

6 Ranking on victory list of all-time major college football coaches.

15 Victories by the Brown football team in 1948-49 while playing quarterback (with 3 losses).

$24⁹⁵ The cost of a stand-up cardboard JoePaterno.

18 Teams in The Associated Press' Top 20.

$59⁹⁵ Cost of 14-inch painted plaster bust of Paterno.

31 Consecutive games without a loss, from Oct. 14, 1967, to Sept. 26, 1970.

36 Jersey number at Brown.

38 Largest margin of defeat (44-6 Nebraska in 1983 Kickoff Classic).

63 Age (birthdate is Dec. 21, 1926).

126 Paterno players to play the NFL (plus four drafted in April, 1990).

8,000 Stand-up cardboard JoePaternos sold to date.

65,000 Copies of "Paterno: By The Book" sold to date.

41 YEARS Number of years at Penn State.

$1,200,000 Amount of money New England Patriots offered to be their head coach in 1973.

$150,000 Amount of money he donated to Penn State library and minority scholarship funds.

9,825,605 Fans to see Penn State play in Beaver Stadium since 1966.

71 Consecutive Beaver Stadium sellouts

3

Showing Penn State Pride

Oo-La-La!

Twins Become Nittany Lion Poster Girls

By LYNDA ROBINSON
Times Staff Writer

When they first arrived at Penn State two summers ago, they were known as the "Oo-la-la Twins." But that nickname for Amy and Beth Sax may have to be modified to the "Oo-la-la Poster Twins."

The 19-year-old identical twins from Pittsburgh posed with the Nittany Lion shrine for a poster that appeared last week in several State College store windows.

The poster, which sells for $3.50, is the brainchild of 23-year-old Greg Woodman, a student at the University and president of Happy Valley Promotions, a company specializing in T-shirts for special events and organizations.

Mr. Woodman said he has been considering doing a poster for a long time and insisted his idea was not inspired by last year's photograph of a nude woman leaning against the Nittany Lion.

"I just thought the students needed a poster to buy," he said. "I saw a void there. I thought a poster could sell."

To fill the void, Mr. Woodman purchased two football jerseys and enlisted the aid of the Sax twins who earned their nickname during last Summer Term.

"I used to walk through the (Pollock) quad and I'd hear 'oo-la-la,' Amy said. "It was pretty funny."

Both young women said they posed for the poster, which they said is a football poster rather than a cheesecake pin-up, because they thought it would be fun.

"It's just reflecting the idea of Penn State being into football," Beth said.

But both sisters admitted that while the shrine, the football jerseys and the fall colors all have a connection with football, their own appearance in the poster has little to do with sports.

The poster has made the twins instant local celebrities — with all the pitfalls stardom entails.

"Most people don't walk into a bookstore and see themselves on a poster," Amy said. "You just kind of look the other way."

But the twins can't escape the people who call or knock on the door seeking autographs for their posters.

"It's interrupting things," Amy, a business major,

said. "Just all the time, they're calling us fun."

"But sometimes you need a break," letters, arts and sciences major.

If Mr. Woodman sells all 2,000 copies twins may have difficulty meeting autograph

Without any advertising, more than posters were sold last week, Mr. Woodm tisements for the poster began on Frida expected to increase.

Most of the purchasers are male, some women are buying the poster fo brothers for Christmas.

Duane Liput, a 21-year-old accoun Versailles, said he intends to buy the good," he said. "It's appealing to the ey

Not everyone finds the poster app taste. University administrators expre the use of the shrine for commercial little could be done to prevent it.

Richard E. Grubb, senior vice pre tration, said the University is explorir registering Penn State as a trademark the University to control the use of it of symbolic representations of the U shrine.

"A lot of universities are movin Mr. Grubb said. But there are disa advantages in following the trend.

Registering the University's na would generate money for the Univ royalties, Mr. Grubb said. Any o State's name on a product would ha and then pay for the privilege.

However, Mr. Grubb pointed ou would then be responsible for mak bearing the Penn State name are au

Another disadvantage of registe the loss of free publicity the allowing companies to use its name

But the University has not decided whether benefits of registering would outweigh the costs. And in the meantime, Mr. Woodman said he plans to print as many posters as he can sell.

Chapter 3: Showing Penn State Pride

bringing *PENN STATE* to you

1984-'85
Catalog of Licensed products for the Penn Stater

HAPPY VALLEY
HVP
PROMOTIONS

PENN STATE BLUE BAND PLAYS SCHOOL SONGS.
Eight marching songs that capture the spirit of the Nittany Lions by Penn State's impressive Blue Band.
X48 .... $ 3.00

HAPPY VALLEY POSTER.
A comic illustrated Full-Color Poster that shows scenes of campus and town.
HVP01 .... $ 4.00

PRIDE AND BEAUTY POSTER.
Sensational color poster is full of Penn State nostalgia with Fall's bright highlights. 18" x 24". features two Penn State sophomore twins posing at famed Nittany Lion Shrine.
HVP02 .... $ 4.00

1982 HIGHLIGHT BOOK
The special Collector's Edition of the Nittany Lions' Championship season. This color magazine includes a game-by-game chronology, 21" x 16" full-color pull-out poster, over 80 photos and special feature articles.
HVP04 .... $ 4.99

1984 FOOTBALL ANNUAL.
64-page Annual Football Edition filled with exclusive photos and articles that preview the 1984 season and take you behind the scenes for a close-up look at the "Beast of the East."
HVP05 .... $ 3.50

Merry Christmas

Merry Christmas

FORD TEE SHIRT by Russell
dard athletic tee shirt in Oxford Grey. 50/50
s. S, M, L, XL
S-81 .... $ 7.75

FORD TEE SHIRT, YOUTH by Russell
to tie 50/4
th Sizes: S, M, L
.... $ 6.50

ALL SPORT JERSEY by Medallion
White heavy weight sport jersey with navy striped trim.
Sizes: S, M, L, XL
S-81 .... $10.50

ALL SPORT JERSEY, YOUTH by Medallion
Same as S-81
Youth Sizes: S, M, L
S-82 .... $ 9.00

GAME JERSEY by Jerico
Heavy nylon mesh football game jersey with 3/4 sleeves. These are pre-cut for pads. Includes your choice of numbers on front, back & sleeves.
Colors: Navy or White.
Sizes: S(34-36), M(38-40), L(42-44), XL(46)
S-80 .... $29.
(Also available in XXL(50)) .... 28.

PENN STATE'S WHY

From the author: I started Happy Valley Promotions by selling T-shirts out of the trunk of my car at home games when I was a student. Pretty soon, we had a great team of Penn Staters working together in a house on Nittany Avenue, capturing the spirit of the '80s with posters and shirts, the "Are You a Penn Stater" book, and the football annuals that are featured here. Putting "Why Penn State" together has been a great look back of the formative decade of the '80s at Penn State. -GJW

Dear Penn Stater:

Hello from Happy Valley!

I'm happy to report that we're still tailgating, eating at "the diner," hanging out on the wall and doing "case studies" at "the Skeller". . . when we're not processing your order.

We at Happy Valley Promotions continue to specialize in capturing the feelings and emotions that are unique to the total Penn State experience. We are dedicated to fulfilling our company slogan, "Bringing Penn State to You!."

In keeping with the spirit of Happy Valley we offer Penn State merchandise with a light, collegiate flair. Whether you purchase our sportswear with an imprinted design, or enjoy the sophomoric humor of the "Are You A Penn Stater Guidebook," our spirit and attention to quality is evident.

We realize that without you there wouldn't be a Happy Valley Promotions. To satisfy your need for quality we draw upon experienced manufacturers like RUSSELL, HANES, UNION, JESCO and JANSPORT, and as always, every product is guaranteed.

Please don't hesitate to suggest new products or request items not shown or just drop us a "lion".

Who Loves Ya,

Greg J Woodman

Greg Woodman

P.S.: We also have group rates for Alumni Clubs.

HAPPY VALLEY PRO

BOROUGH OF STATE COLLEGE

TRANSIENT RETAIL DEALER'S LICENSE

Date: 12/18/79

Permit No. 031-79

Fee Charged: $3⁰⁰

GREG J WOODMAN

Address: 420 E. PROSPECT AVENUE — Business Address: — SAME —

Height: 6'3" Weight: 195 — Color of Hair: BLONDE — Color of Eyes: GREEN

University graduate Greg Woodman (right), owner of Happy Valley Promotions, talks shop with Tom Mosser, another graduate, and Pam Howells (senior-accounting). Woodman says he expects his company's sales to gross more than $100,000 this year.

Photo by Suzanne Tyrrel

...g Woodman, owner and operator of Happy Valley Promotions, tosses examples of his livelihood — T-shirts — into the air in ...apartment, which he has turned into the company's headquarters. Woodman is also well-known for his enterprising poster ...Amy and Beth Sax.

another fine t-shirt from "WHO LOVES YA BABY !"

The latest in "T-shirts for Penn State" this week is a comment on the Pinchot Hall elevator fire. The T-shirts, sold by 5th floor Sproul Hall as a fund raiser, read "Elevator, Elevator — Pinchot, We Got The Shaft."

The shirts are the idea of Greg Woodman (8th-food service and housing administration), who runs his own T-shirt corporation "Who Loves Ya, Baby, Inc." out of the Kappa Delta Rho fraternity.

Woodman has marketed several other Penn State-related T-shirts ("Sooner or Later, Oklahoma," "1979 Sugar Bowl, How Sweet It Is," and others) this year.

Woodman said he had 144 Pinchot shirts printed, but he added he'll probably order more because sales are going well.

His idea's on the button, but it has its ups and downs.

Greg Woodman with his mother and sisters in the '80s (top left) and with his brother and sisters at a recent game, decades later (bottom left). L-R: Steve, Bonnie, Greg and Alicia. Greg and his wife Anita Woodman (above) with their sons (L-R) Brad, Nate and Joe.

NOW JO PA CAN SHOW UP AT YOUR PLACE.

Flaunt your blue and white spirit, or maybe even coach the coach on strategies. Only $19.95 puts Joe where you want him with this life-size, full-color cut-out. Of sturdy corrogated paper, it's perfect for tailgates, parties or as a gift for an out-of-town fan.

We'll deliver him **free** in the State College area, or send him anywhere for a modest shipping fee. He's also available in local book and variety stores.

To order "Joe To Go" just call (8

Crazy idea turns Joe Paterno into life-size, color poster

Stand-up Joe

Only $19.95

- Tailgate with "Joe."
- Let "Joe" greet your party guests.
- Take "Joe" to work with you.

"Stand-up Joe" is a sturdy, life-sized, full-color likeness of legendary Penn State football coach Joe Paterno. "Joe" stands 5'10" tall, has a reinforced brace that lets you stand him up anywhere, and is so life-like that you'll find yourself saying "hello" every time you see him.

"Joe" is the ultimate gift for the Penn Staters in your life. Immediate shipment via U.P.S. guarantees that if you receive your order before December 1st, you can have "Joe" home for the holidays.

HVPIO _____ $19.95

By LORI GOLDBACH
Collegian Staff Writer

Suddenly Joe Paterno is turning up in the strangest places — at tailgates, in dorm rooms, in fraternities and across State College.

Happy Valley Promotions, designer of the "Are You A Penn Stater?" poster, has created the Joe Paterno stand-in. This life-size, full-color picture of the Nittany Lions's head football coach, first seen on Oct. 3, is being sold in several stores on- and off-campus.

"We started this way back in August and it finally came out two weeks ago," said Greg Woodman, founder of Happy Valley Promotions and 1983 University graduate.

"I've got a lot of crazy friends and that's where a lot of these ideas come from. They're real die-hard fans," he said.

Some of the stories his friends told contributed to the conception of the idea, Woodman said.

For example, a friend jokingly mentioned that he would like to have Joe Paterno as a best man at his wedding. Or, that with his busy schedule, it wasn't possible for Paterno to appear at all of the alumni and University functions.

As a result, Woodman thought, "There's got to be some way Joe could appear. And it gradually progressed into a life-size, full-color Joe Paterno."

"Joe thought it was a silly idea, but he's a good sport," Woodman said.

"Personally I find it ludicrous that people would buy a poster of me. Now, if it were Mark Spitz in a bathing suit, maybe," Paterno said.

> **'Personally I find it ludicrous that people would buy a poster of me. Now, if it were Mark Spitz in a bathing suit, maybe.'**
>
> —Joe Paterno

Paterno agreed to participate with the condition that his 6 percent of the profits be donated to the Joe Paterno Library Book Endowment Fund.

Since the fund is relatively new and not yet well-known, Paterno said he thought that the poster would be a good way to raise some money and to bring publicity to the project.

Elizabeth Wilson, of the Penn State Bookstore on Campus, said the bookstore sold the 36 stand-ins it had, but said there will be at least 24 on sale at the concession stands at Beaver Stadium.

Woodman said, "So far there's been a real positive reaction. Everybody's getting a kick out of it.

Woodman laughed when he described the final delivery of the stand-ins.

"It was just a funny sight," he said.

"We had a tractor trailer deliver these. There were 2,500 Joe Paternos in there. The shipment weighed 5,500 pounds. I've never seen anything like it," he said. "This thing just pulled up out front, and it was just the scariest sight I've ever seen."

PennState

December 12, 1984

Mr. Greg Woodman
Happy Valley Promotions
P. O. Box 1201
State College, PA 16801

Dear Greg:

It was great to hear we have $1000 for the Library Fund and I am
pleased the clones are selling.

All the best.

Sincerely,

Joseph V. Paterno
Head Football Coach

DG4/3

Joe Paterno gives money to book fund

When Joe Paterno, Nittany Lions head football coach, agreed to do the life-size, full-color stand-in of himself, he did under the condition that his 6 percent of the profits be donated to the Joe Paterno Library Book Endowment Fund.

Last summer, Paterno donated $20,000 to the University to start the fund to finance the purchase of new materials for the library.

"Mr. Paterno has had a strong interest in the continuing academic excellence of this institution. One of his real areas of interest has been strengthening the library," said Gerald Beaver, University director of Development.

After Paterno's initial gift, the University sent letters to more than 60 of his friends inviting them to contribute.

"We have not asked other people to add to (the fund) at this point. From here on in, though, anyone who wishes to honor Coach Paterno at any time would be welcome to make a gift to the fund," he said.

"This will be a permanent fund," Beaver added, "with the income to be used every year to purchase new acquisitions for the library. The ultimate goal is an endowment of a million dollars, but that will take a while."

Paterno said he stongly believes that a good library is one of a university's greatest assents.

"We will loose some people we should get if we don't have a good library," he said in reference to the professors and students who look to the library for research and teaching.

—by Lori Goldbach

Collegian Photo / Lisa Suseni

Joe Paterno and . . . Joe

Sports Illustrated

December 22-29, 1986 — Volume 65, No. 27

CONTENTS

Cover photograph by Ronald C. Modra

JOES TO GO
More than once our Sportsman of the Year (page 64) has shown that he can't be bought, but life-size likenesses of him can. The Paterno cutouts are $24.95 near the Penn State campus.

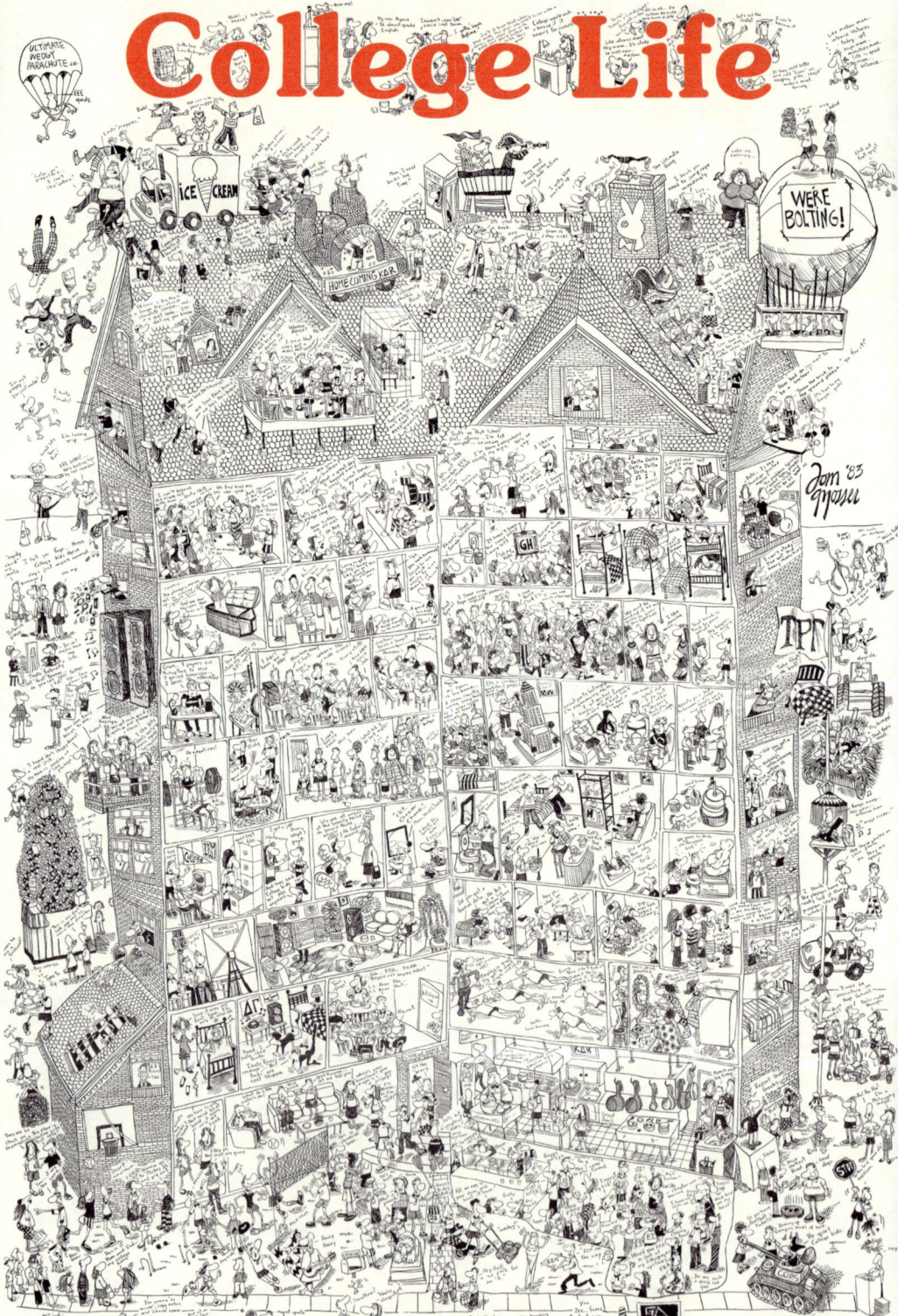

Are You a Penn Stater?

$4.50

A GUIDEBOOK TO LIFE AND TIMES IN HAPPY VALLEY

Also from Happy Valley Promotions:

Nittany Lions, 1982 National Champions Football Yearbook

Are You A Penn Stater? poster

Penn State Twins poster

PENN STATE'S WHY

Happy Valley Promotions was led by alumni who knew that Penn Staters were a breed unto themselves with values, cherished traditions, and inside jokes that no one outside of Happy Valley would understand.

In 1982, the "Are You a Penn Stater" guidebook was published, thanks in large part to the ingenuity and hard work of Tom Mosser and Mike Poorman.

PENN STATE'S WHY

This intro to "Are you a Penn Stater" was written forty years ago, but its sentiments are timeless.

University Park

Dear Fellow Penn Stater:

"To hear students talk, particularly recent alumni, Penn State is simply the best of all possible worlds... Penn State has an almost magnetic attraction that not only gets, but holds. Even after graduation, herds of kids find it difficult to leave the area that's almost free from crime, pollution and turmoil. And many won't."

"Those who have to leave are almost sure to make it back for at least one weekend a year. It is Utopia..."

"In the Phyrst one night last September, somebody mentioned a television news story that told about the *National Enquirer* reporter who was given $10,000 to spend searching for Utopia. Everyone at the table smirked. They'd already found it."

The above excerpt appeared in the November 1977 issue of *Philadelphia Magazine* in an article written by Janice Selinger. As a freshman enrolled at University Park the same year, I was given the article by my sister Bonnie, who had just graduated from Penn State. She suggested that I save the article because I would appreciate it even more after I entered the "real world."

Well, it is now 1983 and I have yet to enter the "real world." Instead, I remain here in "Happy Valley," fighting for the survival of a small business called Happy Valley Promotions. We specialize in those feelings and emotions that are unique to the total Penn State experience.

It is with great pride, and the help of many fellow Penn Staters, that Happy Valley Promotions is able to welcome you to our latest and greatest venture—the "Are You a Penn Stater?" guidebook. Hopefully, the list of 80 activities in the succeeding pages will serve as either a guide to your Happy Valley future or as a key to your treasure chest full of Penn State memories. Each item in the guidebook includes an accompanying box for actually checking upon completion of the designated activity, so you can see how close you are to being the ultimate Penn Stater.

In the process of producing this guidebook, we conjured up some exciting and happy memories of our years in Happy Valley, drawing upon a "think tank" that included the likes of some very special Penn Staters: "Special K," "Stampy," Patty, Pam, Laurie, Carrie, Sharon, Jane, "Dill," "Burkey," "Ads," "Pooh," and the truest Penn Stater of them all, Rich "Sab" Sabatine. The brunt of the research and writing for this guidebook was done by Mike Poorman, who spent many hours gleaning volumes of information at the Penn State Room in Pattee and asking questions like, "Who is Old Coaley, exactly?"

What we've come up with may not be the exact Penn State you know or remember; the Penn State experience is different to different people. You can put as much as you want into your years at Penn State, with the certainty being that you'll get at least twice as much back. That's definitely the case with me.

My first exposure to the feeling that this place must be something special came in 1975 when I was a junior in high school. That spring I visited Penn State for the first time. It was the weekend of the Blue-White Game and I had come along with my family to visit my brother, Steve, and sister, Bonnie, both Penn State students at the time. In just two days, I decided I wanted to become a Penn Stater forever.

I was in heaven when I saw there were playing fields and basketball and tennis courts with games going on everywhere! I was amazed when the soda machine at my brother's fraternity delivered cold Bud when you pressed Pepsi. I couldn't believe the beautiful women my sister had as sorority sisters. (I couldn't talk to them either; I was too shy… and still am.) I had found my paradise. That Monday I wore my new Penn State T-shirt to high school and haven't stopped talking Blue and White since.

Eight years have passed since that first visit, and in that time I have experienced the best and worst that Penn State has to offer— socially and academically. I had A's and a few F's, and I've taken a few terms off. I was there in the New Orleans Superdome when Penn State won its first national football championship and I literally cried after too many losses to Alabama. I'll remember that win against Nebraska in '82 for as long as I live. And I've spent many a Friday afternoon at the Skeller only to spend many a Saturday morning telling myself to "grow up."

For me, Penn State has been a combination country club, playground, giant lecture hall and family dining room table. Penn State is all of the 80 things listed in this guidebook and much, much more.

To me, Happy Valley is:

- **Sports at Penn State.** The Nittany Lions and Lady Lions annually challenge for a national title in over half of their 29 varsity sports. There are better sports here than in a big city, beginning with the football team, which draws better than most professional teams and has a record under Joe Paterno that is tops both on and off the field.

- **Culture.** There are foreign films, classic films and a beautiful art museum on campus. In Eisenhower, there's theatre, ballet and nationally-known speakers, as well as music of all kinds.

- **The downtown area, which has shops, stores and restaurants that cater strictly to students.** Everything is just a short walk away. Where else can you go out to eat at 3 a.m. and have a choice of fast food places as well as being able to order a sit-down breakfast or dinner? And the town is an arcade fanatic's paradise.

- Kappa Delta Rho fraternity, where I had 40 brothers and 30 little sisters for family and constant company.

- **A giant health club.** For a paltry $2,100 for tuition, you can have a year's access to racquet and basketball courts, swimming pools, running tracks, weight machines, golf courses, playing fields, bowling lanes and Phys. Ed. classes with top notch instructors.

- **Bowl games.** Twelve of us crowded into a van for 24 hours to go to the 1983 Sugar Bowl and then the same 12 of us crowded into a single room at the Quality Inn for four days waiting for the game to start. "Dill" didn't drive down, though; he didn't have any vacation time left at work so he paid $600 to fly to New Orleans for one day. He said it was worth every penny. I had four live telephone hook-ups from the Superdome to "Ads" and "Sab" back in Pittsburgh because they deserved to be there more than I did.

- **Homecoming.** Seventeen alumni buddies slept on my floor (I'm the only one still here) last Homecoming weekend. And "Ads" (honestly has the Nittany Lion tattooed on his rear end) slept curled up on the three-foot by three-foot landing leading up to the attic.

- Hundreds of excellent and reputable organizations and activities from Greeks to intramurals to *The Collegian*, which I think is the best-run and most dedicated group of them all.

- **People.** Many of them are special, like Mike at the post office and Donna at the Student Bookstore. Then there are people all Penn Staters have seen at one time or another—Pink Lady, Sam and his dog and Methuselah (aka Father Time and Vent Man).

- **Professors.** They're people, too. I guess, but many of them actually have helped me learn. Not just memorize, but think and grow and apply the classroom to the real world. This is especially true of those in Liberal Arts and Journalism. They've helped me learn how to "survive." Although I'm still not sure why Prof. Schmalz ate that chalk in Geo. Sci. class.

- **My parents.** They're the real Penn Staters, for putting three kids through here, especially me and my grief. I tended to major in fraternity life and novelty products a bit too much for their nervous systems. One term I invested my tuition and rent money in posters! They weren't pleased.

- **The Penn State family.** Wherever I go, there's a Penn Stater. There are over 260,000 Penn State graduates. One out of every 100 Pennsylvanians is an alumnus(a). And one out of every 100 college graduates in the United States is a Penn Stater. Now you know why I'm really in this business. Penn Staters not only send their kids to Penn State, but they also coax their neighbor's kids to come here too.

- **The raw beauty of Nittany Valley.** Spring, summer and autumn there is no place better. Winter just makes you appreciate the other three even more.

- **The opportunity. Happy Valley is the perfect blend of social and academic worlds.** You can work hard and play hard. Penn State is the place to develop both your personal and professional skills in an atmosphere that allows for learning at all levels, if you have the good sense to take advantage of it.

- **The memories.** The feeling of driving up Route 322 or Route 22 and seeing Mt. Nittany once again … Tell me Pitt graduates (both of them) get just as emotional driving through the Oakland section of Pittsburgh.

That's what Penn State means to me. Now if I could just be lucky enough to find a Penn State woman to marry! Thanks for purchasing this guidebook. By doing so, you've enabled me to extend my stay in Happy Valley one more day. Living on borrowed time…

Who loves ya!

Greg J. Woodman

Greg Woodman,
Class of '83

Are You a Penn Stater?

A guidebook to
life and times
in Happy Valley

EDITED BY MIKE POORMAN

© Happy Valley Promotions

You're Not a Penn Stater Until You:

☑ **1. BUY THIS BOOK**

☐ **2. CLIMB MT. NITTANY.**

It takes about two hours to climb to the peak of Mt. Nittany, which is 2,077 feet above sea level and 1,050 feet above the valley floor. The most widely-trailed path to the top is White Trail, although over 25 trails eventually wind their way there as well. The 535 acres that make up the peak of Mt. Nittany are owned by Lion's Paw, a campus honor society that saved the mountain's timberland from the woodcutter's axe by purchasing Mt. Nittany for $2,000 in 1945.

☐ **3. HANG OUT ON THE WALL.**

The Wall is the unofficial dividing line between the town and the university, and a gathering place for various breeds of people and dogs. A gift from the class of 1915, the Wall is three feet high, made of Centre County limestone and extends along the front of campus by College Avenue (see #49). Although no special skills or tools are needed to hang out on the Wall, the following can enhance the experience: a beverage, a guitar, a friend (you can also make one there), an opinion and lots of free time.

4. FALL ASLEEP IN THE HUB "FISHBOWL."

There's plenty to do inside the Hetzel Union Building (like go to "Dough To Go"), but inevitably you wind up spending some time in the fishbowl — especially if you live off-campus. The fishbowl is the glass-enclosed area on the HUB's first floor where students go to study, relax and, most often, sleep. . .sometimes through class.

5. RIDE THE LONDON DOUBLE-DECKER BUS.

The London bus was built in 1950 and used as a commuter bus in the suburbs of London for over 20 years. It was bought by the university in 1973 and has been used to give tours of the campus ever since. Tour guides on the bus must memorize a 25-page script for the 30-minute tours, which cost 50¢ and are conducted weekdays in the spring, summer and fall. A tip when taking the trip: sit on the lower level because much of the view from the top is of tree branches.

tree branches.

6. POSE ON THE NITTANY LION STATUE. . . CLOTHED.

Located adjacent to Rec Hall, the Nittany Lion Shrine was sculpted from a 13-ton block of Indiana limestone by Heinz Warneke in 1942. Since then, thousands have had their photographs taken while posing on the Lion. The two most famous photos involve beautiful ladies — the first of a woman clad only in red high heels that appeared in *Playboy* magazine and the second of two blonde coed twins that was made into a top-selling poster.

7. BUY AN ICE CREAM CONE AT THE CREAMERY.

Owned and operated by the university, the Creamery is located near the corner of Curtin and Shortlidge roads at the north end of campus. More than a half-million ice cream cones are sold at the Creamery each year, an average of over 1,000 a day that climbs to 5,000 on hot afternoons and football weekends. The most popular flavor at the Creamery is bittersweet mint, followed by vanilla, variegated peanut butter, coconut chip and chocolate chip.

8. TAILGATE AT SOMEONE'S UNCLE'S WINNEBAGO.

The eating and drinking going on outside of Beaver Stadium on fall Saturday afternoons are often more important than the football game itself. To tailgate you needn't be friends with the host personally, you just must have some sort of connection — like knowing someone's uncle. And if you don't know any of the tailgaters, don't worry. With time, they'll forget they don't know you either.

9. KNOW THE GODDAMN WORDS.

Penn State's alma mater, written by Professor "Freddy" Lewis Pattee in 1901, is sung before every home football game, although not everyone knows the words. Here they are:

For the glory of Old State,
For her founders strong and great,
For the future that we wait,
Raise the song, raise the song.
Sing our love and loyalty,
Sing our hopes that bright and free,
Rest, O Mother dear, with thee,
All with thee, all with thee.
When we stood at childhood's gate,
Shapeless in the hands of fate,
Thou didst mold us, dear old State,
Dear old State, dear old State.
May no act of ours bring shame
To one heart that loves thy name,
May our lives but swell thy fame,
Dear old State, dear old State.

Now you know why "We don't know the goddamn words."

10. ACTUALLY GO *INSIDE* OLD MAIN.

Old Main was constructed in 1863 and rebuilt in 1929-30 using many of the original stones. It houses the offices of the President, the Provost (see #69), the Alumni Association and other administrators, in addition to the bell-tower clock, by far the most important occupant of Old Main. Also inside Old Main — on the walls — are colorful frescoes (murals) by Henry Varnum Poor that depict the founding and aspirations of Penn State as a land-grant institution.

11. EAT A SUZIE WONG EGG ROLL.

"Good stuff Suz."

Squeezed in among the many storefront shops and restaurants of East College Avenue is Suzie Wong's Egg Roll Kitchen, home of *the* foreign delicacy of State College — Suzie's famous egg roll.

Chapter 3: Are You a Penn Stater

12. DO A "CASE STUDY" AT THE SKELLER.

As the long lines every Friday afternoon attest, the best case studies at Penn State are done at the All-American Rathskeller, located at the corner of Pugh and East College. Over three percent of the Rolling Rocks sold in the world are purchased at the Skeller, where photos of past Penn State sports greats cover the walls and names of not-so-greats are carved in the tables.

13. CAMP OUT IN A NITTANY LINE.

From your first day at Penn State, when you collect your dorm key, to your last, when you collect your diploma at Beaver Stadium, you must constantly wait in line in Happy Valley. Lines are everywhere — at registration, in the dining hall, at the bookstores, to get into bars, at the post office, at Shields and even when leaving Freddy Pattee's namesake, the library. Why do you think the school mascot is the Nittany Line, anyway?

14. DO THE COLLEGIAN CROSSWORD PUZZLE IN CLASS.

The crossword puzzle is the most popular feature of the nation's top-ranked college newspaper, *The Daily Collegian*. The puzzle appears daily on the second to last page of the paper, next to the comics. Doing the puzzle during class helps prevent "head bobs" (see #74).

15. RUN THE PHI PSI.

The Phi Psi 500 is a 1.1 mile race where the contestants run through the streets of State College every April, stopping at six bars for a quick chug of beer or soda. Sponsored by Phi Kappa Psi fraternity, the race was initiated in 1969 with just 24 runners but has grown to an annual field of over 1,800 runners who raise almost $20,000 a year for charity. The most popular feature of the Phi Psi is the "Almost Anything Goes" category, where teams enter dressed in costumes. Previous winners include the "Hare Krishna High School Marching Band" and "Spermy the Whale."

17. HALLUCINATE DURING THE DANCE MARATHON.

For a 48-hour period every February, hundreds of people pack into White Building to dance themselves silly. So silly that they: think it's autumn and head to Beaver Stadium for a football game; begin to take their clothes off before being stopped by a judge; or imagine that the walls are closing in and the bands all sound like Slim Whitman. But all the hallucinations are for a good cause. In 1983, more than $100,000 was raised for the Four Diamonds Fund at the Milton S. Hershey Medical Center.

16. CASH A CHECK AT McLANAHAN'S.

When you desperately need cash, the banks are closed and you don't have an automatic teller card or a bank account in State College, McLanahan's will gladly cash your check. For 25¢. *After* you record everything short of your blood type (see #23) and your mother's maiden name on the back of the check.

18. DO "IT" ON THE 50-YARD LINE. . . ON THE GOLF COURSE.

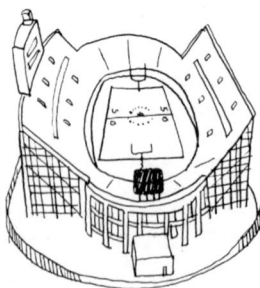

Letters boasting of such exploits by students at "a large Eastern university located in the center of Pennsylvania" have appeared in *Penthouse* magazine, although their validity is best left to the imagination. As should any references to hot spots like the HUB lawn, the CompSci Center, Willard Building or the stacks (see #20). But be careful on the golf course — any good golfer knows it will add a couple of strokes to your score if you get caught in the sand trap.

19. GO TO BELLEFONTE.

In four years at Penn State, it is possible (and maybe even encouraged) to never travel the 12 miles east on Benner Pike to Bellefonte. There are valid reasons for heading to Bellefonte, however, like visiting relatives, going to the county courthouse or getting your photo driver's license at the Department of Transportation office.

20. GET LOST IN THE STACKS AT PATTEE.

Inside the library are more than 1.5 million volumes, 850,000 government documents and a million or so microforms. So it's no wonder that a student is sometimes misplaced there. If you do get lost, at least there's something to do before being found: read if you're alone, or (see #18) if you have company.

21. PULL AN ALL-NIGHTER.

Procrastination and a pot of coffee are the keys to pulling a successful all-nighter. With careful planning and the proper excuses (like defrosting your refrigerator or watching an HBO movie for the fourth time), you don't have to start studying for an 8 o'clock midterm until midnight. Hourly study breaks, a call out for pizza (see #48) and some serious B.S.ing with a fellow all-nighter make the hours till sunrise "speed" by with a minimum of pain. The ritual of pulling an all-nighter is only made complete, though, when you "crash" for 10 straight hours immediately following the exam.

22. SCREAM OUT YOUR DORM WINDOW.

A typical tension releaser, screaming to a captive dormitory audience numbering in the thousands always gets an answer and sometimes leads to the formation of parading, yelling mobs. A certain amount of anonymity goes with screaming out your dorm window, which can further lead to "flashes" of a more personal kind.

23. SELL YOUR PLASMA.

It's two weeks before finals, your checks are made of rubber (don't see #16) and you can't even afford peanut butter and Saltines. That's when you know it's time to sell your plasma. For a good cause, of course . . . drinking money!

25. TAKE THE LOOP.

There are plenty of excuses to ride the loop: it's cold, it's raining, you're on crutches, you're overweight, your arms are full of groceries or you live in East Halls. But the campus buses are used mainly when people are "looped."

24. COME BACK FOR THE ARTS FESTIVAL.

Over 500 craftspeople and thousands of Penn Staters return to Happy Valley every July to take part in a festival that features everything from mime to finger-painting to expensive (and perplexing) sculptures — most of which just wouldn't look right in your dorm room, especially a Noah's Ark made of copper.

26. SAIL AT STONE VALLEY.

The Stone Valley Recreation Area is located 15 miles south of campus, on Route 26 between Pine Grove Mills and Huntingdon. Owned and operated by the university, Stone Valley features a lake, acres of trails and forestland for fishing, hiking and boating (with over 90 sailboats, canoes and rowboats available for renting).

27. COPY SOMEONE'S NOTES ON A HUB XEROX MACHINE.

This is much easier said than done. There are lines (see #13), poorly scribbled notes and broken-down machines to contend with, all of which increase threefold before *your* exam. Meaning that you should have gotten out of bed and went to class, you lazy L.A. major!

28. VISIT THE DEER PENS.

About 100 deer live at the Deer Research Center, located a quarter-mile into the woods past the intersection of Fox Hollow Road and the Route 322 bypass north of campus. The deer, whose habits are studied carefully, are friendly and used to being fed by strangers. They aren't big drinkers, though, which accounts for the pens' lack of red-nosed reindeer.

29. SING ALONG WITH ERNIE AND THE PHYRST PHAMILY.

For over a decade Ernie Oelbermann, owner of The Phyrst and The Brewery, has taken the stage every Saturday night at The Phyrst. Along with his rag-tag "Phamily," Ernie leads a packed house through his repertoire of corny tunes, bad jokes and sing-alongs, including the Phamily's theme song, "We All Get Together on a Saturday Night."

31. GO FOR A SHAKE AT MEYER'S.

It's long been a tradition to head down South Atherton Street (Route 322) to Meyer's Dairy Store for an extra thick shake. The three best times to go: Sunday nights, leaving town for home and coming back from home into town. For those times when your parents are buying, go to Häagen Daz.

30. AVOID A "CANNER" AT THE CORNER OF COLLEGE AND ALLEN.

This particular corner of State College is the busiest in town for pedestrian traffic, which makes it an ideal spot for Greeks and other organizations to solicit donations for charities. Second best place to avoid canners: in front of McLanahan's at the corner of College and Garner.

32. SELL BACK YOUR $25 TEXTBOOK FOR $4.

The college version of new math. One brand-new $25 book minus one semester equals $4. And that's only if the book hasn't already gone into a second printing. If it has, you really wanted a 540-page book detailing matriarchal interactions among the Ukranian peasantry, didn't you?

33. FORGE YOUR ADVISOR'S SIGNATURE.

A necessity if you drop a course or preregister any time other than during office hours, which are usually 8 to 9 a.m. Mondays. Besides, do you think those people in Shields know all the advisors' handwriting? Or that they even care?

34. SEE A PORNO FLICK ON CAMPUS.

Be it the alltime favorite, "Deep Throat," or other Penn State classics like "Debbie Does Dallas," X-rated movies are among the most popular on campus. Sponsored by various student organizations, the films are usually shown in Sparks or the Forum . . . to predominately male audiences. Perhaps the women at Penn State are waiting for "Bobby Does Boalsburg."

35. GET LOCKED OUT OF YOUR ROOM.

It can happen either intentionally (because your roommate got lucky) or unintentionally (you forgot your key), but you're most likely to get locked out of your room right after taking a shower and/or when you're late for class. Thank goodness for the maids and their master keys.

36. PAY YOUR RESPECTS TO "OLD COALY."

Old Coaly was the most popular of the four mules who hauled stone from a nearby quarry to build the original Old Main. Originally purchased for $190 in 1857, Old Coaly remained at Penn State as a pet of the all-male student body until he died in 1893. His bones are preserved in the north lobby of the Agriculture Administration Building, where his memory lives on with the help of the Coaly Society, the honor society for students in the College of Agriculture.

Chapter 3: Are You a Penn Stater

37. LISTEN TO AN EVANGELIST ON THE STEPS OF WILLARD.

The steps of Willard along the Mall are a natural meeting place for both saints and sinners. Through the years, such notables as Bro Cope and Jed Smock have warned the multitudes about the evils of college life. Many have replied to the urgings, but few have actually heeded them.

38. MEMORIZE YOUR SOCIAL SECURITY NUMBER.

At Penn State, it's true: you're not a name, you're a number. At least when taking tests, registering, signing checks and picking up your diploma. There are times when you're lucky and only need to know the last four digits of your Social Security number, kind of like the computer calling you a nickname.

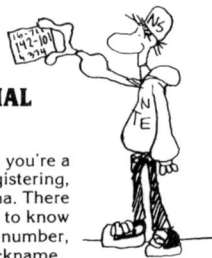

39. HAVE A TA WHO SPEAKS ENGLISH.

Students from 81 countries attend Penn State, many of them graduate students. As grad students, most teach some sections of undergraduate courses, where the students usually have more problems trying to understand the TA than the course content.

40. DODGE A BIKE ON THE MALL.

Although bicycles are prohibited from the main Mall sidewalks, cyclists sometimes use them anyway. Maybe that's because, despite a bike path along the smaller mall by the Human Development Building, there aren't nearly as many targets as on the Mall.

41. FEED A SQUIRREL.

More squirrels than students live on campus. Thanks to free handouts like peanuts, M & Ms, crackers, ice cream cones and gum, the squirrels also eat better than most students. And they're also tamer (although both will sometimes run up your leg).

42. DRINK FROM A KEG ON AN APARTMENT BALCONY.

There are four reasons why the high-rise apartments in State College have balconies: (1) to store bicycles, (2) to store hibachis, (3) so apartment dwellers have a place to keep the keg for their parties, and (4) so apartment dwellers' friends have a place to yell and drop beer from at apartment dwellers' parties.

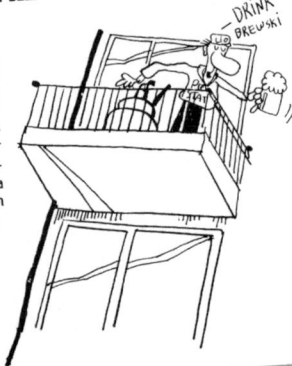

43. SPIN THE WHEEL AT THE DEN.

Every Tuesday night at The Lion's Den the price of a pitcher of beer is left to luck. Customers at the Den, located on Garner Street near College Ave. (see #30), spin the wheel every half hour to determine how much a pitcher will cost for the next 30 minutes.

Chapter 3: Are You a Penn Stater

44. WALK PAST THE OBELISK. . .WITHOUT IT CRUMBLING.

Legend has it that if a virgin walks past the stone obelisk, located between Willard and Sackett buildings along the Mall, the obelisk will crumble to the ground. It hasn't fallen yet, testimony to the fact everyone has been screwed in some way by the university at least once. The Obelisk is 33.7 feet tall and weighs 33.4 tons. It was constructed by the School of Mines in 1896 and contains 281 samples of native Pennsylvania rock, with the oldest (pre-Cambrian) at the base and the youngest (Triassic) at the top. The legend of the crumbling of the Obelisk began shortly after World War II; before then, legend stated that the body of "Old Jerry" — buddy and co-worker of "Old Coaly" (see #36) — was buried at the foot of the Obelisk.

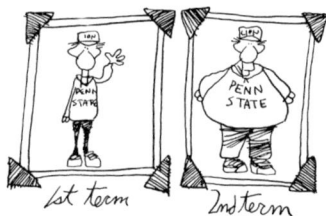

1st term   2nd term

45. GAIN THE DREADED "FRESHMAN 10."

After their first year of college — and with it, starchy dorm food, beer-filled fraternity parties (see #53), tailgates (see #8) and phone calls for pizza (see #48) — most Penn State freshmen are lucky to go home only 10 pounds heavier than when they first arrived at University Park.

46. SAY "HI" TO JOE PATERNO.

Joe Paterno, Penn State's head football coach since 1966, is the most famous personality both on campus and in all of college football today. So it's usually a great thrill to say "Hi" when you see JoPa walking across campus from his home in College Heights to either Rec Hall or his office at the Indoor Sports Complex — especially when you see him for the first time. At least it's something you can tell mom and dad about during your next phone call home.

47. GUARD THE NITTANY LION STATUE AT HOMECOMING.

The statue (see #6) was initially doused with paint the first football season following its construction in 1942. The statue was first guarded before Homecoming in 1951 by the pledges of Pi Lambda Phi. Among those who have painted the Lion is Sue Paterno, who did it before the Syracuse game in husband Joe's first season as head coach (see #46). With help from some assistant coaches' wives, Sue poured orange paint on the Lion in hopes of raising dormant school spirit by pinning the blame on Syracuse. Hey Joe, that's one crazy wife!

48. KNOW THE NUMBER OF DOMINO'S PIZZA BY HEART.

North of campus, it's 237-1414. South of campus, it's 234-5655. They promise to deliver in 30 minutes or less, so don't stand in front of their cars!

49. LOOK THE WRONG WAY ON COLLEGE AVE.

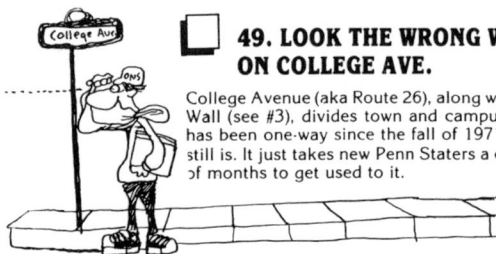

College Avenue (aka Route 26), along with the Wall (see #3), divides town and campus, and has been one-way since the fall of 1971. And still is. It just takes new Penn Staters a couple of months to get used to it.

50. LISTEN TO THE "WITCH DOCTOR" ON WQWK (FM97).

"Mercy, mercy, mercy. It's the man from the street, the man with the funky beat coming at you." Speaking is Warren Coleman, a Penn State professor of physical education who spins records from noon to three o'clock every Sunday afternoon on WQWK. He can "do it with a touch of soul, or do it with a touch of class, or do it with just a touch." Just remember to "Pick up the pieces, uh-huh!"

51. THROW A FRISBEE ON OLD MAIN LAWN.

Or on the HUB lawn, in the quad or in a dorm hallway. You can throw a frisbee anywhere in Happy Valley, but the above four places are distinctly Penn State. Special care should be taken on Old Main lawn —what with two flagpoles, a turtle with a globe on its back and scores of engineering students out surveying.

52. GET A "BACK TO GODHEAD" MAGAZINE FROM A KRISHNA.

"Back to Godhead" is the ideal magazine. It's free, has great distribution (the Mall, the Wall, registration, the HUB) and if you read it, you'll fulfill three credits of "other cultures" requirements.

53. LOSE YOUR COAT . . . OR SOMETHING ELSE . . . AT A FRATERNITY.

Fraternities are best (or worst) known for their parties (see *Animal House*, the movie). At a fraternity party — after a few hours of drink and conversation, and a Lionel Richie song — certain things can happen. Like taking someone else's coat by mistake or . . . (see #18).

54. PASS THE NITTANY LION UP THE STANDS IN BEAVER STADIUM.

Ever since Dick Hoffman donned a Lion costume for the 1922 Penn State-Syracuse game at the Polo Grounds in New York, the Nittany Lion mascot has been a fixture at Penn State football games. So many people "want the Lion" that he now limits his trips up the stands to the first three quarters. That's because by the fourth quarter, there are just too many pinches and grabs from people who really *want* the Lion!

55. SURVIVE REGISTRATION.

Three hours on "the floor" of the IM Building are enough to make a ceramic arts major take BioChem 525 just to get out of the place. The frenzied atmosphere of stepping over people, sorting out No. 6 cards (or is it No. 2 cards?), and dodging information tables and people handing out subscription offers makes registration as painful as a loss to Pitt.

56. CANOE AT THE REGATTA.

Sponsored by Beta Sigma Beta, the Regatta is named for Sy Barash, a former president of Beta Sigma and prominent State College businessman who died of cancer in 1975. The event, which was held at Stone Valley (see #26) for its first eight years before being moved to Bald Eagle State Park in 1983, benefits the American Cancer Society and features canoe races in categories from "blindfold" to "hand paddle."

57. SMUGGLE FOOD OUT OF THE DINING HALL.

Except for a single piece of fruit, sneaking food back to your dorm room is prohibited, which is not to say it doesn't happen. Every smuggler has his or her own technique, from pouring milk into a plastic jug hidden inside a gym bag to tossing a salad into their underwear. The real trick is making sure your Creamsicle doesn't melt before getting back to your room.

58. CHECK THE RIDE BOARD.

If you don't own a car, find hitch-hiking unappealing, hate the sound of Greyhound bus tires squealing and air fares send you reeling, then a check of the ride board is revealing. Whether you're going to the 'Burgh, Philly or Bellefonte (see #19), it's easy finding a ride or a rider.

59. SPEND SPRING BREAK IN FORT LAUDERDALE.

After a winter of books, bundling up (see #67) and boredom, spring break means Fort Lauderdale and the unbridled pursuit of three things: sun, sand and sex. Definite stops in Lauderdale are *The Button*, *Penrod's* (with a free keg in the afternoon), *The Playpen* and *The Candy Store*. Just be careful — Fort Lauderdale is so full of Penn Staters that the person you cavort with on Thursday may be in your English class on Monday.

60. STUDY AT ROY'S.

With a pair of Roy Rogers' on College Avenue, it's hard to not have hit the Happy Trails at least once. The best thing about studying at Roy's (besides the big windows that are ideal for watching people walk by) is that they give refills on coffee and soft drinks, a big plus when you need caffeine running through your veins (see #21).

61. GET A PINK SLIP WITH "ALL SECTIONS FILLED."

After investing hours into studying the schedule of classes, filling out your preregistration form and forging your advisor's signature (see #33), you finally have the perfect schedule. Or so you thought (see #44). In reality the slip often reveals "All sections are filled," forcing you to take first period *and* last period five times a week.

62. STOMACH A TACO DOG.

Where have you gone, taco dog? For incoming Penn Staters, the taco dog is just a legend. But for older Penn Staters and alumni, the memory — and heartburn — of a taco dog lingers for a lifetime. In recent years, such dining hall additions as "weiner wings" and "shrimplets" have come close to rivaling the taco dog, but have yet to reach legendary status.

63. PULL A DORM PRANK.

Dorm pranks are sometimes stupid and sometimes childish, but always funny — at least to the one pulling the prank. Pranks like pennying someone in his room, covering a doorknob with peanut butter or vaseline, "turning a room over," shoving shaving cream under a door with a record album cover and blow-drying baby powder (crop dusting) under a door are all good. Setting your roommate on fire is not.

64. FEED A SQUIRREL (AGAIN).

Squirrels are sometimes even more popular than football players at Penn State. Maybe that's why all the little critters are so upset that it isn't called Squirrel Stadium. After all, how many beavers have you ever fed on campus?

65. BUY A PENN STATE T-SHIRT FOR A RELATIVE.

There are all kinds of Penn State souvenirs: Commemorative chocolate plaques, bumper stickers, authentic jerseys, football highlight books, posters, musical key chains that play the school fight song, Joe Paterno trays, ties, buttons, ashtrays, coffee mugs and...yes, even T-shirts.

66. GET A PERSONAL IN THE *COLLEGIAN*.

It's definitely better to get a personal than give one. It means that at least someone likes/wants you. However, there is always that doubt: "I was there, but do they mean me?"

To the guy with the Penn State sweatshirt and hat. Our eyes met. You're cute.
signed, The gorgeous blonde.

67. WALK ACROSS PARKING LOT 80 IN THE WINTER.

Every November, the parking lot that separates East Halls from the rest of the world turns into the coldest spot in Centre County. Parking Lot 80 in the winter is a good excuse for gaining the dreaded "Freshman 10" (see #45), the survival of the campus Loop (see #25) and moving off-campus.

EAST #80 HALLS →

JOPA.

NUMBA ONE.

LION

SUGAR BOWL

68. GO TO A BOWL GAME.

From 1923 to January 1, 1983, Penn State went to 21 football bowl games, compiling a 13-6-2 record. Under Joe Paterno (see #46) the Nittany Lions have gone 10-4-1, including the 1983 trip to the Sugar Bowl that won us the national title. The results:

- 1983 Sugar Bowl — PSU 27, Georgia 23.
- 1982 Fiesta Bowl — PSU 26, USC 10.
- 1980 Fiesta Bowl — PSU 31, Ohio State 19.
- 1979 Liberty Bowl — PSU 9, Tulane 6.
- 1979 Sugar Bowl — Alabama 14, PSU 7.
- 1977 Fiesta Bowl — PSU 42, Arizona St. 30.
- 1976 Gator Bowl — Notre Dame 20, PSU 9.
- 1975 Sugar Bowl — Alabama 13, PSU 6.

— A preppy Bowl victory!

Ride 'em Jopa!

- 1975 Cotton Bowl — PSU 41, Baylor 20.
- 1974 Orange Bowl — PSU 16, LSU 9.
- 1972 Sugar Bowl — Oklahoma 14, PSU 0.
- 1972 Cotton Bowl — PSU 30, Texas 6.
- 1970 Orange Bowl — PSU 10, Missouri 3.
- 1969 Orange Bowl — PSU 15, Kansas 14.
- 1967 Gator Bowl — PSU 17, Florida St. 17.
- 1962 Gator Bowl — Florida 17, PSU 7.
- 1961 Gator Bowl — PSU 30, Ga. Tech 15.
- 1960 Liberty Bowl — PSU 41, Oregon 12.
- 1959 Liberty Bowl — PSU 7, Alabama 0.
- 1948 Cotton Bowl — PSU 13, SMU 13.
- 1923 Rose Bowl — USC 14, PSU 3.

easy pickins!

KIST

FIESTA BOWL

69. KNOW WHAT A BURSAR IS . . . A PROVOST IS . . . A "BITCH BAG" IS.

The bursar is the officer in charge of funds at the university. The provost is the chief officer for academic affairs at Penn State and is second in command after the university president. A bitch bag is the tote bag imprinted with Greek letters that sorority sisters carry around so they can remember what dorm floor to return to after class and on Sunday mornings when they wake up.

70. PLAY IM'S.

Nearly 35,000 undergrads, grads and faculty members participate in at least one intramural sport every year at Penn State, which has the largest such program in the nation. There are 18 different sports to choose from as well as singles, doubles and coed events. But the best thing about IM's at Penn State is the team names, which over the years have included Siamese Elephants, Muff Divers, IUDs, Lawn Furniture, Gonads and GFY.

71. APPLY FOR A PHEAA LOAN.

Loans from the Pennsylvania Higher Education Assistance Agency are to be used to pay for tuition and room and board. But those fortunate enough to not really need the money for that have been known to use the loan to buy a car, go on a vacation, make an investment or just plain blow it on silly things, like textbooks (see #32).

72. GET YOUR PICTURE IN *LA VIE*.

Candidly speaking, it helps to know a *La Vie* photographer if you want your photo in the yearbook. Or, to be even more certain, you can become a member of a fraternity, sorority, club or sports team. The surest and most satisfying way to get your picture in *La Vie* is to be a graduating senior, but it's a good bet that you won't know either of the two people whose senior pictures are on either side of yours.

73. SUNBATHE IN THE QUAD.

When it's a sunny day in the spring, summer or early fall you know "Surf's up!" all across campus. Each dorm area and fraternity has its own special nick-named beach. The experienced "scopers" have keen eyes for the most scenic beaches (those with the least "beached" whales). No matter what the beach, it's certain the tunes are cranked, frisbees are flying and the smell of sun tan oil permeates the air.

74. EXPERIENCE "HEAD BOBS" IN CLASS.

Head bobs are different things to different people. To the professor in front of the lecture hall, head bobs look like you're nodding "yes" and encourage — rather than discourage — him or her. To the persons sitting behind you, head bobs are both amusing and annoying. And to the head bobber, they're a pain in the neck and a reminder that: (a.) the class is boring, (b.) you need more sleep, or (c.) it's time to do the *Collegian* crossword puzzle (see #14).

75. LEAVE RITENOUR SICKER THAN YOU WENT IN.

While Ritenour is most popular for the PCEP (Peer Contraception and Education Program), some people do go there to see the doctors, who have seen it all before — be it the flu, a broken foot or an ulcer. No matter what you have, it's always something that's "just going around." And it's nothing a little tetracycline or aspirin won't cure... they think.

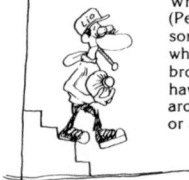

76. EAT A GRILLED STICKY AT 4 A.M.

After studying, hitting the bars, coming home from a party or a date, stopping for a grilled sticky early in the morning (or late at night) will introduce you to another side of State College. Besides yourself, what other normal person would be eating a warm piece of pastry at four in the morning?

77. DIVE OFF THE 10-METER BOARD.

Climbing the diving tower at the outdoor pool next to the Natatorium isn't all that difficult. The true test of courage is what level you choose to dive from — the 1-, 5-, 7½- or 10-meter board. Of course, jumping off the side of the pool would be a lot easier and decrease your chances of doing a belly flop.

78. DANCE TO OLDIES AT THE GAFF.

"There ain't no mountain high enough" to keep dance fans away from the Shandygaff Saloon every Thursday for Oldies' Night. Diana Ross, "Mack the Knife" and Michael Jackson are all regulars at the 'Gaff, located at the rear of the 200 block of East College Ave.

79. GRADUATE WITHIN SIX YEARS.

With some strategy, four years at Penn State can easily be drawn out to six. Some ready-made excuses as to why you're *still* here after four (or five or six) years: "I took some time off to find myself," "I changed majors," "I took a year off to earn some money for tuition," "That time I dropped nine credits really messed me up" and "I had an extra year of athletic (or social) eligibility."

80. GROW UP AND LEAVE HAPPY VALLEY FOR THE REAL WORLD.

Get a job! The vacation is over, so turn in your key. "Club Penn State" must register some new guests. See you on football weekends, Homecoming, the Phi Psi (see #15), the Arts Festival (see #24), at the Skeller (#12) and when you move your kids into East Halls.

WHAT IS A NITTANY, ANYWAY?

Even if you checked all 80 boxes, you can not become an official Penn Stater until you know what a Nittany is. According to regional folklore, Nittany (or Nita-Nee) was a valorous Indian princess in whose honor the Great Spirit caused Mount Nittany to be formed. A later namesake, daughter of Chief O-Ko-Cho who lived near the mouth of Penn's Creek, fell in love with a trader named Malachi Boyer. The tearful maiden and her lost lover became legend and her name was given to the lions that at one time roamed the local mountains. The mountain and the athletic teams at Penn State have since adopted the name Nittany as well.

TOM MOSSER . . .

is a free-lance cartoonist-illustrator-artist who makes his home in Huntingdon, Pa. A diehard Penn Stater down to his blue and white underwear, Tom followed his grandfather, both parents and two sisters to Penn State. While in college, Tom was a member of the Lions' Legion cheerleading squad and staff artist of *The Daily Collegian*. He graduated in 1982 with a B.F.A. in art.

See Tom Mosser's art at
tommosserdesign.com

THE HAPPY VALLEY PROMOTIONS FAMILY

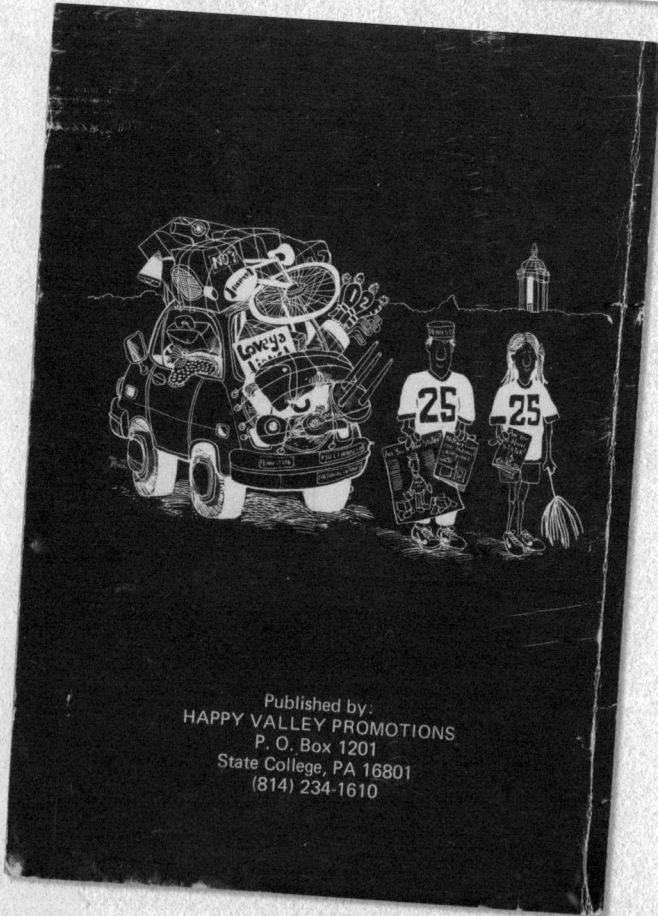

Published by:
HAPPY VALLEY PROMOTIONS
P. O. Box 1201
State College, PA 16801
(814) 234-1610

Are You a Penn Stater?

You're Not a Penn Stater Until You:

☑ 1. Buy this poster.
☐ 2. Climb Mount Nittany.
☐ 3. Hang out on the Wall.
☐ 4. Fall asleep in the HUB "Fishbowl."
☐ 5. Ride the London double-decker bus.
☐ 6. Pose on the Nittany Lion statue...clothed.
☐ 7. Buy an ice cream cone at the Creamery.
☐ 8. Tailgate at someone's uncle's Winebago.
☐ 9. Know the goddamn words.
☐ 10. Actually go *inside* Old Main.
☐ 11. Eat a Suzie Wong egg roll.
☐ 12. Do a "case study" at the Skeller.
☐ 13. Camp out in a "Nittany line."
☐ 14. Do the *Collegian* crossword puzzle in class.
☐ 15. Run the Phi Psi.
☐ 16. Cash a check at McLanahan's.
☐ 17. Hallucinate during the Dance Marathon.
☐ 18. Do "it" on the 50-yard line....on the golf course.
☐ 19. Go to Bellefonte.
☐ 20. Get lost in the stacks at Pattee.
☐ 21. Pull an all-nighter.
☐ 22. Scream out your dorm window.
☐ 23. Sell your plasma.
☐ 24. Come back for the Arts Festival.
☐ 25. Take the Loop.
☐ 26. Sail at Stone Valley.
☐ 27. Copy someone's notes on a HUB Xerox machine.
☐ 28. Visit the deer pens.
☐ 29. Sing along with Ernie and the Phyrst Phamily.
☐ 30. Avoid a "canner" at the corner of College and Allen.
☐ 31. Go for a shake at Meyer's.
☐ 32. Sell back your $25 textbook for $4.
☐ 33. Forge your advisor's signature.
☐ 34. See a porno flick on campus.
☐ 35. Get locked out of your room.
☐ 36. Pay your respects to "Old Coaly."
☐ 37. Listen to an evangelist on the steps of Willard.
☐ 38. Memorize your Social Security number.
☐ 39. Have a TA who speaks English.
☐ 40. Dodge a bike on the Mall.
☐ 41. Feed a squirrel.
☐ 42. Drink from a keg on an apartment balcony.
☐ 43. Spin the wheel at the Lion's Den.
☐ 44. Walk past the Obelisk....without it crumbling.
☐ 45. Gain the dreaded "Freshman 10."
☐ 46. Say "Hi" to Joe Paterno.
☐ 47. Guard the Nittany Lion statue at Homecoming.
☐ 48. Know the number of Domino's Pizza by heart.
☐ 49. Look the wrong way on College Ave.
☐ 50. Listen to the "Witch Doctor" on WQWK (FM97).
☐ 51. Throw a frisbee on Old Main lawn....on the HUB lawn....in the quad....in a dorm hallway.
☐ 52. Get a "Back to Godhead" magazine from a Krishna.
☐ 53. Lose your coat....or something else...at a fraternity.
☐ 54. Pass the Nittany Lion up the stands in Beaver Stadium.
☐ 55. Survive registration.
☐ 56. Canoe at the Regatta.
☐ 57. Smuggle food out of the dining hall.
☐ 58. Check the ride board.
☐ 59. Spend spring break in Ft. Lauderdale.
☐ 60. Study at Roy's.
☐ 61. Get a pink slip with "All sections filled."
☐ 62. Stomach a taco dog.
☐ 63. Pull a dorm prank.
☐ 64. Feed a squirrel (again).
☐ 65. Buy a Penn State t-shirt for a relative.
☐ 66. Get a personal in the *Collegian*.
☐ 67. Walk across Parking Lot 80 in the winter.
☐ 68. Go to a bowl game.
☐ 69. Know what a bursar is...a provost is...a "bitch bag" is.
☐ 70. Play IM's.
☐ 71. Apply for a PHEAA loan.
☐ 72. Get your picture in *La Vie*.
☐ 73. Sunbathe in the quad.
☐ 74. Experience "head bobs" in class.
☐ 75. Leave Ritenour sicker than you went in.
☐ 76. Eat a grilled sticky at 4 a.m.
☐ 77. Dive off the 10-meter board.
☐ 78. Dance to oldies at the Gaff.
☐ 79. Graduate within six years.
☐ 80. Grow up and leave Happy Valley for the real world.

Chapter 3: Are You a Penn Stater

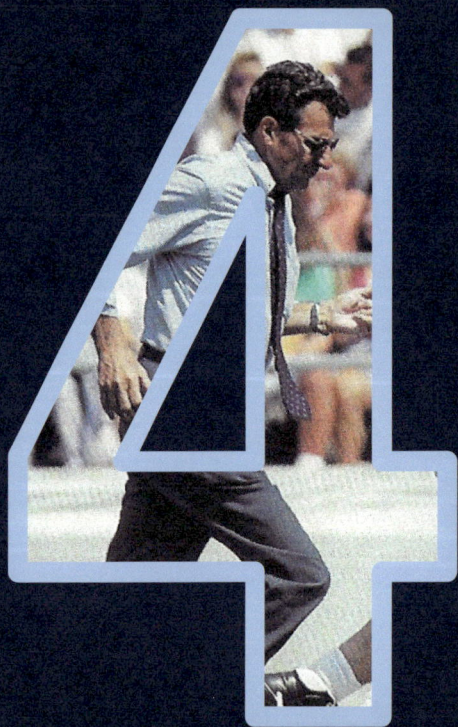

4

A Final Look

Paterno: Preparing Students for Life

1966

Jack Curry, split end, insurance and real estate broker, Danville, Pa.

"Joe's speeches were such that you felt like running through a brick wall when he was finished. **If you came to a game not really ready to play, by the time he got finally finished with his little pre-game pep talk you felt like you could conquer the world.**

1967

Steve Smear, defensive tackle, insurance agent, Annapolis, Md.

"He always cared about your education, making sure you graduated. He believed in the total concept of an education. He wanted you to get out and not be in a football dorm…

"He used to tell us if you keep hustling, something good will happen. And he used to say that you either get better or worse; you never stay the same. You always have to keep working to get better.

1968

Charlie Pittman, running back, newspaper promotion, Erie, Pa.

"**Joe Paterno is like a fine wine; he betters with age.** He's just like a parent. You don't appreciate your parents until you are older, and the older you become, the wiser they become. In other words, the things they tell you when you're younger don't start making sense until you get a little older.

"A lot of the lessons Joe tried to instill in us as players are things we can carry with us in life today. Things he tried to get us to do and understand didn't make sense to us, but what does make sense when you're 18, 19 or 20.

"I have a son who plays for Joe Paterno now and I'm happy. When he says he cares about his players for more than just football players, that's absolutely true. I'm fortunate to have had the opportunity to play for him."

1970

Jack Ham, linebacker, salesman and sportscaster, Sewickley, Pa.

"When you're an 18-, 19-year-old kid in college, you're going in a lot of different directions. I didn't realize it at

PENN STATE'S WHY

During his time as coach, Paterno had a direct influence on thousands of young men. By the end of the '80s, he was the winningest active Division I-A football coach, had coached two national champions, six unbeaten teams, 13 bowl winners and more than 50 first-team All-Americans.

But Paterno took more satisfaction from his 19 first-team Academic All-Americans, 14 NCAA postgraduate scholarship winners and 10 Hall of Fame Scholar-Athletes.

As President Ronald Reagan said about Paterno at a White House ceremony honoring the 1986 national champs:

(continued)

"He's never forgotten he's a teacher who's preparing his students not just for the season, but for life."

His players agreed, and during his silver anniversary season, they shared how Penn State's values had changed their lives.

Jack Ham

the time, but to have a guy like Joe Paterno as your head football coach—a guy who is concerned about football, but also how you turn out as a man—was important to me. He's concerned about your education and how you progress as a person, along with trying to be a good football player. I was lucky to have four years with Coach Paterno, and that's probably one of the reasons why I chose him to introduce me at the Pro Football Hall of Fame, because he probably had more of an impact on my life than anyone else.

"He was a coach who emphasized detail. **His whole philosophy was to do the little things right, and the big things will take care of themselves.**"

1972

Chuck Herd, wide receiver, Penn State conference coordinator, State College, Pa.

"He talks a lot about keeping your poise, and that's one thing I've always carried with me. **No matter what situation you're confronted with, you've got to maintain your poise and deal with the situation as well as you can.** That's something that extends beyond a football game that you can apply to life in general.

"We were going to the Sugar Bowl, and everybody wanted white shoes. So we had the captains confront Joe about this, because Joe was pretty much straight up and down with the uniform. And as it turned out, his comment was 'If we needed white shoes to win this game, we're in pretty bad shape.' We didn't get white shoes, and I think we won the game, so… I think he does a better job recruiting the parents than he does recruiting the kids. I grew up in northern New Jersey, and he came up and sat in the house and talked to mom and dad. The four of us were there, and I think he directed more of his thoughts and comments to mom and dad. Paterno walked out the door, and they said 'That's where you want to go, isn't it?'"

1980

Chet Parlavecchio, linebacker, high school teacher, Basking Ridge, N.J.

"I think the greatest testimony to Coach is that he teaches you to be a man. The sad part of that is you don't realize that until you graduate. I'll never forget when Sean Farrell and I were at a banquet prior to the Fiesta Bowl game against Southern Cal. Our team was there in coats and ties, and Southern Cal came walking in in T-shirts, flip-flops and shorts. At the same time, Sean and I said, 'You know, I understood what he was after. We are different.' And I think that's a testimony to him. There is nothing wrong with a clean-cut look. It doesn't mean you're any less of a football player or any less tough.

"I am a high school coach, and I have found myself so much like him it's incredible. I also believe in a suit and tie before the game. I believe in life you have to answer to somebody, being a disciplined individual and not being afraid to sacrifice.

"I took over a team that hadn't won a game in four years. And in a short two-and-a-half years we went to the sectional finals. And I find the discipline and commitment we forced out of our players is what changed them, and these are the things I got from Coach.

"One day a guy walked into a meeting late, and Coach said 'You're two minutes late. You don't know how late you really are. You're 200 minutes late.' Everybody looked at him as if he were out of his mind. But it was true. He took two minutes out of everybody's time, and there were 100 guys in the room. He was a stickler to that.

"When you're done with football you're going to have to get a job and you're going to have to go to meetings and be at places. You're going to have to be a company individual who is used to commitment and sacrifice. He was more concerned with the things you can take on in life. I knew in his heart he believed these things."

1981

Greg Gattuso, defensive tackle, policeman, Pittsburgh, Pa.

"He teaches you a lot about growing up, about responsibilities. You kind of go in there thinking about having fun and not really about your future, and by the time you're a junior, he's got you thinking about your grades and how important they are and about your future, about your family and things like that. He helps football players mature. We're not just there to play football and put money into people's pockets. He teaches you what the important things are in life, and that's a testament to him and the influence he has on people.

"I'm a football coach now and he's been a big influence on me in that way also. The things that he taught us I try to teach to them, stressing academics, behavior, making them look good all the time by wearing shirts and ties on the road. And it's been very successful for me. It's really helped turn our program around.

"I can remember all the way back to the first day we were on the field as freshmen. We were all stretching and I was sitting there and I was looking and he was walking around, and I was surprised his feet even touched the ground. He was a legend, and I remember looking at him and I was totally petrified. I have never been intimidated in my life like I was by him that first day.

"But one of the great things about him is that he's just a regular person. That nervousness goes away so fast, he just makes you relax, except when he's yelling at you, which with me seemed to be pretty often.

"I didn't finish my degree, and I got cut by the Redskins, and I was sitting there wondering what I was going to do. I needed to graduate and I didn't have any money. I was really in trouble. My father kept saying, 'Call Coach Paterno. He'll help you out.' And I said 'No, he isn't going to help me out.' So finally we called him, and I was enrolled a couple days later and I was a graduate assistant coach. That was something really important for me, because it got me to graduate. It made me understand that he really does care about his football players."

1982

Kenny Jackson, wide receiver, pro football player and restaurateur, Cherry Hill, N.J.

Kenny Jackson

"I didn't have a typical player-coach relationship with Joe. I think we were a little closer in a sense that he helped me in a lot of ways. The most memorable way he helped me was when I was graduating and ready to be drafted by the NFL.

"My mother needed open heart surgery, and he called some people and made sure it got done for me. I didn't pay any money. He told the guy I was worth 'X' amount of dollars and that I would be able to take care of it. And that was something you can't repay. You just thank him for it. And when you do something like that, you never forget it.

"I have a small caricature of Joe in my office. I look at it every day, and probably not a day goes by that I don't think of something he told me.

"Joe Paterno could have been a multi-millionaire if he took more interest in his individual goals than his goals as far as educating kids, and that's all people have to look at."

1985

Keith Radecic, center, financial consultant, Brentwood, Pa.

"Recruiting was an interesting situation because I had a brother (Scott) who was up there at the time. And people might think Joe neglected me in the recruiting, that the family connection would do it. But he really didn't do that. He maintained a very close relationship with me, and tried to overly recruit where he probably didn't have to.

"**Commitment, basically, is what he tries to get across—the commitment to put forth the effort to be the best at whatever you do.** He was very academically oriented. The year of the last national championship was the 100th year of Penn State football.

"We went 11-0 and on top of that we graduated 100

percent of the freshman players who came in with me. Joe found a way to make everything work together and have total success, whereas most other programs fall short in one area or another."

1987

Kurt Bernier, defensive end, production supervisor, Owings Mills, Md.

"If I had to wrap up what I gained from playing football at Penn State, it would be contact with Joe Paterno. Everything he did and everything he said, there was a reason behind it. A lot of times you didn't realize it until a day later, a week later, a year later, and in my case I'm still realizing and picking up on things he said now.

"Even when he was upset with you, the way he communicated was in a way that he was trying to teach you something. He was always trying to guide us in the right direction, not only football-wise, but with school and our personal life.

"He was always in control. He was never a rah-rah type coach. He expected things of you, and you went out on the field trying to fulfill his expectations.

"He would just sit back and watch the game. He never became emotionally excited. You kept thinking, one of these times he's going to burst out and dance around or something, but it never happened. **And that was part of the way he taught us to win gracefully.** Winning was just a pleasure; you didn't need to get super excited about it."

1988

Bob Mrosko, defensive tackle, pro football player, Wickliffe, Ohio.

"I have a lot of respect for Coach Paterno. He influences you on the field, but I think he influences you more off the field to do well and what to expect outside of football.

"A lot of the things he said have really helped. He works hard with his players in a lot of ways. It's not always easy playing for him at the time, he works you hard. But I see why he does it and I'm happy for having the experience. He stressed academics and football together, and he showed me how they can work together and enhance my future."

The Interview: Joe Paterno

BY SCOTT OTT

Reprinted from 1992 Penn State Football Annual

Note from the editor: On the ten year anniversary of Penn State's first national championship, Scott Ott, a writer for Penn State Football Annual, sat down with Joe Paterno to talk about the year. The interview that resulted was about much more than football. Paterno talked about growing up in Brooklyn, the value of learning poetry and the philosophy of sports. The resulting article gives a glimpse into the mind of the coach, and has remained one of our very favorite interviews with him.

The football office is in shambles when I arrive on May 19.

Coach Paterno's secretary wears a dust mask as she types a letter. Receptionist Mel Capobianco apologizes for the mess.

"They're tearing up the carpet, painting. We're getting all new furniture," she says.

I point to one of the world's longest sectional sofas and ask if this is the new stuff.

"No, that's the old stuff," she says smiling.

"I'll buy it," I say.

"You're about the 100th person to say that," Mel says. "I'd like to take it home too."

Sometimes, I think you need to do a renovation, even when there's nothing wrong with the old stuff. Why wait until it's out of date.

Joe Paterno ambles toward me. He steps quickly, leading me silently past the misplaced upholstery to his modest office.

Photos of the 1982 and '86 National Championship teams grace one wall,

along with a bright painting of a Penn State offensive play—a gift from some PSU trustees.

The coach's hair is still black, with a little salt. His thick lenses make his eyes alternately large and invisible. He sits in a low up-holstered chair; elbows on knees, hands clasped, head down. Later in our talk, he'll lean back and put his feet up on the coffee table.

Though he's done thousands of interviews, you can see a sincere effort to treat this one as special—not for the reporter's sake, but for the fans'.

He tells Mel to hold all calls, and to interrupt him only if Reggie Givens comes in.

He speaks quietly, almost too softly for the tape recorder. He fields the traditional questions with the traditional answers.

He is most animated and enthusiastic when he reminisces about concerts, about poetry, about how God has blessed his family, about what Penn State football means to the fan.

Yes, he's even excited about the offense this year.

He's telling recruits he'll stay until he's 70, maybe 74 if he feels good and is doing a good job.

He talks about how he'll know when it's time to go, and what he'll do when he does.

He says Penn State's bureaucracy has frustrated him to the

point where he has had to threaten "I won't take 'no' for an answer" on some issues. But not often.

The overall impression Paterno gives is that of a regular guy—literally embarrassed by all the attention he gets—who loves his job, and has a hard time imagining doing anything else.

He jokes that he's afraid one of his kids will write a "Mommy Dearest"-type book about him.

He says he takes his job seriously, but he doesn't take himself seriously.

He would go to Mass more often if it were still in Latin. He loves tradition.

After 42 years coaching at Penn State, his office got another renovation. Joe Paterno loves it here. He's in no hurry to leave.

He concedes that if he sticks around until age 74, some of his current assistants may be too old to take over.

Annual: What are you most excited about right now?

Paterno: I'm excited because I think it's a good bunch of kids. They've been fun to work with—not a lot of problems, minimal amount of problems actually. I think it's a young team. They're enthusiastic. They're anxious to get good, so they're fun to work with. I think there's some potential on the football team if we keep everybody healthy and have a couple of breaks and everybody's around in the fall—it's a team that can be good. It's not very good right now, but it can be a good team. And it's fun to be around them.

Annual: How do you gauge the attitude of a player?

Paterno: There are a lot of things. Off the field, by his attitude toward his school work. If the kid is conscientious about his studies, discipline, about his appearance; things like that. A little pride, a little self-esteem, the way he handles himself around his teammates, whether he's sensitive to them. And whether he's the kind of kid who reaches out and takes part in some things around the campus.

And the way he practices. The way he does things when he's out on the field. When there's a little enthusiasm. When he's trying to get better. Listens to his coaches and tries to do what his coaches tell him. Coachable. Off-season—whether he's in the weight room. Whether he's doing some conditioning, running, so that when it does come time to practice, he's ready to go.

There's all kinds of things; the way he handles himself, his poise, language—being able to go out on the field and not having to use four-letter words every time something goes wrong. A lot of things as far as what I think are important in their attitude that we want in our players. Now, some other people may not think that that's the attitude they want. They may want somebody that's a little bit more flamboyant; have a different approach to things. I don't. I like a kid to be disciplined…concerned; has respect for his teammates, his coaches; has respect for the tradition of Penn State.

Annual: Do you recruit for that or do you feel you can take somebody who's a natural athlete—maybe a little cocky or flamboyant—and can teach him that?

Paterno: I don't mind if they're a little cocky, as long as they're not showboaters. (Former UCLA basketball coach) John Wooden used to say he doesn't want fancy people, he wants quick people or something to that effect. I think when we recruit kids it becomes quite obvious when they're looking over Penn State that there's a certain type of individual who gets along better here than another type. That's why we've kept our uniforms simple; don't put names on the backs, they're not flashy and I think that gives a message to the kid coming in that this is a disciplined, conservative program. There are certain things we think are important.

I want to make sure he understands what we expect of him, as well as what he should expect from us. It's a statement that's made very early in our recruiting, and if a kid comes he should come in with his eyes open as to what is going to be expected of him.

Annual: Because Penn State doesn't plan to change for that kid's personality.

Paterno: Absolutely. I don't think there's anybody that good.

Annual: Has Tony Sacca changed your attitude about how you deal with quarterbacks?

Paterno: No…I treated Tony as a person, not as a quarterback. He happened to be a person who had a lot of responsibility for the success of the football team. He came in literally a boy, who was very immature; who was put under a tremendous amount of pressure very, very early, when none of us expected him to have that kind of pressure put on him. We had intended just to redshirt him, let him become a normal freshman, get into the feel of college and get a sense of what he wanted to get out of college before he got wrapped up into having to run the whole show out there and be the focal point of literally millions of people as to what Penn State football was going to be. So that was very difficult for him.

It was a tough job to get him not to be so defensive all the time. He was angry about his lack of success at times. Like a lot of young people, he struck out at the system. That was the type

> 66
> *I think when we recruit kids it becomes quite obvious when they're looking over Penn State that there's a certain type of individual who gets along better here than another type. That's why we've kept our uniforms simple; don't put names on the backs, they're not flashy and I think that gives a message to the kid coming in that this is a disciplined, conservative program.*
> 99

of thing he'd do. I thought I had to be firm with him. Yet I didn't want to kill his spirit. I don't think that's what I wanted…I don't think that would have been the way to do it. I had to take him on a couple of times, but never to the point where he thought I'd lost confidence in him. And then he grew up. He matured. For the last two years, he's been a wonderful person to have around. He's been a great quarterback.

Annual: I guess it's kind of a father role. You have to be willing to have them not like you all of the time.

Paterno: I think "liking" is the worst thing you can do. If you're going out there to try to be popular, I think you gotta know what you're all about. You gotta believe in your program and you gotta be strong. You can't let the fans tell you what plays to call and who to play. You can't let the kids tell you what kind of rules you oughta have and not have. I think they should have some kind of say about them. Remember, it's their football team and we're getting paid to coach them; to help make them as good as they want to be. You want to keep that in the back of your mind, but there are certain things you really believe in, that if you can't sell it to the kids, you've gotta make them do it out of fear or discipline or the threat they won't play, or do something. But you've got to be able to stick to what you believe in.

You can't change (so that) one week you believe something, next week you believe something else. They don't need me for that. And a lot of times you do things that are very unpopular, and a lot of times kids resent it. But you hope that you're as fair as you can be. I'd love to say to every kid 'You've gotten a fair deal,' but that's not life. That's impossible when you've got as many kids as we have to say everyone has gotten exactly the same shake. It doesn't happen that way. So sometimes you have some misgivings as to how you handle a kid. But overall, you try to be fair and do what's best for him and the program.

" But you've got to be able to stick to what you believe in. "

Annual: Most of your players aren't going to play pro ball. I imagine most of them have hopes of doing that.

Paterno: Most of them come here with the idea of doing that.

Annual: How good have you been at predicting who really has the pro stuff when they come in?

Paterno: Well, there's some you know have the potential. They're big. They can do certain things. They're quick. Whether they can stay the course, and whether they're willing to work at it to get better and better—none of them are good enough, at least I haven't had one that's been good enough to be a pro after a year or two. Maybe after three years.

It's hard until you've seen whether they can handle some

adversity, how they handle pressure. Are they physically tough enough? Can they play then they're bumped up a little; things that they've got to be able to do in order to be a professional football player. There's no way of telling that until you've been around them a while. You can look at the physical…and just the talent, and say, 'Hey, that kid's got enough talent to be a pro someday.' But all of the other things that make up a professional football player; say the ability to practice and play when you've got aches and pains, the ability to handle tremendous pressure, the ability to make plays when they've got to be made. Those things you can't tell until you've been around a kid a while.

Annual: Does there come a point where you recognize that?

Paterno: Oh, sure.

Annual: It's not the day of the draft?

Paterno: Oh, no, no. You can tell that…maybe not his freshman year, but by the time you get through some practice. Freshman year, sometimes you can tell, but usually you can't.

Annual: Can you tell more quickly when they're definitely not pro material?

Paterno: Oh yeah.

Annual: Do you sit down with these kids and discuss their future?

Paterno: Well, I never talk about pro football with them until it becomes obvious that it is something that they're going to have to be concerned about. We talk to them all the time about staying away from agents even when they just come in. We tell them to stay away from people who just want to be your buddy for no apparent reason except they just want to be around you. We try all the time to talk about their grades, and getting an education. And then everything else is gravy.

If you get your education, what happens happens. If you get to be a pro player, fine. But I very rarely talk to them about what kind of player they're going to be beyond college. Once in a while I will, particularly if I'm going to make a position switch. I may look at a kid—particularly when he gets older, maybe going into his junior year or senior year—and he may like the position he's playing, but it looks to me like if he's got any aspirations to be a professional football player, and he has the ability, that maybe he oughta be playing another position. And then I'll sit him down and say, 'Look, you want to make pro football?' He says 'Yes.' I say you're not going to make it as an offensive guard, you oughta be a defensive end or something like that. And we move him.

Annual: You rarely have to sit somebody down and break it to him that he doesn't have it?

Paterno: No, no. They know. There's no need to. But I'm not

sure. These pros, they're crazy. They draft guys I wouldn't believe they would even look at.

I try to be realistic with (players) about graduate school and 'Are you looking around for a job? What do you want to do?' And some will say 'I want to play pro football.' And I'll say 'Ah, you're kidding yourself.' But a lot of guys won't pay any attention to me.

Annual: What are you reading now?

Paterno: I'm reading a book by the guy who wrote *The Best and the Brightest*. It's called *The Next Century*. I'm just getting into it. I just finished a great book I think every young person ought to read called *Lincoln on Leadership*. Just a little book, but it shows how Lincoln … what kind of leader he was and how he handled certain situations.

Annual: Is it new?

Paterno: It's by a guy by the name of Philipps. In fact, when he was writing it…he used to be with an oil company that I had spoken to their group a couple of times on motivation and things like that…I think it's Don Philipps. He asked me to make a comment. So he sent me the draft. And I made a little comment. I just gave it a quick perusal, and then I made a couple notes and sent them back to him. And then he sent me an autographed copy. I just got finished with it. It's been a while ago, about three months ago. I'm one of those guys that has trouble with finishing a book.

> **"** *I just finished a great book I think every young person ought to read called Lincoln on Leadership. Just a little book, but it shows how Lincoln … what kind of leader he was and how he handled certain situations.* **"**

I have about six things I'm reading at the same time. This one I'm going to finish. I'm enjoying this one…I start on one read a chapter here, another chapter there. I get bored with one, go back to another one.

Annual: Do you have a favorite?

Paterno: Not really. Oh, I used to read so much. I would read a book every two days at one time in my life. But I was very fortunate when I was a kid at a Jesuit high school, a fellow by the name of Dr. Fitzgerald, the librarian, who was really a great guy; he taught a lot of us speed-reading back in the '40s. So I read quickly, and I enjoyed it. But I've read…I mean I couldn't tell you which one I liked the best. But anyway, there are a lot of books I thoroughly enjoyed.

Annual: How important is reading to your personal growth?

Paterno: I think it's absolutely vital to the quality of your life. To watch the television—it's so instant. Sure I know now people tape things and go back and look it over, and maybe that's the answer to it/ But to sit down and read and to have your mind and your imagination take part in some things. The subtleties of good writing… Sometimes I'll read a couple of paragraphs, and go back and read them again.

Poetry; I mean, people don't read poetry…the sense of words… as I've said making speeches, when I'm talking about coaches: you know good coaches should remind you that English teachers showed you how poetry is so concise. The choice of words is so important; the discipline that goes into a good poem. I don't know where we get them anymore, unless we read.

Annual: Have you been able to transfer that passion to your kids?

Paterno: My own kids?

Annual: Your children as well as your players.

Paterno: Oh, sure. My children have all been pretty good readers. The engineer (David) isn't a great reader. He's never been that interested in it. But all of the others have been avid readers, actually. My wife is an English literature major and she reads all of the time. She used to read to them. So we've worked at it. And they read.

It's hard for me to tell whether the people on the squad read that much anymore. I don't know. We have some, Rudy Glocker and I used to talk once in a while. He was taking a course. He was reading one of Hemingway's books—*The Sun Also Rises*—and he didn't like the ending. So I told him to see Phil Young who was an expert in Hemingway. So I said, 'Why don't you call up and talk it over with Phil. You might enjoy it.' I hadn't read the book in 25 or 30 years. I really couldn't tell him why it had ended the way it did.

But anyway. I know some of our kids read a lot. We have a big kid, Mark Flythe, a prodigious reader. I never saw him without a book. He was always reading. He enjoyed it. In fact, he wrote a little poetry himself. Interesting guy. He's 6'6", 290 pounds. He has hands like that [indicates huge hands]. Okay. Go ahead. You're getting a sermon here.

Annual: You seem to have the ideal life—great job, great pay, great marriage, great kids, great attitude. Is everything really that great?

Paterno: I've been awfully lucky. I've been very, very fortunate. I worry about my kids; a couple of them, you know. I got one just married. She's (been) married a year. You know, it looks like it's going really well. Another girl…eh, she's up and down. Another kid who's a freshman at Penn. Overall, we've been very fortunate. They've all been healthy kids. I don't have any complaints. My big problem is, you wonder why you're so lucky, so fortunate. I go to bed at night sometimes and think, 'God, is there something you want me to do. I owe you so much.' You try to give some of it back in different ways. Whether you write a card to somebody that's sick, or whether you give some money to something. You try to share it. But we've been very fortunate.

Annual: Do you have a sense that God has a mission for your life?

Paterno: Well, I've never felt that I was that important [laughs]. I think there's a reason why He does things and hopefully He wants me to do certain things and hopefully I'm doing what He wants me to do. I'm not a born-again. I've got a strong religious nature. But I'm not consistent a church-goer as I used to be. My wife's on my back all of the time about that; go to Mass more often. And I should. I really should, because I enjoy it when I do. I got a little turned off for a while because it was tough for me to go to Mass and see the way some of these kids were dressed, and the folk music, and all that stuff bothered me. I've got to forget about that. That's the way kids are today. Churches accept it. I should accept it.

Annual: You want it to still be in Latin?

Paterno: Absolutely. I get sick when I hear it in English. As an altar boy I had to struggle for two months to learn the Latin to help serve the Mass. So I resent the fact that anybody can become an instant altar boy. I think it oughta be in the Latin. I really do. And I'm not comfortable with some of the liberal attitudes about certain things that the church is taking in order to be a little bit more popular.

Annual: What kind of issues?

Paterno: I don't want to get into all that stuff.

Annual: How do you feel about the fact that thousands of people base their opinions of you on interviews like this, which is really an artificial, structured, cautious relationship?

Paterno: How do I feel about it? Well, I fight like the dickens to try not to be a phony. I don't want to be a hypocrite. Which, as a matter of fact, is one of the reasons I got involved in this last book, because there were some things I felt were getting a little bit out of hand, as to what we were doing…what we were all about. I try all the time to say, 'Hey, I'm not that good. I'm not either that bad, or I'm not that good. I'm just another guy, trying to get in there and do a decent job and make a go of things.'

I'm embarrassed sometimes by going places where people want autographs and things like that. I'm a little embarrassed. I was embarrassed when I went back to my 25th reunion and I get an honorary doctorate degree from Brown, when I had classmates who had done so much more than what I had done. I'm just a coach. I had a couple of guys in my class who were great surgeons. One guy was the first guy ever to be able to implant teeth. And here I'm getting the honorary doctor degree and they're out in the audience. Well, that kind of gets to me a little bit…obviously, I was proud. I didn't turn it down. But I'm not comfortable with either extreme. Some people get on my back about things that I had nothing to do with or I don't even believe in some things that they think I do.

Annual: What's it like to have spent 42 years working to do a good job, and have your decisions criticized and second-guessed by a writer who never played, never coached, never managed anything?

Paterno: [laughs] I don't mind them. Sometimes, you should be second-guessed. You know sometimes you get caught up. I think criticism is good for you. If it's an honest attempt to assess what I've done, I don't have any problems with criticism. Because sometimes I deserve it. I take my job very seriously, but I don't take myself very seriously. I try to keep that kind of attitude about it. The second-guessing doesn't bother me. The fans don't bother me. I think so much of it is because they're so interested in it [laughs], and they're so frustrated sometimes when things don't go well that they just… 'Why'd he do that? Why didn't he do this?'

Annual: You're a fan of Penn State basketball.

Paterno: Absolutely.

Annual: Do you go to the games often?

Paterno: As often as I can.

Annual: When you're a fan, do you ever sit back in the stands and...

Paterno: Absolutely.

Annual: ...and say, 'Parkhill, you idiot. What are you doing?'

Paterno: I'll sit there and say once in a while, to (Athletic Director) Jim Tarman, 'I hope he gets that kid out of there pretty quick.' Like, 'Bruce, get him out. Put someone...'. But that's all part of the fun of going to a game. If I'm going to sit up there, I want to get into the game. And that's why I appreciate the fans. Vince Lombardi grew up in the next parish to me in Brooklyn. And here he was winning those Super Bowls, and I went to a game with my high school coach one time to watch the Packers play New York. My high school coach and I were second-guessing Lombardi the whole day [laughs]. That all goes with the game, and I'm mature enough to understand that. That doesn't bother me.

Annual: What's the role of the sports reporter in the big picture?

Paterno: It's changed obviously. Unfortunately the sports reporters are just like the rest of the media right now. They get into things that, really, I'm not so sure they should; like peoples' personal lives. The off-the-field stuff becomes much more sellable. That's the only way I can describe it. I think the sports reporter ought to go and report what he sees. He ought to try to catch the drama of the game, the excitement of the game; give an accurate description of what happened. Now, that's hard to do these days, because a lot of those games have been on television. So now they want to get the players... 'How come you didn't carry the ball more? Are you in Paterno's doghouse?' [laughs]

It's always so much of the negative to it now. It isn't a question of stressing the guy who won. So much of it is the guy who lost; who blew it. You know, 'Why'd he do that dumb thing.' Instead of, 'Hey, boy, wasn't that a great play. Wasn't it a great game. At a key spot, second and two, so-and-so came up with that great defensive play.' Not that somebody fumbled the ball. Somebody really hit him hard and created the fumble. Things like the positive would be my way of reporting. But I don't have to go out and be responsible to a sports editor who's gotta sell papers. So they gotta do what they have to do.

Annual: What's the role of the fan in the game? What should the fan do?

Paterno: I think a fan oughta do whatever he wants to do. I

> *Vince Lombardi grew up in the next parish to me in Brooklyn. And here he was winning those Super Bowls, and I went to a game with my high school coach one time to watch the Packers play New York. My high school coach and I were second-guessing Lombardi the whole day [laughs]. That all goes with the game, and I'm mature enough to understand that. That doesn't bother me.*

> **❝**
> *When I was a
> kid I used to go
> up to Tanglewood,
> the summer home
> of the Boston
> Symphony... And
> they used to have
> these concerts in
> a big open shed
> and it was great.
> It would make
> me feel good. I
> would go and buy
> a record of it and
> put the record on.*
> **❞**

> **❝**
> *It shouldn't be
> what we've got
> where people try to
> identify with the
> gladiator. They
> come up here, or
> a lot of places,
> and they're anti
> the other team.
> They boo the other
> team. I hate people
> booing people. I
> mean, why?*
> **❞**

don't think there should be any prescribed way a person should act when they go to a game. I think he's a fan; whatever the definition of fan would be. I think you go to the game to enjoy it. I've always thought that an athletic event for a true fan is like going to a concert.

When I was a kid I used to go up to Tanglewood, the summer home of the Boston Symphony. The drive up from New York was beautiful. It was in the summertime, up through the mountains, the Berkshires. And they used to have these concerts in a big open shed. You'd sit down on the lawn. It was great. I used to look forward to it. There would be two or three concerts on a weekend. And I would come home and I would think of...whether it was a violin concerto, or whether it was a Mozart symphony or something...and I would remember it, think about it. It would make me feel good. I would go and buy a record of it and put the record on. It would bring back things. See, I think that a fan should go to a football game at Penn State; drive up on a beautiful day, appreciate the whole bit. Go on to the game, and just enjoy the game. And if there's a play that excites him, go back home and think about it.

I once had an alumnus who was a very, very successful businessman, who was really caught up in football. And he used to say to me, 'You know, some nights I can't sleep. I sit back and think about somebody's great play or a kickoff return and it really adds some quality to my life. It gets me out of the syndrome that I'm in when I've got a lot of problems that carry over from the business day.'

And that's what I think that a fan should get out of a concert. I think a fan should come up, and even if the team gets licked, if it's a really good football game, not if the team doesn't hustle and it's sloppy, which sometimes happens, you know, poorly coached... sure then you oughta be angry, because you paid and you came to see something. It's just like if you went to see a concert and it was a lousy concert; somebody wasn't prepared. You'd be angry about that. So I think that it's something that should add to the quality of the life of the fan.

It shouldn't be what we've got where people try to identify with the gladiator. They come up here, or a lot of places, and they're anti the other team. They boo the other team. I hate people booing people. I mean, why?

I used to have a guy around here by the name of Aaron Druckman who was a philosopher. And he got into sports philosophy. He came to my office. He was a guy with a beard, long hair... he looked like a mountain man. One day he came in and said, 'I just came back from skiing. I had the greatest ski run. I came down from that mountain and I looked at the mountain and said, 'Mountain, I love you. I love you.' He said, 'Because if that mountain hadn't been there, I could not have skied it. And that's the way the competition oughta be. If the other guy isn't good, there's no fun to it.'

You need somebody to make it worthwhile. And fans don't appreciate that. It's like, 'To heck with that.' They want a rout. They want it 60 to nothing. I don't know what the devil they get out of a 60-nothing game.

Annual: Like the, what was it, 81-nothing game last year (against Cincinnati)?

Paterno: Aw, that's the most horrible experience I've ever been through.

Annual: That's not even fun to coach?

Paterno: Nah. Nobody gets any good out of it. You don't get anything out of it when you win and the other guy gets embarrassed. You're not out there to embarrass anybody.

Annual: Why do you think Bruce Parkhill interviewed with Villanova on the eve of Penn State's entry into the Big Ten and the construction of the new arena?

Paterno: That wouldn't be fair for me…I think you oughta ask Parkhill that. There's a lot of reasons. There might be personal reasons. I don't know. I think the important thing is that he's not gone. He stayed. I think that's the important thing as far as Penn State is concerned, and I'm delighted. But I think he's got a tough job and I think he's aware of that. We have to upgrade. We gotta get two or three great players. I mean really great players. Not good ones. I'm talking about as good as anybody has, if we're going to compete in the Big Ten successfully. I don't mean win the championship every year. He's got a tough job ahead of him. I think everybody's got to go to bat and help him to put that program at the next level. Because he's right there now. He's close. So I'm glad he stayed, because I think if we all get behind him, it can be done.

Annual: Will the Big Ten require "going to the next level" for the football team too? Do you have to notch up a bit?

Paterno: Well, we'll see. You know, our recruiting is a lot easier than Bruce's. We can recruit against anybody…and he has not…I think he brought in two kids…but again I think you oughta talk to him. But I think for him to (recruit) one-on-one with, say, a Villanova in Philadelphia, is tough, or against North Carolina. Right now he's not in that position where he's going to be in the four or five visits the kid's going to make.

Annual: You've been talking about retiring [Paterno laughs] at least since 1980. Why bother retiring? Isn't it more glorious for the warrior to die in battle?

Paterno: That's fine if the warrior can still warrior.

Well, I think you've got to be more realistic. I don't want to be in this job unless I can do a good job. If I don't think I can do a big league job, I don't want to be. One of the reasons I started putting in time modules—right now I'm talking about going until I'm 70. Otherwise, I'd just go year to year to year. But people use it against you when you're recruiting.

Bobby Bowden just signed a contract to coach until he's 70. Hayden Fry just signed a contract to coach until he's 70. Because of the very reason I just stated, I say 70. I may get to be 68, 69 and feel really good and say, 'I'm going to coach, if the university will

> **Annual:** *You've been talking about retiring at least since 1980. Why bother retiring? Isn't it more glorious for the warrior to die in battle?*
>
> **Paterno:** *That's fine if the warrior can still warrior.*

let me, until 74.'

I don't see any reason I have to retire if I feel like I'm doing a good job.

But you always hope that somebody's going to whisper in your ear. Like when the Roman conquerors used to come home. When they come down into Rome there used to be a guy riding alongside of him whispering in his ear, 'Fame is fleeting. Fame is fleeting.' You get yourself humbled. I hope there's somebody whispering in my ear, 'Hey, you've had it.'

Annual: Who do you trust who could honestly tell you, 'Look Joe, that's it. You've had enough?'

Paterno: If it were this year, I'd sit down with a couple of guys on the staff and say, 'Look, what do you think'. Let's say this year we're having a bad year and next year we have a bad year. I'd sit down with the staff and say, 'Is it me? I want an honest opinion.' I'd figure out a way that I would get an opinion from them, because they would know better than anyone.

Annual: But you're their boss, Joe.

Paterno: I'd maybe tell them, 'I want you all to go home and type a letter up. I don't want to see any names on it. Nine letters.' You know, I'd do it that way. I'd find out. I'd find out.

Annual: Is there anybody who really knows you?

Paterno: I think my family knows me. They know all of the warts [laughs]. I'm always afraid one of them is going to write one of those books like *Mommy Dearest*. That'll be the end of it. I think my family knows me well enough. I think Sue knows me. She's praying for me. She has a feel for those things. The girls are starting to get a little bit of a sense of where I'm coming from.

Annual: Do you get to spend more time with the kids?

Paterno: Ah, well, it's more meaningful time. You know, conversation. We've been fortunate in that we've been able to get them home fairly frequently. And when we're home we get into all kinds of discussions.

Annual: Johnny Carson spent two years grooming a successor who's completely changed the show. Do you have that obligation to groom somebody?

Paterno: Absolutely. The last time I talked about staying on, I was supposed to consult with the people at the university about whom I would think could step in. I think there are several key people on the staff that would be ready to step in and take over. I've tried to give them the type of responsibility that they could be heard by coaches. So I would be comfortable if it were tomorrow.

Now if I go much longer; if I go to 72, 73, some of them may

> *But you always hope that somebody's going to whisper in your ear. Like when the Roman conquerors used to come home. When they come down into Rome there used to be a guy riding alongside of him whispering in his ear, 'Fame is fleeting. Fame is fleeting.' You get yourself humbled. I hope there's somebody whispering in my ear, 'Hey, you've had it.'*

be too old or may not even want it. But I would feel comfortable right now. When I turn it over, I want to turn it over. Give the person coming in a good shot. I want to leave some meat on the bones. I don't want to leave the cupboard bare when I go.

Annual: No matter how well you set up your successor, isn't there bound to be a letdown for a couple of years?

Paterno: Well, I don't know about that. I look at the Michigan situation. And I look at Gary Moeller slowly starting to (build a program). The Rose Bowl is maybe two or three years if Michigan football continues to be as good as it's been the past couple of years, and Gary will continue working hard to improve morale. He's got a feel for what Michigan football is all about. He's not trying to push Bo Schembechler out of it, and Bo's not trying to stick his two cents in it. Bo wanted Gary to do well. Gary appreciated what Bo's done and tried not to do a lot of things that would be a little bit different than the Michigan tradition that had been built up.

I think that's what would happen here. I think the guys who would take over would do well. If the university would ever accept somebody from the staff and would go along with what I

CHAPTER 4: The Interview: Joe Paterno

think should be done, there wouldn't have to be a big turnover in the staff. I think they would carry on. As soon as they have had some success, after a couple of years; people will still remember Paterno, I hope. But Paterno isn't going to be sitting around second-guessing anybody.

Annual: You're not going to be the athletic director?

Paterno: No way. No way. I'm going to do just like Rip Engle did when he turned (it) over. He never second-guessed me. All he ever did was help. And if they want me to help, I'd never turn them down.

Annual: Paint me a picture of Joe retired-guy; What do you do?

Paterno: That's my problem; I don't know what I'd do.

I know I'll read. I'll go down to the ocean and walk the beach. I love to go to the shore. I don't want to get into that golf syndrome where you get up in the morning and play golf, then go to a cocktail party, eat dinner, go to bed, get up in the morning and play golf. I'd try to find something to do that I was physically able to do.

I'm very sensitive to what's going on in the inner cities, having grown up in the Bedford-Stuyvesant section of Brooklyn. I've thought if you had the kind of money you'd like to have, you'd like to go in there and do what some of the business people have done, and adopt a class in a school. Spend time with them.

So you would wake up in the morning where you…you don't have an eight-to-five job, but you're going to visit the school, spend some time. You're going to take some of the kids, maybe, on a trip. You're going to take them to a museum. You're going to take them to New York's public library. Whet their appetites and try to create a whole different projection of what they can do with their lives. Create new horizons for them.

Because basically I'm an egghead. I'm always on stage teaching, selling. And I would enjoy that. And I think my wife and I could do that together, because she enjoys that. I mean something like that. I just would not want to just go to pasture.

Annual: How has it been working with the Penn State bureaucracy?

Paterno: It's a bureaucracy. I try to work within the kit. I've always felt that I want to go by the rules, chain of authority; go to Jim Tarman. Jim goes to Steve Garban. Work with the trustees, the president, the faculty senate, if it's something they should have a say about, work through them.

But every once in a while the bureaucracy gets a little bit overbearing. And every once in a while, I'll be very frank with you, I'll threaten. 'Hey, enough's enough. We gotta get this thing moving.

> **Annual:** *Paint me a picture of Joe retired-guy; What do you do?*
>
> **Paterno:** *That's my problem; I don't know what I'd do.*

It's a question of whether you guys are right or I'm right. And I feel, with my experience, my feelings are that we gotta do this, and I really can't take no for an answer.'

I've done that a couple of times. Very infrequently. Not very often…maybe three, four times in the 26 years I've been head coach. Because I don't like to do that. I think everybody's got responsibility and I want to be a company/team player. But I think there comes a time every once in a while that you gotta try to do some things that are outside the bureaucracy.

Annual: What would be a thing you'd have to do for that?

Paterno: Let's take the Big Ten. When we made up our minds that we wanted to get into the Big Ten, if we had gone to the president or the faculty senate, and they had said, 'No.' Maybe not the faculty senate, but the president, said, 'I think we're better off as an independent football team,' and gives me good reason. Then I would do everything I could to say, 'Hey, believe me, this is the best. We can't take 'no' for an answer.' Something like that.

Annual: Did you have to do it on that issue?

Paterno: Oh, no. Dr. (Bryce) Jordan was delighted. So was the faculty. No. That's why I brought it up. It would have to be something very important to the whole program, not just football.

Annual: Will entering the Big Ten dispel the criticism that Penn State plays a weak schedule?

Paterno: No. I know a lot of people think the Big Ten doesn't have a lot; just a couple of tough teams. I think it will make things a lot tougher than a lot of people realize. We have a lot of people who think we'll go into the Big Ten and get clobbered.

I don't think that's a fair criticism. There are a couple of things where perception becomes reality. We won the national championship in 1982 playing what at that time was evaluated as the toughest schedule in the country.

I don't think people really know how tough this schedule is. Some years it plays easy. Some years it plays a lot tougher than people will give it credit.

Same way that people like to think I'm conservative. I am not conservative. I'm not a conservative football coach.

Annual: But you want the Latin back in Mass.

Paterno: I create the perception. That doesn't bother me (for people to say) we won't take chances.

Annual: Does that allow you to do something wild then if you have to?

Paterno: I like to tease people. If they want to think that, fine. But when you're talking about how much you throw the ball.

There are some schools out there, when they're trying to recruit some quarterback, they'll say we don't throw the football.

So I sat down with the kid and I said, 'Now, you tell me. We played Maryland—who threw the ball more, Maryland or Penn State? Penn State. When we played Virginia, who threw the ball more. We played Pitt. Who threw the ball more?'

I went through four or five teams who have the reputation of being wide-open, throw the ball all over the place. And we had thrown the ball more times in the game we played than they had thrown against us. So that broke down that thing.

Annual: You'd just as soon have other teams believe you don't throw the ball much?

Paterno: Certainly. Let them think we're conservative. It makes it easier to be successful when you're un-conservative.

Annual: This is the 10th edition of the Penn State Football Annual. Thousands of readers own every issue. What would you like to tell these loyal fans to look forward to in '92?

Paterno: I think it's going to be an exciting team to watch. I think we have a chance to be a good offensive team. I'm a little concerned about us defensively. We did not come out of spring practice with a defensive unit that I'm comfortable with yet.

Now we have a lot of kids that weren't out there. Derek Bochna wasn't out there. Chris Cisar wasn't out there. We have two really fine young players who didn't practice; Willie Smith and Cisar. Brian Gelzheiser was not out there. So there's a lot of players that were not out there. Richard McKenzie wasn't out there.

Annual: Were those players injured?

Paterno: Cisar and Bochna were out for baseball. Smith had been injured. McKenzie out: we wanted him to concentrate on his studies. Gelzheiser had gone through a problem; suspended for the semester.

But I think offensively we're going to be an exciting football team. A young team. I think they'll enjoy it. I really do. I think the schedule is challenging, regardless of what people say. I think all the teams in the east are going to be better. BC's going to be better. West Virginia's going to be better. Pitt's going to be better. I think Boston College is going to be a tough football team. Rutgers, Temple…all bright young coaches who recruited well. Plus we gotta play Miami. Gotta play Notre Dame. We gotta go out to BYU. I think it will be a tough schedule, but I think it will be a fun season.

REMEMBERING A DECADE OF
PENN STATE'S 'WHY'

VALUES

FAMILY

FESTIVALS

TRIUMPH

... AND UNFORGETTABLE
MEMORIES